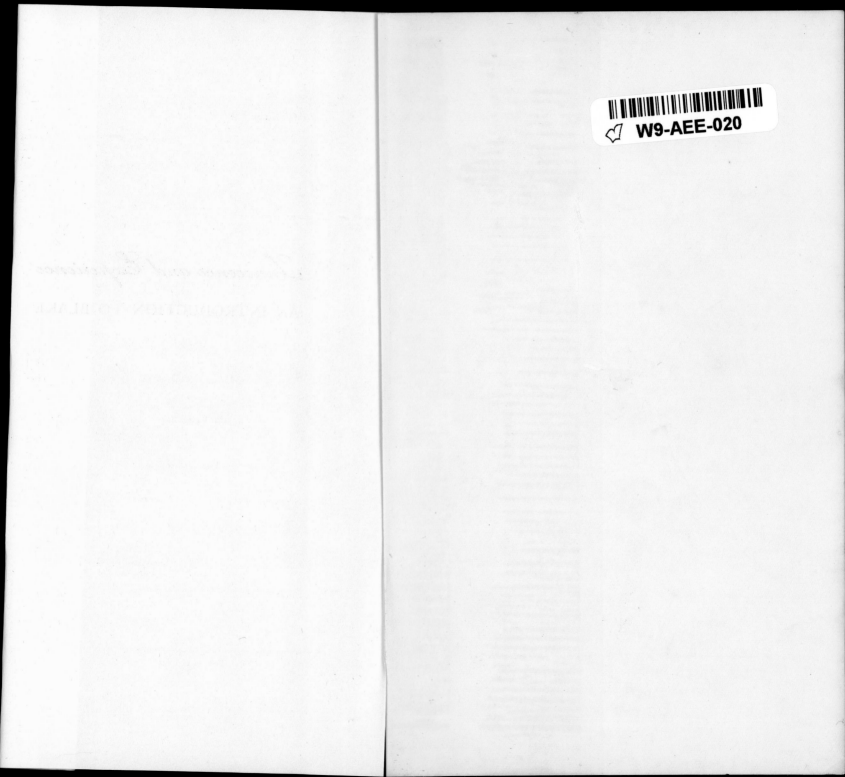

*Innocence and Exp*

AN INTRODUCTION TO

# Innocence and Experience: An Introduction to Blake

E. D. HIRSCH, JR.

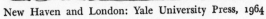

New Haven and London: Yale University Press, 1964

FOR POLLY

*Preface*

Much that has been obscure in Blake's poetry can be illuminated by taking into account the radical changes that occurred in his ideas and attitudes during the course of his creative life. In the past, scholars like D. J. Sloss, J. P. R. Wallis, Mark Schorer, D. G. James, F. W. Bateson, and H. M. Margoliouth have alluded to some of these changes or to the contradictory motifs they produced in Blake's work, but the most widely established view has been that each of Blake's etched works "whatever its date not only belongs in a unified scheme but is in accord with a permanent structure of ideas" (Northrop Frye, *Fearful Symmetry*, Princeton University Press, 1947, p. 14). This systematic conception of Blake's poetry has obscured the fact that Blake not only changed his views radically but also made these changes, and what they symbolized to him, the subject matter of his later poetry. It has been obvious that *Milton* is an autobiographical poem, but far less obvious that Blake's own tumultuous spiritual history is a central theme of *The Four Zoas* and *Jerusalem*. The same is true of the poems in the Pickering Manuscript, which, because of their brevity, I have been able to discuss in some detail.

vii

## Preface

This book focuses on Blake's central major work, the *Songs of Innocence and of Experience,* a work that spans the whole course of Blake's poetical maturity. (He composed the earliest poems of the *Songs* around 1784, and did not cease to alter the character and significance of the work until 1818.) I have elected to emphasize this slowly evolving masterpiece for two reasons. The first is that an expansive, general study of Blake's poetry would have to scurry over too many details and problems to stand, in the present context of conflicting opinions about Blake, as anything more than another assertive commentary. I have tried to raise the argument of this book above the level of mere assertion by confronting all the cruxes in the *Songs,* whether or not I could certainly explain them, and by trying to account for all the relevant facts, including chronological and bibliographical ones. I have taken into account for the first time evidence that has long been available in the bibliographical studies of Sir Geoffrey Keynes. No one can claim certainty in textual interpretation, but one can claim probability, and an interpretation, like any other hypothesis, is more probable than another when it accounts for more facts and explains more relevant data than another.

My second reason for focusing on the *Songs* is that a poem-by-poem commentary is seriously needed. Although the *Songs* is Blake's most widely read, studied, and admired work, it is surrounded by obscurities and eccentric critical opinions that raise obstacles to an appreciative reading and teaching of the poetry. The popularity of this work makes it no less deserving of careful study than Blake's powerful but infrequently read late mythological epics. In fact, quite apart from its intrinsic value as Blake's most successful major work, the *Songs* is the best introduction to those difficult epics because it embodies concretely the personal, spiritual history to which they consistently allude.

My debts to other scholars have been great. I have already mentioned the greatest one—that which I owe Sir Geoffrey Keynes. His *Bibliography of William Blake* (New York, 1921), his more recent *William Blake's Illuminated Books: A Census* (New York, 1953), done in collaboration with Edwin Wolf 2nd, and his chronological edition of *The Complete Writings of William Blake* (London, The Nonesuch Press, 1957) have been indispensable. The last named has been the source of my quotations from Blake, and is referred to throughout this book by the symbol "K." For the most part I have followed Keynes' dates, and have ventured to differ only in those rare instances where the internal evidence seemed to demand it. The dates cannot usually be definitive in any case, and are primarily important in establishing a relative chronology. In general, the important problem is to determine not the precise date of a work but rather the period to which it belongs, the span of time long or short in which Blake preserved a particular outlook. An arrangement of Blake's work by period will be found in Appendix IV.

In coming to understand *The Four Zoas,* the unfinished epic that Blake composed and drastically altered during his public silence of 1795–1805, I have been greatly helped by the work of D. J. Sloss, J. P. R. Wallis, and H. M. Margoliouth. I had already written my account of *The Four Zoas* when the fine edition of G. E. Bentley appeared (*Vala, or The Four Zoas. A Facsimile of the Manuscript, a Transcript of the Poem, and a Study of Its Growth and Significance,* Oxford, Clarendon Press, 1963). Bentley's authoritative introduction is a welcome corroboration of the conjectures I formulated on sparser and less certain evidence.

## Preface

I am indebted also to many Blake scholars whose views I have implicitly or explicitly attacked in this book. Among these I would include Foster Damon, Northrop Frye, David Erdman, the late Peter Fisher, Harold Bloom, J. E. Grant, Robert Gleckner, and Hazard Adams. I have learned a great deal—as have all students of Blake—from these advocates of a systematic approach to Blake's writings.

Among those scholars with whom I have been able to discuss my ideas in person, my greatest debt is to W. K. Wimsatt, who criticized and encouraged me from the time I wrote an anticipatory essay, "The Two Blakes" (*Review of English Studies,* 1960), until the time I completed this book. I gratefully acknowledge, too, the stimulation I gained from conversations about Blake with Geoffrey Hartman, Garry Haupt, Alice Miskimin, Martin Price, Harvey Simon, and Ann Watts. In bibliographical matters I benefited from the knowledge and advice of Marjorie Wynne and Willis Van Devanter. John Hobbs energetically helped me prepare the manuscript for publication, and Louis Martz was kind enough to read it through and make suggestions for its improvement.

The ideas in this book were first conceived while I enjoyed a year's freedom from teaching duties as a Morse Fellow. The Morse Fund generously made an additional grant to defray the costs of typing the manuscript.

For her help at every stage of writing this book my profoundest debt of all is to my wife.

E.D.H.

*New Haven, Connecticut*
*February 1964*

# *Contents*

# Contents

# Contents

# Contents

# Contents

## APPENDIXES

# PART ONE

## The Course of Blake's Poetry

# 1. On Systematizing Blake

At the present time the standard way of reading Blake's work is to relate every part of it to one of the systems he developed in *The Four Zoas, Milton,* or *Jerusalem.* Since each of Blake's systems, including the one he enunciated in *The Marriage of Heaven and Hell,* accounts for everything in the material and spiritual cosmos, it is not implausible to interpret his poetry in terms of one of them: the dialectical principles called "Prolific" and "Devourer," the human aspects called "Tharmas," "Urthona," "Urizen," and "Luvah," the psycho-cosmological states of being called "Ulro," "Generation" "Beulah," and "Eternity," or even in terms of some amalgamation of these formulated by the critic. Certainly it is plausible to utilize the schema of Blake's last long work, *Jerusalem,* for in it Blake attempted to embrace all of his earlier viewpoints within a single comprehensive account. But this late Olympian comprehensiveness was not present to Blake when he composed his earlier works, and there is an obvious and fundamental difference between the

3

vigorous advocacy of a view of life and a later retrospective evaluation of its place in the system.

To the larger part of Blake's work—to the *Poetical Sketches, The Book of Thel,* the tractates on religion, the *Songs of Innocence, The Marriage of Heaven and Hell,* the *Visions of the Daughters of Albion, America,* the *Songs of Experience, The Book of Urizen, Europe, The Song of Los, The Book of Ahania, The Book of Los* —Blake's schemes and categories in the later epics are largely extrinsic. Blake preserved a great deal of his earlier thought by transforming it, but he was not a poet who developed and refined with varying emphases a single fundamental interpretation of reality. He was a poet who changed his interpretation of reality as radically as any figure in English letters. It is difficult, in fact, to think of any other poet who approaches him in this, for the familiar palinodes of Chaucer, Spenser, Coleridge, Wordsworth, and Yeats are temperate in comparison with Blake's recurrent self-repudiations and self-satires. About God, Man, and Nature Blake fundamentally changed his mind not once but twice, and he recorded those changes in his work not by unconscious implication but by deliberate choice. The substance of his work from 1790 to the end of his life consists largely of self-commentary. Consequently, the application of Blake's later systems to his earlier works on the assumption that whole corpus constitutes a monumental unity not only falsifies the earlier works but also falsifies the later epics by leaving out of account the intensely confessional spirit that pervades them and gives them their vitality.

On the more particular issue of detailed textual explication, the systematic conception proliferates error by causing the critic to explain Blake's images in one period by his use of them in another. Blake was attached to favorite words, phrases, and images, and therefore used them, as he used recurrent motifs in his pictorial art, to serve varied purposes. The phrase "infant joy" does not have the same meaning in the *Songs of Innocence* (1789), *Visions of the Daughters of Albion* (1793), *The Book of Los* (1795), *The Four Zoas* (ca. 1800), and *Jerusalem* (ca. 1810). Every time Blake mentions a star, a predatory animal, or a fiery forge, he does not necessarily mean the same thing, and there is no reason that he should. The theory that his work constitutes a single corpus was not Blake's own, and at times he refused to offer certain of his etched works—notably *The Marriage of Heaven and Hell,* and *Milton*—for sale.[1] Nor did he, in general, import his mythological personages into his lyric poetry, being sensitive not only to the proprieties of genre but also to the autonomy of an individual work of art. Each poem was for him a new start, and while he quite naturally borrowed from his earlier work whatever suited his present purpose, he did not assume that what he borrowed had to be used in the same way as before. The critic has a right to illuminate a problematical passage in Blake by comparing it with similar passages elsewhere; he needs to seek illumination where he can. But he ought to avoid, and this is more emphatically the case with Blake than with many other poets, facile equations between one work and another.

1. In his last years, Blake answered two requests for lists of the works he had for sale (letter to Turner, 9 June 1818, K.867; letter to Cumberland, 12 April 1827, K.878). Both lists omit to mention *The Song of Los, The Book of Ahania,* and *The Book of Los.* These works, as I point out below, pp. 81–87, reflect a despondency and uncertainty which gave the later Blake a low opinion of them. Of *The Song of Los* and *The Book of Ahania* he apparently etched only one copy (K.896). In the second list *Milton* is replaced by *Jerusalem.* The most striking fact is that *The Marriage of Heaven and Hell* is missing from both lists. Blake felt, I think, that the work pronounced too obviously in his own voice a view he had repudiated.

The favored ground for the systematization of Blake has been the *Songs of Innocence and of Experience,* for the very good reason that Blake himself, with his penchant for consolidation as well as self-repudiation, systematized the *Songs.* He did so by the simple act of adding in the second (extant) issue of the *Songs* a general title page that bore the subtitle, "Shewing the Two Contrary States of the Human Soul." While Blake did not, as I shall show in some detail, originally compose these poems as elements in a larger philosophical scheme, he did schematize them after the fact, just as he later schematized his past viewpoints in *Jerusalem.* But the schema Blake imposed on the *Songs* changed significantly in the course of his life. Which ex post facto system are we to take as the basis for our interpretation? That of 1794? That of 1800? The two different schemes imposed during the period of *Milton?* The scheme imposed during the period of *Jerusalem?* When Blake added "To Tirzah" in 1805, he radically altered the larger meaning of the *Songs.* When he placed "A Dream" or "The Schoolboy" or "The Voice of the Ancient Bard" in *Experience,* the systematic intention was different from the one that had preserved these poems in *Innocence.* Blake's systematic purpose in placing "To Tirzah" in the middle of *Experience* was radically different from his purpose in placing it last.

The basis on which Blake made these changes was his knowledge that Innocence and Experience were two mutually exclusive states of his own soul corresponding to two different periods of his life. His subsequent changes in the order and classification of the *Songs* reflected his changing evaluation of those two moments in his spiritual history. To perceive this is to grasp the unchanging substance underlying the changing systems, and also to grasp what is needful for understanding the *Songs* in their intensity, namely that they are not intellectual counters within a dialectic, but poems that express two distinct outlooks that Blake in each case held with an unqualified vigor and fervor of belief. Because of this alone the poems have life and intensity, and their larger, systematic implications force and validity.

While every critic of Blake has commented with varying expansiveness on the *Songs,* only two have devoted full-scale studies to them, and of these, only one critic, Wicksteed, has provided a poem-by-poem commentary.[2] On the whole Wicksteed's book has been the most valuable single aid to understanding them. For all the old-fashioned flavor of his enthusiasm, Wicksteed is often a most sensible and sensitive critic who in spite of his conviction that the *Songs* are built upon a dialectical system, is willing, for example, to say of "The Lamb": "There is almost nothing cryptic about this lyrical gem. Deeper knowledge of Blake will reveal no darkly buried meaning, only a deeper sense in the meaning obvious to all." [3] Yet this welcome disclaimer is necessary only because Wicksteed does frequently try to exhume what he supposes to be darkly buried. He finds hidden meanings in the *Songs* on the assumption that their "system" is based on the doctrine of sexual emancipation enunciated by Blake in the 90s. Thus about "Infant Joy":

> "I have no name:
> "I am but two days old."
> What shall I call thee?
> "I happy am.
> "Joy is my name."
> Sweet joy befall thee!
>
> Pretty joy!
> Sweet joy but two days old,

2. J. H. Wicksteed, *Blake's Innocence and Experience, A Study of the Songs and Manuscripts "Shewing the Two Contrary States of the Human Soul"* (London, Dent, 1928).
3. Ibid., p. 91.

Sweet joy I call thee:
Thou dost smile,
I sing the while,
Sweet joy befall thee!

Wicksteed remarks that the second line implies: "In my journey through Time I have only reached the moment of impregnation, of 'holy Generation' in the body." Now Wicksteed could hardly have made this remark and others like it unless he were convinced that Blake's "system" required esoteric meanings. Indeed his preconception is quite apparent in his introduction to the foregoing interpretation: "The esoteric meaning of a lyric so perfect in its simple meaning as 'Infant Joy' can only be regarded as finally established if a very definite inner meaning can be found for the second line, 'I am but two days old.' " [4]

The other full-length study of the *Songs* is that of Mr. Robert Gleckner, whose purpose is not to discuss them poem by poem (though he does provide full commentaries on some of them) but to explain the system developed in the *Songs* as a whole.[5] While his comments are cast in a more modern and tough-minded mold than Wicksteed's, and while he, too, makes numerous helpful remarks, his study is even more rigorously schematic than Wicksteed's. According to Mr. Gleckner, the *Songs* are built upon the idea that the soul moves from "unorganiz'd innocence" to "experience" to "the higher innocence." Therefore he has this to say of "Infant Joy":

The essence and symbol of the infant joy, intensified to the point of syntactical obscurity, is established in the poem of that title. Without reference to its enigmatic punctuation and confusing dialog-monolog form I hazard here a·

4. *Ibid.*, p. 124 n.
5. R. F. Gleckner, *The Piper and the Bard, a Study of William Blake* (Detroit, Wayne State, 1959).

8

very tentative partial paraphrase to point up the essential "thoughtlessness" of the Blakean innocent. "I am, I exist," says the infant joy; "and since I am happy in that existence happiness or joy must be my name." The adjective merely becomes a noun; the quality assumes concrete symbolic form; the essence achieves identity. The Piper, aware of impending experience but unable to do anything directly for the infant innocent, speaks in the final lines the supreme prayer of the state of innocence: "Sweet joy" (Christ, higher innocence, imagination, wisdom) "befall thee." [6]

The poem implicitly contains the entire scheme; "The infant joy" is "unorganiz'd innocence" about to embark on "experience" and therefore needs to be wished well on its journey to the "higher innocence." I submit that no critic would come to quite this conclusion unless he were convinced that each song has its appropriate and necessary place in the "system."

The impropriety of viewing the *Songs* and Blake's other works within a single, unvarying systematic context may be suggested in a preliminary way by examining a short work Blake composed at the time he was writing the *Songs of Innocence* and which he subsequently revised shortly before he wrote the *Songs of Experience*. The work is the little tractate called *There Is No Natural Religion*. It exists in two etched versions. No one has explained why Blake undertook to revise this carefully composed, laboriously etched, and minutely colored little work. Clearly some dissatisfaction must have compelled him to recast the work entirely, illustrate, etch, and color it anew, but there is no reason to believe that he was dissatisfied with the formal effectiveness of the first version, which is a satirical masterpiece that brilliantly demolishes the opposition. The second version, on the other hand, is less an attack on

6. Ibid., pp. 298–99.

9

natural religion than a vigorous affirmation of a newly found confidence in the natural world. The clear implication is that Blake was dissatisfied with his first version because he had changed his ideas.

The first version of *There Is No Natural Religion* is probably Blake's earliest experiment in "Illuminated Printing," and since he stated at the end of *The Ghost of Abel* that his "Original Stereotype was 1788," this is the accepted date of the work. Internal evidence confirms that the date is probably correct. The hand Blake used is the same as that in the *Songs of Innocence* (1789), and his designs represent the same kind of pastoral scenes. More important, his emphasis in the first tractate is on the special suprasensible and visionary faculty that is celebrated in the *Songs of Innocence*.

Blake's procedure is to refute natural religion by showing the logical impossibility of its assertion that the religious sense in all men is built up from sense impressions.[7] He attacks that Eighteenth Century form of deism which was built upon the psychology of Locke and specifically upon the notion that all ideas, including the idea of God, are built up from sense data alone. Blake's strategy in attacking this position is the quietly satirical one of adopting the opponent's own premises and then disclosing the dead end to which they lead. This logical dead end is exposed in the third proposition: "From a perception of only 3 senses or 3 elements none could deduce a fourth or fifth." That is, given sense data alone, no one could deduce a nonsensible reality, since all ideas, according to Locke, are compounded of elements from sense perception: "None could have other than natural or organic thoughts if he had none but organic perceptions." But since men do have moral and religious ideas, it follows that they must have extra-organic per-

7. In this section I avoid a detailed discussion of the intricacies in Blake's argument. A full discussion will be found in Appendix I.

ceptions deriving from an extra-organic sensibility which Blake calls "the Poetic or Prophetic character."

In identifying man's special, extra-organic sense with the faculty that produces poetry and prophecy, Blake implies that religion and morality derive from the same spiritual capacity as poetry. Thus the poetic and the prophetic have the same source. But what is the source of the prophetic faculty? It is quite literally the divine influx, the breath and being of the Lord in man. The "Poetic or Prophetic character" is Blake's version (as it was Akenside's) of the "inward light" tradition in dissenting Protestantism, and it is a central idea in the *Songs of Innocence*. Children possess this faculty unconsciously but in unclouded purity, and it was this faculty that inspired the Piper of the *Songs* to "Sing a song about a Lamb."

The second version of *There Is No Natural Religion* is generally given the same dates as the first, 1788, but this date is almost certainly incorrect. Some time must have elapsed (though perhaps not very much) before Blake became dissatisfied with his earlier accomplishment, and even though the elapsed time could have occurred within the year 1788, the bulk of relevant evidence makes this most unlikely. In the first place, there are numerous indications that Blake did not begin to look with disfavor on his earlier works until the latter part of 1789. In the second place, the revised version is lacking in the pastoral scenes that characterized the etched work of the 80s and is written in the script characteristic of the 90s. But quite apart from these external clues, the thematic content of the revised version has more affinities with *The Marriage, America,* and the *Songs of Experience* than with anything Blake had composed before 1790.

The new version represents a shift in the emphases of Blake's religious ideas. He now insists that man's religious perceptions are not "other than natural or organic," but "more than sense (tho' ever so acute) can discover." He has no inclination to make a sharp separation between what is "natural" and what is beyond sense; his distinction is entirely between limited or bounded sense perception and the perception of the infinite in all things: "He who sees the Infinite in all things, sees God." That is to say, man gains access to God not by a special pipeline to the spiritual realm but by an expanded perception of the actual world. Blake's new emphasis is on "possession" rather than "perception," on the actual experience of the "Infinite" both in man and in the world.

This affirmation of an immanent divinity in the natural world corresponding to the infinite in man himself appears to lack any significant kinship with the bitter satires of the *Songs of Experience,* but a closer look will disclose that this is precisely the kind of implicit affirmation which the *Songs of Experience* (1794) make. One of the points I shall develop will be that Experience, for all its satirical bitterness, implies a far more hopeful and optimistic view of the natural world than Innocence does. Innocence places implicit trust in ultimate divine beneficence, but it invests very little hope or trust in the actual world. Consequently, one of the difficulties that any systematization of the *Songs* must encounter is that Innocence is not simple-minded and illusioned while Experience is mature and disillusioned; with respect to natural life Innocence is less illusioned and trustful than Experience. Although no systematization of the *Songs* can explain this apparent inversion of the "system," anyone could explain it by acknowledging the change that occurred in Blake's attitude to the natural world between the composition of *Innocence* and the composition of *Experience.* And in Blake's later years, when he returned to some of his earlier beliefs and repudiated his temporary flirtation with the natural world, he came to feel that it was *Experience,* not *Innocence,* which implied the more illusioned state of the soul.[8] Nothing more clearly refutes the idea that Blake's works entail a rigorous system than Blake's own changing conception of the *Songs* and his continual manipulation of their order and classification. The soundest interpretation of the *Songs* and of all works by Blake is one that attempts to understand them in relation to the original impulse out of which they were composed.

8. See below, pp. 106–65.

# 2. The Independence of the Songs of Innocence

The history of commentary on Blake's *Songs* shows that the critic's conception of their general character plays a larger role in his interpretations than the actual words of the individual poems. This is not altogether surprising. All lyric poetry, when it is good, means a great deal more than it explicitly says, and the way we understand the unsaid meanings of Blake's *Songs* depends less on our grammatical construction of their words than on our conception of Blake's unspoken attitudes and intentions. In reading the *Songs* the one idea that most influences our general notion of Blake's attitudes and intentions is our conception of the relationship he conceived to exist between *Innocence* and *Experience*.

In very general terms the accounts that have been given of this relationship have taken two forms: the systematic and the biographical. The systematic account is, briefly, that *Innocence* was deliberately composed to represent a state of the soul which is inadequate by itself and requires for completion a representation of the contrary state, Experience. The various versions of this account differ in details but have in common the idea (probably derived from Blake's general title page) that each group of poems is incomplete without the other, thus making the two works stand to one another as *L'Allegro* stands to *Il Penseroso*; each opposes and corrects the other, and both are necessary to an adequate conception of the "human soul." The biographical account, on the other hand, is that Blake originally wrote the *Songs of Innocence* as a complete and independent work. Later he changed his viewpoint so radically that he felt impelled to compose a contrary self-satirical group of poems. On this view, *Innocence* stands to *Experience* as Spenser's *Hymne in Honour of Love* stands to his *Hymne of Heavenly Love*, the later work relating to the earlier more as a palinodic recantation (a contrary state of the soul) than as a philosophic completion implied from the beginning. The biographical account implies that if the *Songs of Innocence* were originally composed as a complete and independent work they should be understood as such before they are placed in any larger schematic context.

That more is at stake here than the mere determination of biographical facts is evident from the use made of the systematic account in interpreting the *Songs of Innocence*. Of all Blake's poems, these have suffered most from the intricacies of systematic criticism. The most extreme view makes them out to be deliberate exercises in naive illusion, fragile and vulnerable to their own implicit ironies. The least extreme systematic view regards them as both targets for *Experience* and implicit satires of *Experience*. This view has the virtue that it sets up a genuine dialectic in which Innocence has a value beyond its mere vulnerability, but it has also the vice common to all systematic interpretations of the *Songs of Innocence*. It makes them intellectual counters in a secular dialectic rather than poems which demand a repudiation of both the intellectual and the secular. The main poetic value of these simple poems, apart from their felicity of language, resides in the emotional intensity of the religious vision they express. Religious affirmations are absolute, not dialectical. If these poems are to have any real significance when they are subsequently viewed (if that be desired) within a larger dialectic, they must be sympathetically experienced apart from any dialectic. This was the pattern of Blake's own experience of them, and it was the way they had to be understood during the five years (1789–94) when Blake issued them as a separate, complete, and independent work.

This curious bibliographical fact is even more remarkable when it is coupled with another: Blake not only waited until 1794 to etch his contrary poems, he apparently waited until 1793 to compose them.[1] These are, quite naturally, disconcerting facts for the critics who hold that Blake had his sequel in mind from the start. Consequently arguments have been marshaled against attaching much significance to these facts. The arguments may be summarized as follows: (1) The whole corpus of Blake's work shows that he would not have composed in deadly and unqualified earnestness such simple and gentle ("namby-pamby") poems. (2) The presence of three poems of *Innocence* in an early satirical manuscript called *An Island in the Moon* proves that Blake associated these poems with satire from the beginning. (3) The independent validity of *Innocence* is

1. The *Songs of Experience* exist in first draft in a notebook called the Rossetti Manuscript. Blake's editors Sampson and Keynes both conclude that these drafts were composed in 1793. See John Sampson, ed., *The Poetical Works of William Blake* (London, 1913), p. xxxiv, and Keynes, ed., *The Complete Writings*, p. 889. Their estimate receives support from David Erdman who finds allusions in the Manuscript to events of late 1792 and early 1793: *Blake, Prophet against Empire* (Princeton, Princeton University Press, 1954), pp. 167, 174.

denied within the poems themselves, particularly in their use of such words as "stain'd" ("Introduction"), "wands" ("Holy Thursday"), "my father sold me" ("The Chimney Sweeper"), etc.

This, to my knowledge, is a summary of all the arguments that have been adduced in favor of the idea that Blake always intended to compose *Experience* and always considered *Innocence* to be incomplete. Even without the citing of contrary evidence, these arguments are open to grave objections. Blake did, after all, have a decided taste in the 8os for what could conceivably be called the namby-pamby. Besides the *Songs of Innocence,* the best examples of this are the early pastorals and *The Book of Thel.* Secondly, it is not self-evident that Blake was subjecting to satire every poem (or any poem) he included in his satirical miscellany, *An Island in the Moon.* In fact, the way in which the recitation of "Holy Thursday" puts an end to foolish conversation ("After this they all sat silent for a quarter of an hour") suggests that the poem is more an agent than an object of satire. On the whole, the example from this manuscript which most clearly favors the systematic argument is the poem that, after a pause, follows "The Little Boy Lost":

> I say, you Joe
> Throw us the ball.
> I've a good mind to go
> And leave you all.
>
> I never saw such a bowler
> To bowl the ball in a [turd *del.*] tansey,
> And to clean it in my handkercher
> Without saying a word.          [K.6o–61]

"Here a laugh began," but after most careful consideration I cannot perceive that this poem is a satire of "O father, father, where are you going?" Indeed, I can't see that anything of the desired kind can be proved by the entire manuscript unless it be that Blake had a penchant for satire and a sense of humor.

The most compelling argument for the idea that the poems of *Innocence* implied a contrary set of poems from the beginning is that they themselves intentionally suggest their own inadequacy and incompleteness: How can we confront images of school wardens with sticks or of fathers selling their small children without perceiving that the complacent tone of these apparently simple poems is deliberately undercut by their subject matter? In a poetic world that contains chimney sweepers, slavery ("The Little Black Boy"), and cruelty (wolves and tygers howl for prey") how can we read straightforwardly such lines as:

> Can I see another's woe
> And not be in sorrow too?
>
> . . .
>
> O no never can it be
> Never, never can it be!

The lines are clearly ironical and self-accusing, for the very facts instanced within the poems of Innocence show that "it" certainly can be.

This argument, which is not necessarily based on a systematic idea, makes the apparently reasonable assumption that Blake was not, after all, either a fool or a knave, and would not have looked indifferently upon the existence of cruelty and injustice. Clearly, he must have made an implicit moral judgment on cruelty and injustice which was at odds with the benign and accepting surface tone of his poems. Blake's poems of Innocence must therefore be ironical, or what is essentially the same—deliberately inadequate. For no human being, as Blake well knew, can remain in Innocence within this human world. Even the attempt to remain in Innocence by refusing to pass moral judgment implies just the opposite of Innocence, a guilty abandonment of human responsibilities. To be human requires a moral engagement with the world. Yet this very insight is clearly implied within the poems of *Innocence*. Take, for example, "The Chimney Sweeper." The poem certainly contains an implicit moral judgment, if not against the sweep's father, then certainly against a society in which such things "can be." That is precisely why the poem alludes to such things; it does not try to deny them; it tries to imply through its tone that ideas like pity and forgiveness are higher and more important than ideas of moral judgment. The deliberate transcendence of moral judgment in order to effect a moral transformation of men is no more the mark of a fool or knave than the possession of childlike faith is the mark of an ignorant child.[2]

The way we read a poem is not self-authenticating. If we try to deduce Blake's "system" or his original intentions from the way we read his *Songs,* we are arguing in a circle. We are saying, for example, that Blake must have intended to write a sequel because the *Songs of Innocence* are ironical, and that the *Songs of Innocence* are ironical because Blake always intended to compose a sequel. If a knowledge of Blake's original intentions is important in deciding how to read the *Songs* (and all critics agree that it is—if only by their arguments about Blake's intentions), then clearly something more than a merely assertive reading will be required in order to determine those intentions.

There is one troublesome, if merely bibliographical, fact which I have not yet mentioned. It is that most of the twenty odd separate issues of the *Songs of Innocence* do not belong to the five-year period between the pub-

---

2. Blake did, however, come to believe that *Innocence* had not sufficiently committed itself to moral action. See the discussion of *Jerusalem,* below, pp. 162–65, and of *The Book of Thel* in Appendix II.

lication of *Innocence* and the publication of the combined *Songs*. That is to say, Blake issued most of the separate copies of *Innocence* when he could have added *Experience* if he had wanted to. By contrast, Blake never, according to Keynes, issued *Experience* as a separate work.[3] And if Blake regarded *Innocence* in this way after he had etched *Experience*, it is hard to disbelieve that he so regarded it before. The most obvious implication of this evidence is that Blake continued to issue the *Songs of Innocence* as an independent work because he had regarded it as such from the beginning, and that he failed to issue the *Songs of Experience* separately because he had conceived of them as ex post facto contraries to *Innocence*. This evidence conforms so perfectly with the evidence of a change in Blake's outlook between *Innocence* and *Experience* that the burden of proof must rest with those who consider the late appearance of *Experience* to be a mere chronological accident having no significant bearing on the relationships between the two works.

3. See K.893, and Geoffrey Keynes and Edwin Wolf 2nd, *William Blake's Illuminated Books, a Census* (New York, Grolier Club, 1953), pp. 9–18, hereafter referred to as "Keynes and Wolf." Of the twenty-one copies of *Innocence* of which details are known, only the first eight (copies A–I) belong to the period 1789–94. The rest (copies J–U) were issued after the combined *Songs* had been published. "The Little Girl Lost" and "The Little Girl Found" (transferred to *Experience* from the beginning) are invariably missing from these copies, some of which bear watermarks proving their lateness: Copy O, "1802," Copy P, "1802," Copy Q, "1804," Copy S, "1808."

# 3. The Songs of Innocence

The *Songs of Innocence* are highly original poems that have no true counterpart in English literature, or, to my knowledge, any other literature. They are not simply religious poems for children—that was the kind of poetry which Dr. Watts, not Blake, "condescended" to write. They are religious poems for children and adults. They address childlike percipience in the adult and adult percipience in the child. Their childish simplicity of language belies their adult profundity of insight, but their symbolic implications tend to resolve rather than manufacture complexities. Their intricate identifications of man and God, Earth and Heaven, Child and Man, are accomplished without paradox or irony. Their only paradox is the one that deliberately undercuts all self-conscious elaboration of paradoxes: "If any man seemeth to be wise in this world, let him become a fool that he may be wise." The critic of these poems should accordingly retain what Professor Abrams happily calls a "keen eye for the obvious," which is the Christian paradox of wise innocence translated into criticism.[1] Although most of the poems were undoubtedly composed in 1788 and 1789, three of them—the ones that appear in *An Island in the Moon*—were written by 1784, and another, "Laughing Song," by 1787. Thus, while Blake did not begin to etch the poems before 1788, he composed them over a period of at least five years, an indication that the continuity of his early poetry was great enough to permit the inclusion of poems not originally intended for the *Songs*. This suggests that the *Songs of Innocence* are the direct culmination of Blake's early work in lyric poetry.

While the *Poetical Sketches* (1783) are, by comparison with Blake's later achievements, 'prentice work, they have a consistency of tone which shows a consistency in Blake's early conception of the lyric mode. While Blake made various kinds of experiments in the Elizabethan manner, most of his attempts in this vein are set in an idealized version of the countryside, and celebrate emotions and activities which, like those of the *Songs of Innocence,* tend to be purified of all complexity and taint. Frequently Blake's images are taken from the standard landscape of heaven. Spring, for instance, has "angel eyes" and "holy feet"; Summer pitches a "golden tent" by "waters clear as heaven"; the Evening Star is a "fair hair'd angel," and Morning a "holy virgin clad in purest white." This semitranscendent world is also the usual world of his love lyrics:

> My feet are wing'd while o'er the dewy lawn
> I meet my maiden, risen like the morn:
> Oh bless those holy feet, like angels' feet;
> Oh bless those limbs, beaming with heav'nly light!
>
> Like as an angel glitt'ring in the sky
> In times of innocence and holy joy;

1. M. H. Abrams, "Five Types of *Lycidas*," in C. A. Patrides, ed., *Milton's "Lycidas," The Tradition and the Poem* (New York, Holt, 1961), p. 231.

## Songs of Innocence

> The joyful shepherd stops his grateful song
> To hear the music of an angel's tongue.

> So when she speaks, the voice of Heaven I hear:
> So when we walk, nothing impure comes near;
> Each field seems Eden, and each calm retreat;
> Each village seems the haunt of holy feet.      [K.9]

The association of "innocence" with "holy joy" is suggestive, but it would be a mistake to stress the religious implications of these fundamentally secular early poems. The general collapsing of the religious into the secular was a characteristic of late eighteenth-century poetry, as the word studies of Professor Josephine Miles have shown, and Blake in *Poetical Sketches* is a characteristic and derivative poet.[2] But his fashionable vocabulary is, nevertheless, suggestive in another way; words like "holy," "heaven," and "angel" do not raise the mind to the realm of religious orthodoxy, but they do evoke an experience in which "nothing impure comes near." The world of these lyrics is the deliberately purified realm of the idealizing imagination. Blake conceived of the pastoral mode as filtering out everything that is "ting'd with the village smoke," and of the pastoral landscape as ᷍epresenting the spiritual domain of poetry itself. That domain was, from the first, associated with "innocence":

> I love the pleasant cot,
>   I love the innocent bow'r,
> Where white and brown is our lot,
>   Or fruit in the mid-day hour.      [K.8]

That this early, Edenic version of innocence is several points of the spiritual compass away from the *Songs of Innocence* is clearly indicated by Blake's correlation of

2. See Josephine Miles, *The Primary Language of Poetry in the 1740's and 1840's* (Berkeley, University of California, 1950).

23

the word "innocence" with the sternly secular word "virtue":

> Joys upon our branches sit,
> Chirping loud and singing sweet;
> Like gentle streams beneath our feet
> Innocence and virtue meet.                    [K.7]

This secular and didactic element in *Poetical Sketches* ("for ignorance is Folly's leasing nurse") is associated with a landscape that welcomes "Heaven" and "Angels" as well as "Pan," "Mercurius," "Pallas," and "Minerva."

After *Poetical Sketches* Blake continued to write this kind of secular and didactic pastoral poetry. Three of these slightly later poems survive in the margins of a copy of *Poetical Sketches,* and show that Blake's emphasis on the ethical dimension of "innocence" was, if anything, more pronounced than before:

> Song 1st By a Shepherd
>
> Welcome, stranger, to this place,
> Where joy doth sit on every bough,
> Paleness flies from every face;
> We reap not what we do not sow.
>
> Innocence doth like a rose
> Bloom on every maiden's cheek;
> Honour twines around her brows,
> The jewel health adorns her neck.             [K.63]

The place to which the "stranger" is so didactically welcomed remains the no-man's-land of the earlier pastorals —a fenced-off segment of the secular world from which the impurities but not the benefits of that world have been excluded. Joy and honor are the just rewards of moral probity; the jewel health is spiritual well-being and a rosy complexion.

Quite significantly, however, Blake departs from this

ambiguous conception in the last poem of this group, the "Song by an Old Shepherd." In all the previous pastorals he had symbolized moral innocence by a benign and purified landscape that was half in the world and half out; in this poem he presents a deliberate and self-conscious opposition between moral innocence and the external setting:

> When silver snow decks Sylvio's clothes
> And jewel hangs at shepherd's nose,
> We can abide life's pelting storm
> That makes our limbs quake, if our hearts be warm.
>
> Whilst Virtue is our walking-staff
> And Truth a lantern to our path,
> We can abide life's pelting storm
> That makes our limbs quake, if our hearts be warm.
>
> Blow, boisterous wind, stern winter frown,
> Innocence is a winter's gown;
> So clad, we'll abide life's pelting storm
> That makes our limbs quake, if our hearts be warm.

[K.64]

That Blake is here developing a broader conception of the pastoral may be perceived in a comparison of this poem with an earlier poem from *Poetical Sketches,* having an almost identical beginning:

> When silver Snow decks Susan's cloaths,
> And jewel hangs at th' shepherd's nose,
> The blushing bank is all my care,
> With hearth so red, and walls so fair.

In the earlier poem the cold of winter is contrasted with the cosiness of a "sea coal" fire. In the later it is contrasted with a spiritual state. As soon as "moral innocence" is understood as a totally inward condition, entirely independent of the secular world, the merely

moral and secular dimension of "innocence" has begun
to lose its primacy.

If, on the other hand, we compare the "Song by an
Old Shepherd" with one of Blake's best poems of *Innocence,* "The Chimney Sweeper," we can see the direct
lineal descent of the *Songs of Innocence* from the early
pastorals. Like the Old Shepherd, Tom Dacre is attacked
by life's pelting storm, and Tom's dismal city life is carefully set in the winter season. When Tom has a dream-
vision of Eternity, the visionary landscape of Heaven
becomes very like the pastoral landscape of the earlier
poems:

> Then down a green plain leaping, laughing they run,
> And wash in a river, and shine in the Sun.

The consequence to Tom of this prophetic vision is
precisely the same as the consequence to the Old Shepherd of "Virtue," "Truth," and "Innocence":

> Tho' the morning was cold, Tom was happy & warm.

But while Tom's innocence permits him the grace of this
warming vision, it is certainly not his virtue that warms
him against life's pelting storm. He is no more virtuous
after his dream than before. And yet, lapsing momentarily into his earlier conception, Blake adds the jarring
line:

> So if all do their duty they need not fear harm.

The idea jars in this poem, as it does not in the earlier
one, because vision is not the same as virtue. The sweep's
vision and his going to Heaven do not depend on his
dutifully sweeping chimneys. No doubt Blake means by
"duty" something considerably broader than "assigned
task," but the line is a flaw, the one flaw in the poem,
and is clearly a vestigial remnant of Blake's earlier iden-

tification of "innocence" with "virtue." This vestige marks both "The Chimney Sweeper" and "Holy Thursday" as relatively early poems. (We know that "Holy Thursday" was written by 1785.)[3] Blake's impulse to write the *Songs of Innocence* came when he abandoned the limited and secular conception that connected "innocence" with "virtue," and consciously embraced the wider, religious, and visionary conception of "innocence" that informs, except for its last line, "The Chimney Sweeper."

Blake himself seems to describe this development in his "Introduction" to the *Songs of Innocence*. He first presents himself as a poet of secular pastorals:

> Piping down the valleys wild,
> Piping songs of pleasant glee.

The image is of a carefree country swain or even a Pan-figure. Suddenly he receives a new inspiration:

> On a cloud I saw a child,
> And he laughing said to me:
> "Pipe a song about a lamb."

While the new kind of song is to be religious, it is to be played on the same pipe as before and will be written down with the same "rural pen." The inspiration was a brilliant and liberating one which exploited the natural association between pastoral imagery and Christian symbolism and accorded perfectly with Blake's expanding conception of his prophetic vocation in lyric poetry. Blake saw that one great advantage of this new genre over the earlier kind of pastoral was that unfallen spiritual perfection is more profoundly portrayed in the mind and heart of a child than in fields and villages peopled by swains and maidens. By giving his poems this new

3. It appears in *An Island in the Moon* (ca. 1784–85).

center, he could transcend the restrictions of the traditional pastoral, and could even write city poems of innocence.

Having before him the dissenting tradition of children's literature from Bunyan through Watts to Mrs. Barbauld, Blake did not achieve his new inspiration entirely on his own. Of these predecessors, however, only one had an important influence on him: Anna Laetitia Barbauld. From her fine little book, *Hymns in Prose for Children* (1782), Blake borrowed a number of themes and images (at least twelve of the *Songs of Innocence* contain parallels with the *Hymns*), but these isolated images were far less important to Blake than one fundamental conception he gained from Mrs. Barbauld's book. What kindled his imagination may be seen in her variation on the Twenty-Third Psalm:

> Behold the shepherd of the flock. He taketh care for his sheep, he leadeth them among clear brooks, he guideth them to fresh pasture. . . . But who is the shepherd's Shepherd? Who taketh care for him? . . . God is the shepherd's Shepherd. He is Shepherd over all.   [Hymn III]

Mrs. Barbauld departs from the Twenty-Third Psalm in making man as well as God a shepherd, but in her analogy the emphasis is entirely on God: "Who is the shepherd's Shepherd?" "God is the shepherd's Shepherd." The catechism is a hymn of praise. In Blake's analogy between the shepherd and God in the *Songs of Innocence*, the religious affirmation is considerably more complicated:

> How sweet is the Shepherd's sweet lot!
> From the morn to the evening he strays;
> He shall follow his sheep all the day,
> And his tongue shall be filled with praise.

For he hears the lamb's innocent call,
And he hears the ewe's tender reply;
He is watchful while they are in peace,
For they know when their Shepherd is nigh.

["The Shepherd," K.118]

If the shepherd were a symbol only for God, and the sheep only for men, then it ought to be they, not the shepherd, whose "tongue shall be filled with praise." Yet the shepherd is obviously a symbol for God; his sheep are in peace when they know he is nigh. On the other hand, it is the shepherd's lot that is sweet; he follows the sheep all the day. And whom does *he* praise? The shepherd is both shepherd and flock, and is shepherded not only by his Shepherd, but also by his Sheep. God is both Shepherd and Lamb; man is both Lamb and Shepherd. "Thou, Father, art in me, and I in thee, that they also may be one in us. . . . And the glory which thou gavest me I have given them; that they may be one, even as we are one: I in them and thou in me, that they may be made perfect in one" (John 17:21–23). The poem is less simple than it appears because it subtly expresses a religious perspective in which man and God are not simply analogous but essentially one. God became a man; He became a little child; He is a Lamb. Man is a Child, and a Lamb, and to others, a Shepherd. Ultimately, Shepherd and Sheep, Father and Child are the same:

For Mercy, Pity, Peace, and Love
Is God our father dear,
And Mercy, Pity, Peace, and Love
Is Man, his child and care.

["The Divine Image," K.117]

This radically immanental Christianity gives the *Songs of Innocence* their characteristic form and intensity.

Every event and image has sacramental implications because all human relationships are sacramental re-enactments of man's relation to God and God's to man. Every shepherd is a lamb and every lamb a shepherd. These are not merely symbols, they are the thing itself; they partake of the divinity they represent. Blake's affirmation of God's immanence is most profoundly and characteristically expressed in the relationship between Parent and Child, and here again Mrs. Barbauld's *Hymns* were helpful:

> The mother loveth her little child; she bringeth it up on her knees . . . she nurseth it with tender love; she watcheth over it when asleep. . . . But who is the Parent of the Mother? [Hymn III]

And again Blake transforms this pious analogy into literal sacramental truth. In "A Cradle Song," for example, he goes far beyond the expected Christological comparisons:

> Sleep, sleep, happy child,
> All creation slept and smil'd;
> Sleep, sleep, happy sleep,
> While o'er thee thy mother weep.
>
> Sweet babe, in thy face
> Holy image I can trace.
> Sweet babe, once like thee,
> Thy maker lay and wept for me. [K.120]

While the mother sees Christ in her infant, the poet sees Christ in the mother weeping over her child. For Blake every mother is Mary and Christ, and every infant is, like God, the parent's parent.

Man's sacramental re-enactment of Christ's care for man is one of the two principal themes of the *Songs of Innocence*. The child becomes a symbol for man, his parent or guardian a symbol for Christ. Yet the guardian is himself a man, and therefore a child, while the child is also a symbol, or indeed a reincarnation of Christ. The effect of these interchangeable identities is to express man's oneness with God, but this affirmation of the "Divine Humanity" is in no way a celebration of the blessedness of life in the world. On the contrary, nothing can prevent the pain and danger of life's pelting storm. Innocence is spiritual blessedness amid natural bleakness. There is as much weeping as laughter in the *Songs of Innocence,* and weeping is man's natural response to natural life. The whole idea of sacramental guardianship assumes a recognition of man's vulnerability to pain and sorrow in the world.

Thus the mother weeps over her slumbering baby for the same reason Christ wept for her. She weeps for the sorrow her baby must endure. As the baby's human guardian or shepherd, the mother must try her best to avert pain and suffering, but her tears express her recognition that she cannot succeed. She is like the guardian angels in "Night" who are unable to protect the sheep from "wolves and tygers" and can only "pitying stand and weep." That is the best that can be done for man in this world, and that is why within this world the "Divine Image" is "Mercy, Pity, Peace, and Love." It is because the guardian (Shepherd, Parent, Christ) loves his child that he feels Mercy and Pity for his inevitable sorrow; it is because the child (Lamb, Man, Christ) trusts his guardian that he feels peace amid the dangers of life. In the world of *Innocence,* a human or divine guardian always watches as the children sleep or play. On the other side, the human guardian receives back from the child the gift of peace that he gave. The mother's final words as she watches over her child are:

> Infant smiles are his own smiles;
> Heaven & earth to peace beguiles.

This reciprocity between the human guardian and the child is very beautifully expressed in the opening lines of the "Nurse's Song":

> When the voices of children are heard on the green
> And laughing is heard on the hill,
> My heart is at rest within my breast
> And everything else is still.

In her loving sympathy with the children the nurse experiences the complete trust which their laughter unconsciously expresses. The shepherd herself is in peace. All her anxious knowledge of the world's pain and danger is stilled in that moment. Then, in the second stanza, the setting sun reawakens her adult anxieties, and she calls out protectively:

> Then come home my children, the sun is gone down
> And the dews of night arise.

In the disagreement that ensues on the question of bedtime, it is the children who are victorious and the experienced adult who gives way. The children's arguments are unassailable, and the nurse's knowledge that darkness and danger will follow the sunset is for the moment irrelevant, since the light of the sun has not disappeared. Besides, the birds still fly and the sheep still graze, and *they* know when it is time to go to bed, just as they know when their shepherd is nigh. The nurse gives way both to the arguments of the children and to their trust. In her loving sympathy she re-experiences the insight she gained from them at the beginning of the poem, and as the night draws still closer she is again in peace. The poem ends as it began, with the laughing and shouting of children.

The little drama acted out in the "Nurse's Song" shows that Innocence is not merely ignorance of "the dews of night" but is a spiritual condition which an adult can share. While the children may not be aware that their insouciance implies a faith in divine care, the nurse is aware of it and responds, knowing she is herself a child, by feeling the same trust. Blake is careful not to stress the Swedenborgian distinction between the naive innocence of children and the wise innocence of adults; he wants to show the identity of the two, just as he wants to show the identity of child and parent, shepherd and sheep, God and man. The effect of these shifting identities is to build a world in which the basic truth about man is that he is a vulnerable and dependent child and that the innocence of the child is the highest wisdom man can attain. The poems cannot be read sympathetically without a sense of the profundity of the Christian paradox: "Except ye be converted and become as little children ye shall not enter into the kingdom of heaven." The important fact about the child's instinctive wisdom is not his ignorance of the natural world, not his lack of experience (the chimney sweeper does not lack experience), but his trust. In celebrating the divinity of human guardianship, the *Songs of Innocence* celebrate the wisdom of trust, and that wisdom is the final fruit of human guardianship. The mere exercising of Mercy, Pity, and Love is neither efficacious in the world nor spiritually sufficing in the guardian (that would be mere self-gratulation). The fruit of these sacramental emotions is Peace.

The word "Peace" is pivotal in the *Songs of Innocence,* as in the New Testament. Peace is a condition of spiritual blessedness that both reconciles man with this world of sorrow and prefigures the blessedness of the kingdom to come. "These things I have spoken unto you that in me ye may have peace. In the world ye shall have tribulation" (John 16:33). The spiritual peace experienced *in* the world is the same as the peace that will be, "for the kingdom of God is not meat and drink, but righteousness, peace and joy" (Romans 15:17). Thus "Peace" has a double meaning that expresses the doubleness of man's spiritual life, which both acts itself out in the world amid other men, and has "in heaven a better and an enduring substance" (Hebrews 10:34). Peace is therefore not only trust and consolation; it is also visionary joy. And just as the child's implicit trust expresses the profoundest religious insight, so does his joy express the highest prophetic wisdom.

Since neither child nor adult gains trust or inner joy by instruction or experience, their Peace must come from an inborn faculty of religious knowledge. We recall that this faculty was the subject of Blake's first etched work, *There Is No Natural Religion* (1788) and that he called this faculty the "Poetic or Prophetic Character." In the *Songs of Innocence* Blake gives his view a distinctly Wordsworthian flavor by honoring this faculty not only in the poet and prophet but also in the child. (Blake was beside himself with excitement when he first read the "Intimations Ode" and saw that Wordsworth also viewed the child as a "Mighty Prophet" and "Seer Blest." He would have approved also the passage in *The Prelude* where Wordsworth finds in infancy the "first poetic spirit of our human life." [4] The presence of this faculty in the child implies its universal presence in man, and Blake explicitly formulated the connections between poetry, prophecy, and the universal religious instinct in another etched work of 1788, *All Religions Are One*:

> The Religions of all Nations are derived from each Nation's different reception of the Poetic Genius. . . . As all men are alike (tho' infinitely various), So all Religions &, as all similars, have one source. The True Man is the source, he being the Poetic Genius. [K.98]

4. See *Henry Crabb Robinson on Books and Their Writers,* ed. Edith Morley (3 vols. London, Dent, 1938) , *1, 330.*

The "True Man" or "Divine Humanity" is man divested of his "selfhood." Or, to put it differently, it is the child in man, for the "Poetic Genius" in Blake's sense of the term is the great inherited possession of children, the source and explanation of their joy and trust. Transcending the "ratio of the five senses," the "Poetic Genius" brings joy and trust because it brings the "Divine Vision." This is the second of the two principal themes of the *Songs of Innocence*.

The "Divine Vision," bluntly defined, is the perception of a better world beyond this one. Blake had first adumbrated that realm in the never-never land of the early pastorals and would give it minute articulation in his last long work, *Jerusalem;* in the *Songs of Innocence* that transcendent world is a pastoral Heaven instinctively perceived by every child whose joy and trust is nurtured by the watchful care and pity of his human guardian. That care, so thoroughly futile in the natural sphere, is entirely successful in the spiritual, and it succeeds in precisely the way that God's care succeeds: though the human guardian cannot avert pain and disaster, he can preserve the child's trust and joy; though God weeps for man in this world, he brings him blessedness in the next. Ultimately, then, it is the child's faith in God's guardianship, in the reality of that transcendent realm, which the human guardian preserves.

This conception of the guardian's nurture of the "Divine Vision" in the child (besides explaining the whole dissenting tradition of devotional poetry for children) explains a typical pattern in the *Songs of Innocence*. Blake first presents an image of the child's pitiable condition in the world, then an image of the loving guardian who brings him peace, and finally an image of the "Divine Vision" which that guardianship has nurtured. Thus the Chimney Sweep, himself a deprived child like

35

all men in the natural world, plays the part of the guardian to little Tom Dacre:

> Hush, Tom! never mind it, for when your head's bare
> You know that the soot cannot spoil your white hair.

This expression of loving care, so bitterly ineffectual in improving Tom's natural situation, is completely effective in bringing him peace:

> And so he was quiet, & that very night
> As Tom was a-sleeping, he had such a sight!

Tom's "Divine Vision" assures him that the loving guardianship of the Chimney Sweep is an image of God's guardianship both here and in Heaven:

> And the Angel told Tom, if he'd be a good boy,
> He'd have God for his father, & never want joy.

Similarly, the prelude to the "Divine Vision" in "The Little Black Boy" is the description of the child's deprived state in this world:

> But I am black as if bereav'd of light

which is followed by a description of the mother's loving care, and this in turn by an image of the Father's loving care in Eternity:

> She took me on her lap and kissed me,
> And pointing to the east began to say:
> "Look on the rising sun; there God does live."
>
> .        .        .
>
> And thus I say to little English boy:
> "When I from black and he from white cloud free,
> And round the tent of God like lambs we joy,
>
> I'll shade him from the heat, till he can bear
> To lean in joy upon our father's knee."

A particularly effective and subtle use of this pattern occurs in "Holy Thursday" where the Charity School children are first shepherded into St. Paul's by the "grey-headed beadles." Once inside the church, the beadles are seated beneath the children and the church service is transformed into a vision of the "seats of Heaven" as described by John in The Book of Revelation.

Blake's usual images of Heaven are less explicitly biblical than those of "Holy Thursday." More often Heaven is a pastoral landscape like the one in "The Chimney Sweeper" or "The Little Black Boy." But in the *Songs of Innocence* the idealized springtime landscape with its birds, lambs, laughing children, and echoing greens does not hover ambiguously between the actual and the spiritual world; it is very much in the natural world. The village green where the children play is just as much a part of the actual world as the city street where the sweeper cries " 'weep, 'weep," and the actualness of the pastoral setting makes it all the more effectively symbolic of the world beyond. Thus there are no "waters clear as heaven" or holy virgins "clad in purest white"; the fields are simply "green," the fens "lonely," and the hills "all covered with sheep." It is impossible not to feel that this pastoral world is far more real and contemporary than that of the *Poetical Sketches* with its Elizabethan swains and maidens. Yet the very actualness of this landscape affirms the truth of that transcendent world which the "Poetic Genius" perceives in the laughter of real children on a real village green.

Blake's straightforward (though still highly selective) presentation of the landscape is another fruit of the sacramental conception which informs these poems. The echoing green is not simply a symbol of spiritual blessedness but a sacramental experience of what Heaven is really like. And if it was Mrs. Barbauld who suggested to Blake the sacramental presentation of human guardianship, it was Swedenborg who pointed to the sacramental meaning of the natural setting. Swedenborg's doctrine of correspondences was, briefly, that all objects and events in the natural world have a corresponding meaning in the spiritual world. Furthermore, all that we experience in life we shall experience in a transfigured form after death. Blake's attraction to such ideas in Swedenborg's work disposed him to become an active member of the New Church, and he remained a member during the time he composed most of the *Songs of Innocence*. From Swedenborg, Blake may have derived also the idea that "Innocence," especially in children, is a manifestation of heavenly insight, and the idea that the Last Judgment is an inner and visionary as well as a cosmological event. This last idea is important in all the poems of joy because the child's joy (or the adult's) is at once a prefiguration of his happiness in Heaven and an inward experience of Heaven while on earth.[5]

The Swedenborgian doubleness of Blake's landscape is best seen in a simple poem like "Spring," where the interest resides almost entirely in the sacramental meaning. Like the new year they celebrate, the inhabitants of the poem's springtime landscape are newly born: the lamb, the little boy, the little girl. While it is appropriate to the "natural sense" of the poem that these young creatures be the celebrants at the birth of the natural year, it is absolutely essential to the poem's "spiritual sense" that they be newly born, for the poem

5. These doctrines of Swedenborg may be found in the works Blake annotated: *Wisdom of Angels Concerning Divine Love and Divine Wisdom*, and *The Wisdom of Angels Concerning Divine Providence*, as well as in another work he probably read, *Heaven, Its Wonders and Hell*. For a full, though not chronological, account of Blake's debt to Swedenborg and his membership in the New Church see J. G. Davies, *The Theology of William Blake* (Oxford, Clarendon Press, 1948).

is not only about birth but also about rebirth and apocalypse. The opening words:

> Sound the Flute!
> Now it's mute

are a pastoral prophecy of the last trumpet. So is the crowing of the cock, which, in Blake's apocalyptic reading of the Bible, announces the moment when a previous cock-crowing assumes its final significance:

> And immediately the cock crew. Then they led Jesus
> from Caiaphas into the hall of Judgment.   [John 18:27–28]

Similarly the refrain,

> Merrily, Merrily to welcome in the Year,

gives to the word "Year" the same apocalyptic sense it has in Isaiah. And the last stanza, so embarrassing to some readers, carries a weight of apocalyptic meaning in the words:

> Little Lamb
> Here I am.

Probably the most effective fusion of the natural with the prophetic or visionary landscape is accomplished in "The Ecchoing Green," a poem that traces the entire cycle of human life in these two realms. The course of natural life is represented by a natural day, from dawn in stanza one ("The Sun does arise") to dusk in stanza three ("The sun does descend"). In the middle stanza we are in the middle of life in the world, and Blake presents both extremes of worldly life in the words of the "old folks" who watch the children at play:

> "Such, such were the joys
> When we all, girls and boys,

> In our youth time were seen
> On the Ecchoing Green."

But in the last stanza, which immediately follows these lines, it is the poet who speaks, and his words, coming after those of the "old folks," have as much relevance to them as to the children:

> Till the little ones, weary,
> No more can be merry;
> The sun does descend,
> And our sports have an end.

The distancing effect of these lines is achieved not only by the implied physical distance of the poet from the scene but also by the subtle shift from the sports of the "little ones" to "our sports." At this point the "old folks," the "little ones," and all the rest of us have become children playing out their games from morning to evening, when there will be

> sport no more seen
> On the darkening Green.

But in the full cycle of life the setting of this sun is a new and greater sunrise. (Notice Blake's capitalization of one "sun" and not the other.) The end of the poem implies (though it is tactfully reticent in doing so) its beginning:

> The Sun does arise,
> And make happy the skies.

The clearest hint of this prophetic meaning is found in the middle stanza, where Blake, like Wordsworth, finds in our memory of childhood intimations of immortality. The old folk who recollect their natural past in the joy of children see both their source and their rebirth in

40

Eternity. The ability of Old John to "laugh away care" is a sign not that his worldly care is inconsiderable but that he, like the Nurse, finds peace in the laughter of children. His sympathetic recollections of early childhood are prophetic intimations of eternity; in his embers is "something that doth live." The natural harmonies of the echoing green are sacramental. Like human guardianship, the pastoral landscape is at once an occasion for and the content of prophetic vision, and just as a transcendent meaning resides within the natural world, so the realm of eternity also resides within the human breast. Eternity is both within and beyond.

Thus while these poems are not counters in an intellectual exercise, they do resolve with unassuming simplicity a depth and complexity of thought. A poem like "Infant Joy," for instance, does carry "hidden" implications, but these implications arise entirely from the religious perspective that underlies the *Songs of Innocence* as a whole. In that perspective, human life is a circular path from Eternity, through the temporal world, and back to Eternity, and it is always this larger perspective that lends ulterior significance to the literal, natural events of the poems. It is this perspective, for example, which gives implicit meaning to the daringly infantile lines:

> I have no name:
> I am but two days old.

That the infant is too new even to have a name is a literal reason for giving it one (the poem is literally about a mother's naming of her baby), but the baby's newness is also the explanation of its joy. The pure joy in being that is expressed in the smiles of a two-day-old infant ("I happy am") must have a source that is prior to and beyond earthly experience, for the baby (lacking even an earthly name) has had no earthly experience.

It has not yet managed to focus its eyes, and has probably not yet taken milk. As yet it knows nothing of this
earth. Thus the joy of the baby is essentially the same
as the joy which warms poor Tom Dacre; it derives
from a divine spark that is inborn and independent of
experience.

It follows from this that the significance of an infant's
joy appears only in relation to an infant's sorrow. Birth
into this world of suffering brings with it prophetic joy,
but it brings tears as well. Blake consciously neglects to
remind us that the two-day-old came crying upon earth,
because he wants to develop in this poem the symbolic
meaning of joy. However, elsewhere he shows that the
other half of our response to being "put on earth a little
space" is to weep. In "On Another's Sorrow," Christ is
seen as coming to earth to

> Hear the woes that infants bear,
>
> . . .
>
> Weaping tear on infant's tear.

On the other side, infant smiles have an equally sacramental meaning:

> He doth give his joy to all;
> He becomes an infant small.

The present tense suggests the constant re-enactment of
Christ's atoning incarnation, and the two poems together suggest the equal importance of smiles and tears
in the phase of life into which the infant has just been
thrust.

As in the "Cradle Song," the mother in "Infant Joy"
watches over her baby as Christ watches over us. (Both
parts of the dialogue are, of course, taken by the mother
whose loving identification with the infant permits her

to speak for it.) And here, as in other poems, the guardian receives as much as she gives:

> Thou dost smile,
> I sing the while.

When the mother chooses this moment of joy to give the child a name, or, rather, to let it name itself, she is quite aware of the symbolic nature of her act: the name, "Joy," is to be symbolic (hopefully) of the child's course of natural life and also prophetic of the child's goal. The mother's choice of a name corresponds to her hopeful prayer, "Sweet joy befall thee," which is equivalent to "Heaven bless thee—both in life and in Eternity."

Her symbolic act of naming her child becomes in this way a basis for the symbolic meaning of the poem's title. "Infant joy" is inborn joy and is therefore the earliest expression of the "Divine Vision." "Joy" is consistently Blake's word for the emotion that accompanies our direct experience of Eternity, just as "Mercy, Pity, Peace, and Love" are his words for the sacramental emotions that accompany our experience of the natural world. Blake's deliberately one-sided emphasis on Joy in this poem should therefore be set against his one-sided emphasis on Mercy and Pity in "On Another's Sorrow." The "dialectical" meaning of the *Songs of Innocence* (if one wishes to call it that) exists within the poems themselves; that is why they have their fullest impact when they are properly read—seriatim and as an autonomous whole.

Because of their daring simplicities the *Songs of Innocence* place greater demands on the reader than any other work by Blake—not greater intellectual demands, of course, but greater imaginative and emotional ones. Like Wordsworth's self-conscious exercises in deliberate simplicity, these poems demand a depth of response that

43

has no obvious basis in their rhetoric, for that is the whole point of their rhetoric: They invite the reader to see a profound significance in childlike verse that corresponds to the profound significance in children themselves. The poems present themselves quite unconcernedly like the children who play under the watchful eyes of the Nurse, but they demand from the reader the Nurse's sympathetic insight into the identity as well as the difference between the childlike and the adult. In other words, the poems make the difficult demand that the reader be at once a child and an adult, and for some readers that will remain, no doubt, an impossible demand.

But there is one piece of childishness that no reader can fairly accuse these poems of—that they deliberately exclude ideas of cruelty and injustice or fail to pass moral judgment on such evils. The deprived children of these poems are usually victims of a failure of love, a failure of guardianship. The poignancy of "Holy Thursday" and "The Chimney Sweeper" lies partly in the unnaturalness of the beadles and the sweep having to take care of children who have been abandoned through a failure of love and guardianship. If the little English boy had loved the little black boy as he should, there would be no point in saying "and he will then love me," and there would be no slavery either. Yet the poems rightly assume that even without failures of love and guardianship men would still have to exercise the Christological emotions of Mercy and Pity. The ills of life do not arise merely because parents have sold children to be chimney sweeps or slave traders have sold them to be slaves. The human failures in these poems, sometimes avoidable sometimes not, ask us to redeem the failure as far as we can ("Then cherish Pity"), but the failures also stand as symbols of the evils in life that are unavoidable:

44

> When wolves and tygers howl for prey,
> They pitying stand and weep;
> Seeking to drive their thirst away,
> And keeping them from the sheep.

Blake tells us as explicitly as may be that the guardian angels cannot keep away the inevitable wolves and tigers:

> But if they rush dreadful
> The angels, most heedful,
> Receive each mild spirit,
> New worlds to inherit.

It is only in those new worlds that Christ's atonement has its full effect:

> Wrath by his meekness,
> And by his health, sickness
> Is driven away
> From our immortal day.

The two ills Blake speaks of here, "wrath" and "sickness," are significant, for while Mercy, Pity, and Love might conceivably overcome "wrath" in ourselves if not in a tiger, no spiritual virtue will overcome "sickness," or those other built-in ills of life, pain and bereavement. Blake does pass implicit judgment on the human failure that produces orphans, sweeps, and slaves, but the plight of these deprived children is also symbolic of built-in evils that ultimately transcend moral judgment.

Finally, there are three poems from the original canon of the *Songs of Innocence* that do not conform to the general pattern I have traced, and it is significant that Blake later transferred these poems, "The Little Girl Lost (and Found)," "The Schoolboy," and "The Voice of the Ancient Bard," to the *Songs of Experience*. None

45

of these poems is among Blake's best, but as a group they are highly important for the light they shed on Blake's intellectual and poetic development. With the "Introduction" to *Experience* and "Ah! Sun-Flower" they belong to that period in late 1789 when Blake, immensely stirred by the French Revolution, was moving toward the revolutionary and naturalistic outlook that informs the *Songs of Experience*. This transitional group of poems will be considered in the next section.

# 4. Year of Revolution

The *Songs of Innocence* contain Blake's first apocalyptic outburst. Its title, "The Voice of the Ancient Bard," harks back to the Ossianic experiments in *Poetical Sketches*, but the tone is unlike anything to be found in Blake's earlier poetry:

> Youth of delight, come hither,
> And see the opening morn,
> Image of truth new born.
> Doubt is fled, & clouds of reason,
> Dark disputes & artful teazing.
> Folly is an endless maze,
> Tangled roots perplex her ways.
> How many have fallen there!
> They stumble all night over bones of the dead,
> And feel they know not what but care,
> And wish to lead others when they should be led.

The inclusion of this poem in the *Songs of Innocence* is inexplicable except on the assumption that Blake's interest in the unity and coherence of his work was less than his interest in writing and publishing a poem written from a new and exciting vantage point. It is true that the other poems of *Innocence* are prophetic poems—prophetic of a bright world that transcends this one. In contrast, "The Voice of the Ancient Bard" prophesies a new terrestrial era. The figure who symbolizes the transformed world is neither a child nor an adult, as in the other poems, but a "youth." The better world is not a traditional Eden or Heaven but a repudiation of all the old traditions, including traditional pieties: We shall no longer "stumble over bones of the dead." The phrase is redolent of the proverb of Hell: "Drive your cart and your plow over the bones of the dead." The morning that opens is less like the dawn of "The Ecchoing Green" than the dawn of "A Song of Liberty":

> The son of fire in his eastern cloud, while the morning plumes her golden breast, Spurning the clouds written with curses, stamps the stony law to dust, loosing the eternal horses from the dens of night crying:
>
> EMPIRE IS NO MORE! AND NOW THE LION & WOLF SHALL CEASE.

It must be admitted that in "The Voice of the Ancient Bard" the character of the new era is left rather vague. There is no clear image of what will follow the departure of "doubt," "reason," "dark disputes," and "folly," though presumably its lineaments are to be found in the "youth of delight" himself. Now, the word, "delight," is suggestive, for while Blake is not altogether consistent, he tends to use this word to connote pleasure in actual existence ("gave thee clothing of delight"), while he tends to reserve the word "joy" to connote the prophetic experience of Eternity. In the *Songs of Innocence* "joy" outnumbers "delight" by a ratio of four to one; in the *Songs of Experience,* "delight" is preponderant by a ratio of two to one.[1] In the *Songs of Innocence,* "care" is seen to be an inevitable part of life; in this poem, the "youth of delight" will have only scorn for those who "feel they know not what but care."

In later years Blake transferred "The Voice of the Ancient Bard" along with "The Little Girl Lost (and Found)" and "The Schoolboy" to the *Songs of Experience.* All three of these poems celebrate with varying degrees of tentativeness a "delight" that lies entirely within the actual world. Since this aspect of these poems is fully discussed in the commentaries, we may proceed immediately to the problem raised by the new kind of fervor they begin to display. The poems are so fundamentally different from those in the canon of *Innocence* that Blake's inclusion of them must be judged an indication that something had occurred in his attitude toward the actual world which made him confident that the "opening morn" was near at hand.

According to the date on the title page, which cannot, of course, be anything but a *terminus a quo,* the *Songs of Innocence* were published in 1789, the year of the French Revolution. Considering the company Blake kept at the house of the radical bookseller, Johnson— Paine, Priestley, Godwin, and Mary Wolstonecraft—it is hardly surprising that he was infected by the revolutionary ecstasy felt by so many in his generation and permanently recorded by Wordsworth:

> Not favour'd spots alone, but the whole earth
> The beauty wore of promise, that which sets,
> To take an image which was felt, no doubt,
> Among the bowers of paradise itself,

1. I discount the ironic use of joy in the parodic poem "Holy Thursday": "Can it be a song of joy?"

> The budding rose above the rose full blown.
> What temper at the prospect did not wake
> To happiness unthought of? 2

That Blake was caught up in this apocalyptic excitement no one who has read his fragmentary work called *The French Revolution* can doubt. The crash of the Bastille changed the flute of the piper to the trumpet of the bard. And why? Because the millennium, as Wordsworth went on to recall, was at hand here in the actual world:

> Not in Utopia, subterraneous Fields,
> Or some secreted Island, Heaven knows where,
> But in the very world which is the world
> Of all of us, the place in which, in the end,
> We find our happiness, or not at all.

This Wordsworthian repudiation of the blest abodes is found in all the triumphal outbursts of Blake's bard; it is expressed with great irony in *Europe* (1794), where the pastoral Heaven prophesied in *Innocence* has become a sinister priestly delusion which tries to make us believe

> That an Eternal life awaits the worm of sixty winters
> In an allegorical abode where existence hath never come.

> [K.240]

If one imagines the mood of those days in late 1789 and early 1790 it is not difficult to imagine how political chiliasm could transform even fundamental religious beliefs. As Tocqueville and others have noted, the Revolution itself had all the marks of a religious movement. It was a religious movement in which the central idea

2. These lines and the ones that follow below were extracted from *The Prelude* by Wordsworth and published in 1815 under the title "French Revolution as it Appeared to Enthusiasts at its Commencement."

was "Nature." The great apocalyptic event being witnessed was not a sudden incursion of the divine into
human affairs, but a rising up from below of repressed
natural forces, themselves inherently divine. When
Blake wrote:

> O Earth, O Earth, return!
> Arise from out the dewy grass;
> Night is worn,
> And the morn
> Rises from the slumberous mass,

["Introduction" to *Experience*]

he was invoking a process that was "nothing out of
nature's certain course," for, indeed, he had already
witnessed its beginnings. In these lines, as later in his
Lambeth Books, he is "foreseeing" as a prophet something that has already begun to happen before his eyes.

The apocalyptic view of the Revolution as a restitution of repressed "natural" forces makes an implicit
assumption about the natural world which Blake did not
fail to perceive. If the fallen state of the world is the
result of a conspiracy between Kings and Priests, and
if the restitution of the terrestrial paradise may be accomplished merely by breaking "this heavy chain," then
the world in its natural state must be inherently good,
inherently divine. Blake's adjective for these repressed
vital energies is "holy." In other words, when Blake
viewed the Revolution as the herald of apocalypse—the
youth of delight coming hither—he viewed terrestrial
life as inherently blessed. The spark of delight has lain
dormant, and now it is about to burst into flame. And
if that is true, then the whole notion that this world is
inherently suffering and fallen must be enthusiastically
repudiated.

This revolution in Blake's thought was, in one sense,
merely a shift in the focus of his prophetic perception:

He was still the prophet of the blest abodes; he had simply shifted their location. Blake had always associated poetry with prophecy, and in the *Songs of Innocence* his sacramental conception of life had caused him to perceive immense value in the Edenic aspects of the natural world, but it cannot be reasonably doubted that the Revolution of 1789 was the occasion for a radical change in Blake's valuation of actual life.

As a documentation of the way in which the events of that year affected Blake, we are fortunate in having something comparable to a controlled experiment— Blake's annotations to Swedenborg in 1788 and in 1790. Blake begins his notes of 1788 with a comment that is helpful in understanding his conception of the soul's journey through life, a fundamental idea both in the *Songs of Innocence* and *The Book of Thel*. The soul, as Blake put the idea in "The Little Black Boy," must be put "on earth a little space," that it "may learn to bear the beams of love." The crucial word is "learn," and in his note to Swedenborg, Blake equates this learning with the acquiring of "understanding": "If God is anything he is Understanding." "Understanding or Heaven . . . is acquired by Suffering and Distress & Experience" (K.89). Thus Mercy, Pity, Peace, and Love are part of the divine scheme of "soul-making." The assumption is that earthly life breeds suffering, and that this suffering educates the soul. On the other hand, everything pertaining to the "natural" side of man is irrelevant to the education of the soul: "Will, Desire, Love, Pain, Envy & . . . are natural, but Understanding is Acquired" (K.89).

In these comments of 1788, Blake proceeds to annotate the passages in Swedenborg which pertain to his favorite early speculation, the distinction between "poetic" knowledge which is "spiritual" and sense perception which is merely "natural":

SWEDENBORG: . . . a wise man perceiveth not from a
knowledge that Love is the life of man, but from Experience of this fact.

BLAKE: They also perceive this from Knowledge, but not
with the natural part.

SWEDENBORG: God . . . cannot be comprehended by a
natural idea because in that idea there is Space.

BLAKE: What a natural Idea is.

SWEDENBORG: A spiritual Idea doth not derive any Thing
from Space, but it derives every Thing appertaining to
it from State.

BLAKE: Poetic idea.                                    [K.89]

This confrontation between spiritual knowledge and
natural experience is particularly clear in Blake's next
note: "Observe the distinction here between Natural
& Spiritual as seen by Man. Man may comprehend, but
not the natural or external man" (K.90). Throughout
these notes "nature" is consistently disparaged, and
most strikingly in the long remark in which Blake speaks
of the shutting-off of spiritual perceptions as a descent
into "meer Nature or Hell" (K.93).

Blake's notes of 1790 to another work by Swedenborg
are rather cursory and short tempered, but their contrast with the notes of 1788 is striking. Two are particularly significant:

SWEDENBORG: All the grandest and purest Truths of Heaven
must needs seem obscure to the natural Man at first
View—

BLAKE: Lies & Priestcraft. Truth is Nature.

SWEDENBORG (continuing his sentence): until his intellectual Eye becomes accustomed to the Light, and can
thereby behold it with Satisfaction.

BLAKE: that is: till he agrees to the Priests' interest.

[K.131]

Blake's newly acquired distaste for Swedenborg was, we
remember, one of his motivations in writing *The Mar-*

*riage of Heaven and Hell,* where the rejection of the distinction between the spiritual and the natural is stated quite explicitly in the form "Man has no Body distinct from his Soul," and "Energy is the only life and is from the Body." The term "Priestcraft" which Blake associates with the now fallen Swedenborg would have been to him, as a Dissenter, a term of abuse at any time. But the sinister responsibility of the Priests for repressing what is natural in man is an idea that Blake has borrowed from radical propagandists of revolution, like Tom Paine. To convince Blake that the strangling of the last king with the entrails of the last priest would unveil the terrestrial paradise required an apocalyptic event. Nothing less than such an event could have altered "meer Nature or Hell" to "Truth is Nature." The immense importance to the *Songs of Experience* of this change in Blake's views will be described in detail in the next two sections, but in this discussion of the fateful transition period between late 1789 and early 1790 I must not defer mentioning two poems of the *Songs of Experience* which, like the transferred poems of *Innocence,* clearly belong to this period. The internal evidence that this is the case is confirmed by external evidence which, again, has very nearly the force of a controlled experiment. For the only two poems in the *Songs of Experience* which bear the marks of Blake's poise between the pastoral pieties of *Innocence* and the energetic this-worldliness of *Experience* ("Introduction" and "Ah! Sun-Flower") are also the only poems in the original issue of the *Songs of Experience* which do not appear in the Rossetti Manuscript of 1793!

"Ah! Sun-Flower," perhaps Blake's most beautiful lyric poem, is fundamentally a poem of Innocence; that is to say, it looks forward to "that sweet golden clime Where the traveller's journey is done." But it is distinguished from the poems in the canon of *Innocence* by its quite uncharacteristic references to repressed natural life. The human figures in the poem are neither children nor adults but, respectively, a "Youth," as in the "Voice of the Ancient Bard," and a "Virgin," as in "The Little Girl Lost." What makes them "weary of time" is not the built-in sorrow of life but the imposed repression of their love:

> Where the Youth pined away with desire,
> And the pale Virgin shrouded in snow.

"Snow" is the repressive smothering of natural instincts (Urizen in the Lambeth books is consistently associated with snow and hoar frost), and "desire" is natural desire. The poem wonderfully evokes the longing for release, but it is a release from repression as well as from the temporal world. It is a poem that is poised in perfect balance between the desire of the Youth for the Virgin and the desire of the moth for the star. It is a poise that Blake would never again achieve. Much later he would call it, with a touch of disparagement, the state of Beulah.

The second poem of the original *Songs of Experience* that is missing from the Rossetti Manuscript is the "Introduction." Its tone is highly similar to "The Voice of the Ancient Bard," though its prophecy is even more ambivalent. Significantly, the spiritual poise of the poem is precisely the same as in "Ah! Sun-Flower"; the Bard pays his respects to both the natural world and Eternity. He is respectful, for instance, of the orthodox Christian myth of the Fall. When Adam and Eve fell, the Bard was there and heard "The Holy Word That walked among the antient trees." He heard God "Calling the lapsed soul" and "weeping in the evening dew." When, however, the Bard-prophet calls for renewal, *he* does not call to the lapsed soul, but to the earth:

> O Earth, O Earth return!
> Arise from out the dewy grass;
> Night is worn
> And the morn
> Rises from the slumberous mass.

Earth has been sleeping. The Fall has been a lethargic slumber of the natural energies. But the poem is ambivalent; when earth does arise, it is to a merely temporary fulfillment:

> Turn away no more;
> Why wilt thou turn away?
> The starry floor,
> The wat'ry shore,
> Is giv'n thee till the break of day.

Since the morn had already risen in the previous stanza, the "break of day" must be the sunrise of Eternity which Blake had been celebrating in the *Songs of Innocence.* The starry floor and the wat'ry shore are given us until the Last Judgment. The poem is a remarkable fusion of naturalistic affirmation with orthodox prophecy, and could have been written only in late 1789 or early 1790.

This was the reason that Blake, the revolutionary of 1793, the composer of the *Songs of Experience,* was not satisfied with the poem. He used it as his introduction to the *Songs of Experience* mainly in order to answer it by satirizing its orthodox pieties. The companion poem, "Earth's Answer," found in the Rossetti Manuscript, satirically converts the "starry floor" to "starry jealousy," the "wat'ry shore" to a prison, and the "Holy Word" to the "Selfish father of Men":

> Prison'd on wat'ry shore,
> Starry Jealousy does keep my den:
> Cold and hoar,

## Year of Revolution

Weeping o'er
I hear the Father of the ancient men.

Selfish father of men!
Cruel, jealous, selfish fear!
Can delight
Chain'd in night,
The virgins of youth and morning bear?

The satire of the bard's prophecy in "Earth's Answer" is self-satire, and vigorous self-satire is one of the most important elements in the other *Songs of Experience*. As I shall show, the impulse to self-satire was the motivating impulse of their composition.

# 5. Blake in the Nineties

The *Songs of Experience* were composed in the midst of a short period of Blake's creative life (1790–95) whose importance cannot be measured by its span. It is the crucial period in Blake's career. It was signalized by an immense burst of creative activity in which Blake "published" not only the *Songs of Experience* but also *The French Revolution, The Marriage of Heaven and Hell, Visions of the Daughters of Albion, The Gates of Paradise, The Book of Urizen, Europe, The Song of Los, The Book of Ahania,* and *The Book of Los.* For ten years afterward Blake was, as a poet, publicly silent. In number of plates (162), the etched work of this period outweighs all the poetry Blake would subsequently publish, and this is astonishing when we consider that his last long work, *Jerusalem,* alone contains 100 plates, and that Blake continued to publish original work through 1822.

The period of the *Songs of Experience* can and should be called "naturalistic." The word has been avoided by

students of Blake largely because he so frequently
castigated nature as being at best the fallen world of
fools and at worst "meer Hell," best and worst being
approximately the same. But none of these denuncia-
tions is found in Blake's work of the early 90s. His later
outbursts against nature are all the more bitter for
being repudiations of views he himself had vigorously
held.

Blake's penchant for self-satire had been manifest as
early as 1784 in *An Island in the Moon,* and after 1790
a large portion of his work would consist of arguments
with and satires of an earlier self. When, for example,
Blake undertook to satirize Swedenborg in his highly
naturalistic work *The Marriage of Heaven and Hell,* he
was also satirizing his own earlier, Swedenborgian views.
Blake was not disposed in his ruthless honesty to protect
any vested interest in previous expenditures of spirit;
and while he did not physically destroy his earlier
works, he did not hesitate to repudiate them. To this
self-satirical pungency we owe the existence of the *Songs
of Innocence and of Experience,* and also a great deal
in the Lambeth Books, *The Four Zoas, Milton,* and
*Jerusalem.*

Blake's first considerable work of the early 90s, *The
Marriage of Heaven and Hell,* begins in a way that
once again shows the path of his movement from the
dissenting Christianity of *Innocence* to the revolutionary
naturalism of *Experience.* For, oddly enough, this anti-
Christian satire begins with a respectful bow to Christianity. The "Argument" to *The Marriage* is similar in
this to the "Introduction" to *Experience* and probably
belongs to the same transitional period of late 1789 and
early 1790:

> Once meek, and in a perilous path,
> The just man kept his course along
> The vale of death.

> Roses are planted where thorns grow,
> And on the barren heath
> Sing the honey bees.
>
> Then the perilous path was planted,
> And a river and a spring
> On every cliff and tomb,
> And on the bleached bones
> Red clay brought forth.

The spiritual abundance brought forth by meekness and justice out of natural aridity collapses into the spiritual aridity of a cunning and opportunistic priesthood who drive the true Christian to rage like Isaiah and Blake in the disestablished wilderness:

> Till the villain left the paths of ease,
> To walk in perilous paths, and drive
> The just man into barren climes.
>
> Now the sneaking serpent walks
> In mild humility,
> And the just man rages in the wilds
> Where lions roam.

The "Argument" ends as it began with the prophecy of a cleansing fire that will re-establish the primal order and redeem the world:

> Rintrah roars & shakes his fires in the burden'd air;
> Hungry clouds swag on the deep.

I have quoted the "Argument" in full because its pieties so obviously clash with *The Marriage of Heaven and Hell* as a whole, just as the pieties of the "Introduction" clash with the other poems of *Experience*. The subsequent parts of *The Marriage* by no means exhort a return to the spiritual rigor and asceticism of early Christianity. What matters here is that we should understand why Blake felt it possible to use the piece as an introduction, and the answer to this is rather easy. The "Argument" describes the process of the Fall and prophesies the Resurrection in a form which exactly parallels the naturalistic interpretation of Fall and Resurrection in the *Marriage*. Even as a revolutionary naturalist Blake remained true to his origins. The structure of his naturalistic interpretation of the Fall came from the dissenting idea that primal Christianity was corrupted by institutionalized religion. In both Falls the "villain" is the same: the priest who drove the true Christian into barren climes is also the priest who repressed natural desires and chained natural energies. In *The Marriage* Blake says nothing about a return to genuine Christianity, but he does prophesy a return to the primal unity of being which existed before man was fragmented and his natural energies repressed by the establishment of pharisaical religion. Thus the earlier idea of Christianity's corruption and the later idea of man's corruption merge into one another, so that the earlier "Argument" is made to symbolize the later apocalyptic naturalism which is the actual argument of *The Marriage*. In this we have a suggestive picture of the process by which one view changed into the other, for if Blake had felt strongly the clash between the ideal of the "meek" and "just" man within a "vale of death" and the ideal of a world in which "the lust of the goat is the bounty of God," he would not have been inclined to preserve the "Argument."

The best place to observe the radical naturalism of *The Marriage* is in the "Proverbs of Hell" which show quite clearly the completeness with which nature has become the norm for Blake's ideas. Some of the proverbs, for example, are directly authenticated by references to the nonhuman natural order:

> In seed time learn, in harvest teach, in winter enjoy.
> All wholesom food is caught without a net or a trap.

Expect poison from the standing water.
Think in the morning, act in the noon, eat in the evening,
   sleep in the night.

But the great majority of the proverbs take their sanction not from observed facts of nature but from Blake's metaphysical conception of the natural order as a whole. That conception can be summarized in three propositions:

(1) The basis of the natural order (reality) is "life" or "energy," a vital force which is the divine substance. All expressions of "life"—strong emotion, sexual drive, strength, instinctive desires—are therefore holy and their repression evil:

The wrath of the lion is the wisdom of God.
The nakedness of woman is the work of God.
The soul of sweet delight can never be defil'd.
He who desires but acts not breeds pestilence.
Dip him in the river who loves water.
The tigers of wrath are wiser than the horses of instruction.

This principle accounts also for some of Blake's propositions elsewhere in *The Marriage:*

Energy is the only life and is from the Body; and
   Reason is the bound or outward circumference of Energy.
Energy is eternal delight.
The voice of honest indignation is the voice of God.
God only Acts and Is in existing Beings or Men.
All deities reside in the human breast.

(2) The essential characteristic of "life" or "energy" is individuality. The divine substance achieves plenitude of being by realizing itself in the most varied possible

forms, thus making this the best, richest, most vital of possible worlds:

> Bring out number, weight & measure in a year of dearth.
> Let man wear the fell of the lion, woman the fleece of
>   the sheep.
> The cistern contains, the fountain overflows.
> The apple tree never asks the beech how he shall grow;
>   nor the lion the horse how he shall take his prey.
> The best wine is the oldest, the best water the newest.
> Exuberance is Beauty.

And elsewhere in *The Marriage:*

> One Law for the Lion and Ox is Oppression.

(3) The individuality of life makes the order of nature a clash between different selfhoods, each following its own instinctive drives and desires. This clash must be encouraged both because it is in the nature of things and because without it there would be no vitality or progress. In the large view the clash of individuals creates not a chaos but a higher, vibrant order because the natural instincts, being divine, cannot betray. Blake's view of nature is a dynamic, metaphysical version of Mandeville's beehive and Adam Smith's invisible hand. The ruthless self-assertion of different selves creates an autonomous and self-regulating organism. And, even within an individual, the self-regulating character of the divine organism expresses itself by forcing all excess into its opposite:

> The road of excess leads to the palace of wisdom.
> Drive your cart and your plow over the bones of the dead.
> The cut worm forgives the plow.
> No bird soars too high if he soars with his own wings.
> Excess of sorrow laughs. Excess of joy weeps.
> The roaring of lions, the howling of wolves, the raging

of the stormy sea, and the destructive sword are por-
tions of eternity too great for the eye of man.
The weak in courage is strong in cunning.
Enough! or Too much.

And elsewhere:

Without contraries is no progression. Attraction and
Repulsion, Reason and Energy, Love and Hate, are
necessary to Human existence.
One portion of being is the Prolific, the other the Devouring. . . . But the Prolific would cease to be Prolific
unless the Devourer, as a sea, received the excess of his
delights.

The three general propositions taken together explain
why the idea of free sexuality is so important in Blake's
writings of this period. The sexual drive is an expression
of the fundamental divine force, just as the sexes themselves are expressions of the tendency of the divine force
to divide itself into opposite principles. To prevent the
free fulfillment of the sexual drive is to thwart the order
of nature and thereby prevent fruition and progression.
Sexuality is the root metaphor for all of Blake's dialectical oppositions. The Prolific is male, the Devourer
female; Energy is male, Reason female, the Strong are
male, the Cunning female. Blake reduces the forces of
nature to two dialectical principles because he has observed that nature or "life" is sexualized. His advocacy
of free and vigorous sexuality and his recurrent use of
sexual metaphors have fundamentally a religious significance.

There is, however, one sort of proverb in the "Proverbs of Hell" which is not in any obvious way naturalistic:

A fool sees not the same tree that a wise man sees.
One thought fills immensity.

## Blake in the Nineties

Every thing possible to be believ'd is an image of truth.
Where man is not, nature is barren.

In the last proverb, the word "barren" is crucial. Without man, nature cannot bring forth. Without man's
capacity to perceive its inherent divinity, nature remains
a brute impenetrable fact. Indeed, nature remains barren *with* man so long as he fails to achieve "Human
existence" by perceiving the infinitude that lies beneath
the surface fact. That is why the process of relief-etching
is symbolic; it works "by corrosives . . . melting apparent surfaces away and displaying the infinite which was
hid." "All that we saw," Blake tells an Angel whose
world was both horrid and finite, "was owing to your
metaphysics."

In these pronouncements Blake has preserved his
earlier idea of a special faculty of religious perception,
but the significance of the change he has made in his
conception of it should not be overlooked. To see the
infinite *in* the actual world instead of beyond the world
is to alter the character of the special religious faculty.
At all times Blake believed that a "fool sees not the
same tree that a wise man sees," but while Blake's wise
man in the 80s and, later, in the 1800s, might see a
sacramental truth of some kind—the tree of life or the
angelic host crying "Holy! Holy! Holy!"—the wise man
of his naturalistic period sees infinite life within the
tree itself. Religious insight was always for Blake the
perception of a divinity that also resides within man;
only like can know like. But while one kind of vision
is the perception of Eternity, the other is a perception
of the natural-infinite. In the early 90s, man's special
faculty is the fruition of the natural order, nature made
conscious of itself. Without man, nature is barren, because man is the fruition of nature. His perception of
the natural infinite is the outward bound of the divine

natural force, just as the soul is the outward bound of the Body, and Reason "the bound or outward circumference of Energy."

Ultimately, then, Blake's concern with a special, visionary mode of perception is the obverse of his concern with the natural order. Like Wordsworth, he finds the fulfillment of nature in man and the fulfillment of man in nature. That is why the apocalyptic resurrection of the fallen world will be an automatic corollary of imaginative perception: Then "the whole creation will be consumed and appear infinite and holy, whereas it now appears finite & corrupt." The way in which this new way of seeing implies man's fusion with the natural order is given in Blake's next pronouncement: "This will come to pass by an improvement of sensual enjoyment." It will come to pass when man ceases to separate himself from the divine by repressing his natural desires. Life is eternal delight. Sensual enjoyment is a fusion with life, and therefore leads to a perception of the infinite. Sensual enjoyment is expansive, bracing, cleansing. Repression is debilitating, pestilential, contracting. "For man has closed himself up, till he sees all things thro' the narrow chinks of his cavern."

The continued popularity of *The Marriage* is an effect of its vigorous and unambiguous irony, its epigrammatic and proverbial style. It has always been a sourcebook of standard quotations from Blake. But the disjunctive form of the work was an artistic dead end. There was no point in etching another discursive manifesto, and at the end of *The Marriage* Blake announced his intention to publish a "Bible of Hell." Before turning to the first book of that Bible—Blake's most ambitious work of the early 90s, *The Book of Urizen*—I shall glance briefly at the two works that immediately followed *The Marriage of Heaven and Hell*.

The first of them, *Visions of the Daughters of Albion*

(1793), is the first narrative expression of Blake's new naturalism, and the Ossianic flavor of its style shows that Blake had not yet decided upon the appropriate vehicle for his new vision. The tale is a kind of Susanna story given a Blakean moral. The central figure, Oothoon, is the beloved of Theotormon. On her way to him she is raped by the priest, Bromion, who then perfidiously accuses her of harlotry. This indictment of the priesthood plays on one of Blake's favorite themes in 1793— that the "Angels" enjoy in secret and by cunning what they forbid the rest of us. Compare the lines from the Rossetti Manuscript:

> I asked a thief to steal me a peach:
> He turned up his eyes.
> I ask'd a lithe lady to lie her down:
> Holy & meek she cries—
>
> As soon as I went
> An angel came.
> He wink'd at the thief
> And smil'd at the dame.
>
> And without one word said
> Had a peach from the tree
> And still as a maid
> Enjoy'd the lady.              [K.163, 261]

The consequence of Bromion's accusation is Theotormon's spurning of Oothoon. Bromion has laid his curse upon the fairest joys, but Theotormon, a passive figure in the poem, has an equal share of guilt. He is an illusioned innocent, which means in 1793 that he is "guided by men's perceptions" and thinks not for himself.[1] He is Blake's satire of his earlier ideal. Tormented by the priestly code (Theo-tormon) and victimized by priestly pieties, he can only shake his head with Mercy and

1. See "Motto to the Songs of Innocence & of Experience," K.183.

Pity. Consequently, he abandons his beloved, and at the end of the poem sits "conversing with shadows" while the daughters of Albion echo Oothoon's sighs.

The interest of the poem resides in the satirical irony of the situation and the Blakean affirmations contained in the lamentations of Oothoon. She is a free spirit. The force of life in her has overcome not only the priestly code but even the petty jealousy that would keep Theotormon to herself alone:

> Such is self-love that envies all, a creeping skeleton
> With lamplike eyes watching around the frozen marriage
>     bed.
> But silken nets and traps of adamant will Oothoon spread,
> And catch for thee girls of mild silver, or of furious gold.
> I'll lie beside thee on a bank & view their wanton play
> In lovely copulation, bliss on bliss, with Theotormon.

[K.194–95]

The vigor of Blake's opposition to the institution of marriage should not be attributed merely to his rejection of unnatural restrictions and his own supposed marital difficulties. Marriage is a restriction upon instinct, but it is not the central one. Part of the intensity of Blake's attack against the "Marriage hearse" comes from the fact that he, like Swedenborg, had given marriage a profound sacramental significance that was far broader than that of the established church. Blake used the term "marriage love" in this Swedenborgian sense as early as "Then She Bore Pale Desire" (ca. 1777–84), and later looked upon his entire naturalistic period as a capitulation to the "spectrous Fiend" who is "the enemy of conjugal love." [2] The attack on the "Marriage

2. "Then She Bore Pale Desire," K.43. The spectrous fiend who is the enemy of conjugal love is repudiated by Blake in a famous letter to Hayley, 23 October, 1804, K.851–52.

hearse" is central to the attack on pious Innocence, because it had been central in Blake's own period of Innocence. The choice of theme is partly determined by the impulse to self-satire.

The same motivation can be detected in the way Blake presents the speeches of Bromion. The only way priestly repressions can be enforced is by the threat of Hell or the promise of Heaven—places that exist in some never-never land. Here is the way Blake turns upon the central themes of *There is No Natural Religion* (a), and the *Songs of Innocence:*

> But knowest thou that trees and fruits flourish upon the earth
> To gratify senses unknown? trees, beasts and birds unknown;
> Unknown, not unperceived, spread in the infinite microscope,
> In places yet unvisited by the voyager, and in worlds
> Over another kind of seas, and in atmospheres unknown.

[K.192]

Heaven is a priestly delusion and so is the idea of a special faculty beyond sense. And to make the repudiation complete, Blake dissociates these delusions from the idea of *true* innocence, which now has nothing to do with supernatural perception and everything to do with following natural desires. Oothoon considers herself an innocent ("Arise my Theotormon, I am pure.") because she knows that "the soul of sweet delight can never be defiled." [3] The touch of the world, instead of soiling, sanctifies:

3. See also another passage in *Visions,* K.193:
> Infancy! fearless, lustful, happy, nestling for delight
> In laps of pleasure: Innocence! honest, open, seeking
> The vigorous joys of morning light.

> Sweetest the fruit that the worm feeds on, & the soul
> prey'd on by woe,
> The new wash'd lamb ting'd with the village smoke.
>
> [K.191]

In the *Visions* Blake first introduced the name of "Urizen"—a deity residing in the human breast who represents man's projection of an unnatural and impossible demand upon himself:

> O Urizen! Creator of men! mistaken Demon of heaven!
> Thy joys are tears, thy labour vain to form men to thine
> image. [K.192]

In Blake's designs he is always imaged as a hoary Jehovah figure, most strikingly in the plate where he holds the Tables of the Law. His name originated, probably, in one of Blake's most consistent and unchanging attitudes —his dislike of the logic-chopping Lockean mind that cannot see beyond the narrow chinks of its cavern. This is the mind that is fallen in all periods of Blake's life, for it can no more see Eternity by the poetic-prophetic faculty than it can see the natural infinite by an improvement of sensual enjoyment. Blake's arch-villain had an immutable persistence. In 1784, for example, he wrote the following bit of dialogue:

> "Sir," said the Antiquarian, "according to my opinion the author is an errant blockhead."
>
> "Your reason—Your reason?" said Inflammable Gass. "Why—why I think it very abominable to call a man a blockhead that you know nothing of."
>
> "Reason, Sir?" said the Antiquarian. "I'll give you an example for your reason. As I was walking along the street I saw a vast number of swallows on the rails of an old Gothic square. They seem'd to be going on their passage, as Pliny says. As I was looking up, a little *outré* fellow, pulling me by the sleeve, cries, 'Pray, Sir, who do all they

belong to?' I turned myself about with great contempt. Said I, 'Go along you fool!' 'Fool!' said he, 'who do you call fool? I only ask'd you a civil question.' I had a great mind to thrash the fellow, only he was bigger than I."

[*An Island in the Moon;* K.44–45]

The little *outré* fellow, the wise fool, is, of course, the positive norm to be set against "Your Reason" of the Antiquarian and Inflammable Gass. It is useful to keep in mind this probable etymology of "Urizen," since it shows the titanic humor behind the name and also indicates what Urizen represents. He is the separate, isolated rational faculty disconnected from genuine religious perception (as in the passage just quoted) and from natural instinct (as in the Lambeth Books).

Another principal figure in the Lambeth Books is Orc (probably from *Orcus* or *Cor*) who represents in their revolted violence all those natural forces which Urizen's laws cannot permanently bend into conformity. His fire is set against Urizen's snow, his youth against his age, his freedom against his bondage. While Urizen is the god of the status quo and is a kind of death wish in man, Orc is the youthful god of revolution and of the life principle. Because he is the redeemer of earth, Orc is frequently (and satirically) identified with Christ. But this messianic redeemer is the violent expression of a divine force which would not require violent revolution if it had not been unnaturally repressed by Urizen. In other words, Orc is a correlative of Urizen, born out of life's need to reassert life. The violence of Orc is the reaction of nature to an action of isolated, separated man, and the principle involved in this reaction is the self-regulating autonomy of nature. Life re-establishes itself through Orc as soon as Urizenic repression reaches its deadliest intensity, just as the fool persisting in his folly becomes wise.

Orc makes his first appearance in Blake's next work, *America*, which is subtitled "A Prophecy." It is a description of the American Revolution in terms of the conflict between the cosmic forces represented by Urizen-England on the one side and Orc-America on the other. This prophetic interpretation of recent history shows the connection in Blake's own thinking between his new apocalyptic naturalism and the exciting political events which precipitated his conversion. He regards the American Revolution as the precursor of the final Revolution of 1789 whose success had sanctioned his present faith. The last plate of *America* prophesies the apocalyptic finality of that Revolution:

> Till Angels & weak men twelve years should govern o'er
> the strong;
> And then their end should come, when France receiv'd
> the Demon's light.                              [K.203]

The invalidation of this prophecy by actual events was an important cause of Blake's subsequent loss of confidence in the apocalyptic naturalism of *America*. His cognizance of this is recorded in the four lines he later added to the "Preludium":[4]

> The stern Bard ceas'd, asham'd of his own song; enrag'd
> he swung
> His harp aloft sounding, then dash'd its shining frame
> against
> A ruin'd pillar in glitt'ring fragments; silent he turn'd
> away,
> And wander'd down the vales of Kent in sick & drear
> lamentings.                                        [K.196]

4. That these lines were added later, and not, as Keynes suggests, merely deleted in some of the copies is indicated by Keynes' own bibliographical evidence. All the early copies, except those listed in Keynes and Wolf as A and B, lack these lines, lack foliation, and lack watermark dates. They all bear the watermark "E P". Copy A,

## Blake in the Nineties

This is the first example we have encountered of Blake's correcting the viewpoint of an earlier work by changing its text, but it is not the last.

This brief introduction to Urizen and Orc serves to introduce the first book of Blake's promised "Bible of Hell," *The Book of Urizen* (1794). Blake's new Bible was motivated by a straightforward and serious as well as a satirical intention. In a serious sense it was to be a truer account of God, Man, and History than that of the Old and New Testaments, because it was to be based on an awareness, lacking in them, that "all deities reside in the human breast." Man makes his own gods. As soon as that is realized it is possible to write a true, theocratic —which is to say, psychological—account of Man and History. *Visions of the Daughters of Albion* was an ironic drama of man's self-delusion and self-defeat cast on the level of individual psychology. *America* had narrated man's redemption from this bondage in the course of actual historical events. *The Book of Urizen* tells the story of the Fall as the typical history of the way man creates a fallen world out of his self-delusions. It is a chapter in Blake's *Phenomenology of Mind,* written twelve years before the publication of Hegel's work. That is the serious intention of the poem.

On the satirical side it is a parody of The Book of Genesis and of all religious codes that formulate myths of Creation and Fall as literal truths. It is a fundamental mistake to regard this apparently cosmological poem as having any serious concern with cosmology. It is a parody of cosmology. All of the figures in the poem are serious-satirical counters for elements in the human

which contains the lines, has foliation and bears the watermarks "J Whatman" and "1794." With this date, how could Copy A be the first issue of a work that was apparently etched in 1793? On the other hand, all the latest copies of the work—N, O, P, and Q—contain the lines and are foliated.

73

mind. The universe—which is to say, nature—is a given that Blake does not seriously attempt to explain; it is the ground of his explanations. The poem is not about the creation of the world but about the way man, narrowing his perceptions, creates for himself a fallen world out of an inherently divine natural order. It describes man's clouding of the doors of perception; the natural world itself remains what it always was—infinite. This point cannot be overemphasized. It should be kept in mind not only when reading *The Book of Urizen* but also in contrasting it with Blake's last long work, *Jerusalem,* which *is* a genuinely cosmological account of the Creation and Fall.

In 1794, however, the psychological account is the true story of the only kind of fall there is:

> Of the primeval Priest's assum'd power,
> When Eternals spurn'd back his religion
> And gave him a place in the north,
> Obscure, shadowy, void, solitary.          [K.222]

There can be no other kind of Fall because the only element in man's soul that can be separated from natural instinct is the independent rational faculty. In this conception Blake is at one with two other Romantic poets of the 90s, Wordsworth and Coleridge, for whom the rational faculty alone can create a world "disconnected, dead and spiritless." The feelings, on the other hand, unite man with the life of things. Blake, like Wordsworth and Coleridge saw the redemption of the separate rational faculty in its unity with feeling—"feeling intellect." [5] This unity, which brings the whole soul of man into activity, is the Imagination or, in Blake's terminology, "Los," an anagram of "soul" and "sol." In *The Book of Urizen* Blake introduces this important

5. See *The Prelude,* Book XIV, line 226.

figure for the first time to symbolize the ideal fusion of intellect with feeling, Urizen with Orc.

While The Book of Genesis begins with the creation of the world from the void, *The Book of Urizen* begins with the creation of the void from the infinite world:

> Lo, a shadow of horror is risen
> In Eternity! Unknown, unprolific,
> Self-clos'd, all-repelling: what Demon
> Hath form'd this abominable void,
> This soul-shudd'ring vacuum?            [K.222]

The separation of Urizen from the primal unity makes it impossible to answer this question, since no one can give an identity to a "self-contemplating shadow":

> Some said
> "It is Urizen." But unknown, abstracted,
> Brooding, secret, the dark power hid.        [K.222]

Of all the Romantic poets, Blake had the most fully developed sense of humor, and is the only Romantic who instead of attacking the rational faculty head-on consistently satirizes it from the rear.

Having created this nothingness from infinitude, Urizen proceeds to construct a world with the only tools he can use—ruler and compass and chronometer:

> Times on times he divided & measur'd
> Space by space in his ninefold darkness.        [K.222]

The heroism of his deluded activity is measured by the impossibility of his task—the forming of a finite world by abstracting it from the natural infinite:

> Dark, revolving in silent activity:
> Unseen in tormenting passions:
> An activity unknown and horrible,

75

> A self-contemplating shadow,
> In enormous labours occupied. [K.223]

With brilliant irony Blake fills Urizen's description of his fruitless toil with the pride of accomplishment:

> First I fought with the fire, consum'd
> Inwards into a deep world within:
> A void immense, wild, dark & deep,
> Where nothing was: Nature's wide womb;
> And self balanc'd, stretch'd o'er the void,
> I alone, even I! the winds merciless
> Bound; but condensing in torrents
> They fall & fall; strong I repell'd
> The vast waves, & arose on the waters
> A wide world of solid obstruction. [K.224]

This opaque world, seen through the narrow chinks of man's cavern, must now have laws. The world man makes by his isolated reason must have a law-giving god, a *deus absconditus* that only reason could invent. Only Your Reason can ask, "Is there not one law for both the lion and the ox?" for it is dissatisfied until it subsumes everything under a universal law.[6] It is only logical, after all, to insist that the lion shall lie down with the lamb for the sake of peace and order:

> Lo! I unfold my darkness, and on
> This rock place with strong hand the Book
> Of eternal brass, written in my solitude:
> Laws of peace, of love, of unity,
> Of pity, compassion, forgiveness;
> Let each chuse one habitation,
> His ancient infinite mansion,
> One command, one joy, one desire,

6. The satire on the uniform law for lion and ox recurs in *The Marriage* (K.158), and *Tiriel* (K.109). The quoted phrase is from *Visions* (K.192).

> One curse, one weight, one measure,
> One King, one God, one Law. [K.224]

The imposition of these uniform, priestly laws completes the creation of Your Reason's world. Now man has to live in it. Blake's description of the confusion that results from his trying to do so is terrifying and also titanically funny:

> And o'er the dark desarts of Urizen
> Fires pour thro' the void on all sides
> On Urizen's self-begotten armies.
> But no light from the fires: all was darkness
> In the flames of Eternal fury.
> In fierce anguish & quenchless flames
> To the desarts and rocks he ran raging
> To hide; but he could not. [K.225]

Since the story of the Creation-Fall is now complete, Blake proceeds to retell the story from the vantage point of Los, the unifying principle of the soul. The creation of Urizen's separate world implies a separation of reason from the primal unity and is therefore a wrenching apart of Urizen from Los. Blake's model is still The Book of Genesis, and he presents this event as a grisly parody of Eve's creation from Adam's side:

> Los wept, howling round the dark Demon
> And cursing his lot; for in anguish
> Urizen was rent from his side.
>     .     .     .
> Los howl'd in a dismal stupor,
> Groaning, gnashing, groaning,
> Till the wrenching apart was healed.
> But the wrenching of Urizen heal'd not. [K.226]

The unhealed wound of Los is an effective symbol of the spiritual injury which the separation of the rational

77

faculty inflicts upon the soul. The wounding of Los is a wounding of Imagination, and Imagination must fall along with the rest of man's world.

Unfortunately, from an artistic point of view, Blake decided at this point to present a third version of the Fall, in which Urizen instead of being wrenched from Los is forged by him "ages on ages." While this abrupt diversion of the narrative is disconcerting, the designs in which Blake depicted it are among his most powerful, and his reasons for presenting the new version are compelling. The two previous versions of the Fall leave an important problem unresolved. Somehow Blake must explain how it was possible that man's soul could have been divided in the first place. In the primal unity, Urizen has no existence as a separate faculty and therefore no power to separate himself from Los. The *possibility* of Urizen's separation, which is to say his separate existence, must be explained. If Urizen could not make himself, then the only creative power in man, Los, the fusion of intellect and feeling, must have made him. The true beginning of the Fall is not the creation of an opaque world by the isolated reason but the formation of an isolated reason in the first place. There is no evil principle in the natural order, but there is the possibility that man's free, creative capacities will go accidentally awry. That is why Los becomes confused and terrified by *his* creation in the same way that Urizen was terrified by his:

> In terrors Los shrunk from his task:
> His great hammer fell from his hand.
> His fires beheld, and sickening
> Hid their strong limbs in smoke. [K.229]

But the most compelling reason for presenting this final version of the Fall is that Blake has left unexplained the origin of Orc. Orc, like Urizen, has no independent existence in the unfallen unity of man's being. How could he exist separately when the very meaning of the primal unity is the fusion of conscious intellect with vital force? Los cannot *create* Orc, since he is that part of Los himself which is still left when Urizen has been formed and man has fallen. The divine spark cannot be put out: "Another flower shall spring because the soul of sweet delight Can never pass away." [7] The origin of Orc, who is the divine force in its unnaturally repressed or separate form, must be associated with the origin of Urizen. But even Los cannot forge the source of his own creative power. Blake's mythical solution to this problem is highly ingenious: When Los perceives Urizen's painful and unnatural state within his self-made world, he begins to feel pity, and since "pity divides the soul" (another thrust at *Innocence*) part of Los becomes a pitying, female principle, Enitharmon. The existence of this delusive and debilitating principle had already been represented in the Urizenic code of "pity, compassion, and forgiveness," but Blake now gives the principle a mythical identity as the female subversion of male strength and vitality. She is the "first female now separate" (K.231), by which Blake means the archetype of female cunning, coyness, secrecy, and false modesty. She is the opposite of Oothoon, the female not separated from the life force. When Los attempted to embrace Enitharmon,

> she wept, she refus'd
> In perverse and cruel delight
> She fled from his arms. [K.231]

One cannot but admire Blake's success in coalescing his favorite themes. Los finally does beget a child upon Enitharmon because, in spite of her perversity, natural

7. *Visions*, K.189.

desire cannot be totally repressed, and out of this union is born Orc. This is no victorious birth, but another separation from man's unified, natural, and unfallen state. The corollary of Orc's separate existence is the usurping victory of Urizen. For Orc's nurture by Enitharmon can be nothing but a cunning restriction:

> A tight'ning girdle grew
> Around his bosom. In sobbings
> He burst the girdle in twain;
> But still another girdle
> Opress'd his bosom. [K.233]

When Orc, like Prometheus, is chained to a rock, the story of the Fall has not really advanced beyond what was implicit in the opening lines of the poem. Blake is making explicit the implications of those lines and is explaining how the seed of redemption (Orc) was planted within the Fall itself. The guiding principle of Blake's account is here again the self-regulating capacity of the natural order. The story of the Fall, involving as it does the binding of Orc, is little different from the story of the fool who persists in his folly.

This positive implication in the story of the Fall is suggested at the end of the poem where Blake returns to Urizen and to his actual subject: man as he exists in his fallen state. The parody of Genesis is continued by equating man's psychological bondage ("bound down to earth by their narrowing perceptions," K.236) with the bondage of the Jews in Egypt. The poem ends with the promise of an apocalypse, which will be the departure of Urizen's children from the psychological Egpyt. Man cannot live forever in the unnatural bondage he has created for himself, and Urizen has discovered his fated incapacity to make the real world into the kind of world he had intended:

He in darkness clos'd view'd all his race,
And his soul sicken'd! He curs'd
Both sons and daughters; for he saw
That no flesh nor spirit could keep
His iron laws one moment.                    [K.235]

Late in 1794 and early in 1795 Blake etched two more
illuminated poems, *Europe* and *The Song of Los*. Since
the latter contains two series of plates titled "Africa"
and "Asia," these works, with *America*, embraced all
four continents and completed the prophecy of the social
and political redemption of the entire world. In both
these works the French Revolution continues to be the
crucial and redemptive event in human history, and
Orc continues to be the saving agent of apocalypse. As
before, the Fall is described as the instituting of a
Urizenic order and the clouding over of the doors of
perception. The millennium which Blake prophesies is
still man's perception of the infinite world as it really
is. In *Europe* this natural paradise is adumbrated on
the first plate, and it is significant that Blake, in the
same disenchanted mood reflected in the four lines added
to *America*, subsequently removed this plate from
*Europe*:[8]

"Then tell me, what is the material world, and is it dead?"
He, laughing, answer'd: "I will write a book on leaves of
    flowers,
"If you will feed me on love-thoughts & give me now and
    then
"A cup of sparkling poetic fancies; so, when I am tipsie,

8. Keynes, disagreeing with Damon (Keynes and Wolf, p. 79), argues
that the lines were not suppressed but were added later. On consideration, I now believe that Keynes has the stronger argument. In
any case, great emphasis should not be laid on the changes in *Europe*, since the lines at issue exist only in copies H and K. The importance of the lines added to *America* is far greater, and is quite
sufficient to carry the burden of the argument.

I'll sing to you to this soft lute, and shew you all alive
The world, where every particle of dust breathes forth its
    joy."                                 [K.237]

In *The Song of Los* this inherent natural paradise is
perceived by the risen man in a parody of biblical prophecy similar to one that occurs in *America:*

Forth from the dead dust, rattling bones to bones
Join; shaking convuls'd, the shiv'ring clay breathes,
And all flesh naked stands: Fathers and Friends,
Mothers Infants, Kings & Warriors.

The Grave shrieks with delight & shakes
Her hollow womb & clasps the solid stem:
Her bosom swells with wild desire,
And milk & blood & glandous wine
In rivers rush & shout & dance,
On mountain, dale and plain.

    The SONG of LOS is Ended.

    Urizen Wept.                           [K.248]

In 1795 Blake etched two more works, *The Book of
Ahania* and *The Book of Los.* To read them is to understand why this year marked the end of Blake's most
vigorous and productive period. His faith in the apocalyptic finality of the French Revolution had faded, and
with it the sanguine vigor of his visionary naturalism.
Orc appears in neither work. Both are pervaded by a
discouraged tone which makes 1795 a likely date for the
despondent additions to *America* and the removal of
the confident first plate of *Europe.*

*The Book of Ahania* is a brilliantly imaginative story
of the failure of all man's revolutionary hopes. It is
divided into chapters and verses and is meant to be the
sequel to *The Book of Urizen,* but it is no longer part
of the optimistic "Bible of Hell" Blake had originally

planned. Blake's Genesis had carried the "theocratic" history of man up to the flight out of Egypt. This, his Exodus, tells the story of mankind being led out of bondage only to wander in the wilderness and to find, instead of the promised land, another kind of bondage. This identification of the Exodus story with the failure of the French Revolution is more than a striking metaphor for a contemporary event. It typifies, through a new myth, the recurrent pattern of man's failed hopes. The archetypal Moses, here called "Fuzon," is not only Robespierre but also Christ. Fuzon's wounding of Urizen is at once Moses' defeat of Pharaoh, Christ's defeat of the Pharisees, and France's defeat of Kings and Priests. But the ephemerality of all these hopeful victories is represented by Urizen's counter victory, and his nailing of Fuzon to the Tree of Mystery. Blake is not implying that the forces of Urizen always directly defeat the forces of life. His implication is even more pessimistic. The forces of life always collapse into the forces of Urizen. Fuzon in his brief moment of victory has already had time to fall:

> "I am God," said he, "eldest of things."     [K.251]

The defeat of one oppressive god is merely the occasion for the institution of another. Moses the great liberator brings Israel not freedom but the Tables of the Law. Christ after defeating the Pharisees is the agent of a religion more pharasaical than the last. The French revolutionists overcame tyranny only to become tyrants themselves:

> The hand of Vengeance found the Bed
> To which the Purple Tyrant fled.
> The iron hand crush'd the Tyrant's head
> And became a Tyrant in his stead.

> ["The Grey Monk," K.431]

If *The Book of Ahania* may be regarded as a revision
of the apocalyptic history presented in *America, Europe,*
and *The Song of Los,* Blake's last etched work of 1795,
*The Book of Los,* may be regarded as a revision or correction of *The Book of Urizen.* It is not a discouraged
sequel to that work, like *The Book of Ahania,* but a
completely new start that tells the same story in a different way and gives it a different interpretation. It, too,
is a parody of Genesis:

> Then Light first began; from the fires,
> Beams, conducted by fluids so pure,
> Flow'd around the Immense. Los beheld
> Forthwith, writhing upon the dark void,
> The Back bone of Urizen appear.          [K.259]

Los is regarded no longer as the eternal prophet who
fuses Urizen and Orc in man's primal unity of being,
but as the eternal prophet impotently raging in the
wilderness. As the creative principle in man, he once
again forges Urizen, but not until he himself has fallen.
Even before he creates Urizen he creates a finite, fallen
world:

> Then aloft his head rear'd in the Abyss
> And his downward-borne fall chang'd oblique
> Many ages of groans, till there grew
> Branchy forms organizing the Human
> Into finite inflexible organs;
> Till in process from falling he bore
> Sidelong on the purple air, wafting
> The weak breeze in efforts o'erwearied.
> Incessant the falling Mind labour'd,
> Organizing itself, till the Vacuum
> Became element, pliant to rise
> Or to fall or to swim or to fly,
> With ease searching the dire vacuity.          [K.258]

Associated with this event is the stifling of the visionary and imaginative principle, which is another way of describing the fall of Los:

> The Immortal stood frozen amidst
> The vast rock of eternity times
> And times, a night of vast durance,
> Impatient, stifled, stiffen'd, hard'ned.　　[K.257]

In this new version of the story, the most important change Blake has made is to view the Fall not as the binding of the vital principle, Orc, but as the binding of the imaginative principle, Los: "The eternal prophet bound in a chain" (K.256). It is not Orc, but Los who

> no longer could bear
> The hard bondage, rent, rent the vast solid
> With a crash from immense to immense,
> Crack'd across into numberless fragments,
> The prophetic wrath struggling for vent.　　[K.257]

The saving principle is no longer the inherent capacity of life to revolt and achieve its own redemption. The failure of the Revolution has proved that. If the resurrection of the fallen world is to be achieved at all, it must be achieved by the imaginative faculty; not by revolution and not by sensual enjoyment but by vision. Blake has by no means abandoned his faith in the inherent divinity of the natural order, but he no longer believes in its capacity to redeem itself. Blake has started on his tortured journey back to Innocence.

In the works of 1795, however, he has hardly taken the first step. The paradise he envisages is still the natural, terrestrial paradise, and if he is no longer confident of its imminent descent, he still believes in its inherent existence. Blake set no date for the victory of imaginative perception, and there is something rather poignant in the way his millennium of the future has now become a golden age of the past. It is as though Blake were lamenting the passing of his own optimistic naturalism. *The Book of Ahania* ends on a note of nostalgia:

> O eternal births sung round Ahania
> In interchange sweet of their joys!
> Swell'd with ripeness & fat with fatness,
> Bursting on winds, my odors,
> My ripe figs and rich pomegranates
> In infant joy at thy feet,
> O Urizen, sported and sang.
> Then thou with thy lap full of seed,
> With thy hand full of generous fire
> Walked forth from the clouds of morning.
>
> .     .     .
>
> But now alone over rocks, mountains,
> Cast out from thy lovely bosom,
> Cruel jealousy! selfish fear!
> Self-destroying, how can delight
> Renew in these chains of darkness,
> Where bones of beasts are strown
> On the bleak and snowy mountains,
> Where bones from the birth are buried
> Before they see the light?
>
> FINIS                          [K.255]

And *The Book of Los* begins with this same nostalgia:

> Eno, aged Mother,
> Who the chariot of Leutha guides
> Since the day of thunders in old time,
> Sitting beneath the eternal Oak
> Trembled and shook the steadfast Earth,
> And thus her speech broke forth:
> "O Times remote!
> "When love and joy were adoration,
> And none impure were deem'd:

Not Eyeless Covet,
Nor Thin-lip'd Envy,
Nor Bristled Wrath,
Nor Curled Wantonness."                    [K.255–56]

The *Songs of Experience* were composed about 1793 in
the full bloom of Blake's revolutionary fervor and optimistic naturalism. The golden age they implicitly
prophesy is still in the hopeful future.

# 6. The Songs of Experience

In this section I propose to show that the *Songs of Experience,* composed about 1793 and published in 1794, display the same kind of self-satire and revolutionary naturalism found in the Lambeth Books of 1793 and 1794. The most important source of materials for studying the *Songs of Experience* is Blake's notebook, generally called the Rossetti Manuscript. Except for the two poems already discussed in Section 4 above, all of the poems contained in the first issue of *Experience* are found in the Rossetti Manuscript. Though Blake used this notebook over a long period (from ca. 1793 to ca. 1811) it is possible, thanks to the labors of Professor Sampson and Sir Geoffrey Keynes, to study separately the portion Blake used in 1793. All references to the Rossetti Manuscript will be to this portion of it.

The most interesting and informative feature of the Manuscript is the unity of its contents. All the pieces in it are poems of revolutionary naturalism having a common array of images and a common set of values. For this reason, the Manuscript is an invaluable aid to the interpretation of individual poems in *Experience*. If, for example, a reader is puzzled by the symbolism of Blake's brilliant little poem "The Sick Rose," he need merely turn to the other poems of the Manuscript to discover the Blakean connotations of "night," "crimson joy," "invisible worm," and "dark secret love," and he will discover them with a certainty that no amount of isolated analysis could attain. I shall first quote the poem as it appears in *Experience*, and then quote a series of extracts from the Rossetti Manuscript which illuminate its meaning:

> O Rose, thou art sick!
> The invisible worm
> That flies in the night
> In the howling storm,
>
> Has found out thy bed
> Of crimson joy,
> And his dark secret love
> Does thy life destroy.

The following Manuscript passages, numbered according to Keynes, are quoted in the order in which they occur:

2.

> I told my love, I told my love,
> I told her all my heart,
> Trembling, cold in ghastly fears
> Ah she doth depart
>
> Soon as she was gone from me
> A traveller came by
> Silently, invisibly—
> O, was no deny. [lines 5–13, K.161]

89

13.

Like to holy men by day
Underneath the vines they lay
Like to serpents in the night
They embraced my blossoms bright.

[lines 36–40, K.167]

20.

I slept in the dark
In the silent night
I murmured my fears
And I felt delight.

In the morning I went
As rosy as morn
To seek for new Joy
But I met with scorn.                    [K.170–71]

21.

Why darkness and obscurity
In all thy words & laws,
That none dare eat the fruit but from
The wily serpents jaws?
Or is it because Secrecy gains
     females' loud applause?

[lines 5–9, K.171]

22.

The modest rose puts forth a thorn
The humble sheep a threat'ning horn
While the lilly white shall in love delight
Nor a thorn, nor a threat, stain her beauty bright.

[draft of "The Lilly," K.171]

29.

Love to faults is always blind
Always is to joy inclin'd,
Lawless, wing'd, & unconfin'd,
And breaks all chains from every mind.

Deceit to secrecy confin'd
Lawful, cautious & refin'd
To everything but interest blind
And forges fetters for the mind.                    [K.175]

31.

O Rose thou art sick;
The invisible worm
That flies in the night
In the howling storm

Hath found out thy bed
Of crimson joy.
O, dark secret love
Doth life destroy.

[first draft of "The Sick Rose," K.175]

The negative, Urizenic values Blake satirizes in the
poems of the Rossetti Manuscript and the positive,
Orcan values he celebrates are precisely those he satirizes
and celebrates in the *Visions, America,* and *The Book of
Urizen.* This is easily shown by aligning the positive
images to be found in the Manuscript against the negative images. The words are Blake's:

| *Negative* | *Positive* |
|------------|------------|
| Death | Life |
| Lawful | Lawless |
| Secret | Open |
| Age | Youth |
| Dark | Light |
| Female | Male |
| Invisible | Honest |
| Night | Morning |
| Chaste | Casting Seed |
| Abstinence | Gratified Desire |
| Cold | Fire |
| Winter | Spring |
| Weeds | Flowers, Fruits |

| Negative | Positive |
|----------|----------|
| Serpent | Eagle |
| Sickness | Health |
| Indolence | Play |
| Desart | Harvest |
| England | America |
| Bound | Free |
| Chain'd | Unconfin'd |
| Charter'd | Wing'd |
| Marriage | Free Love |

Lest this very incomplete list appear misleading in its symmetry, I quote as a representative poem number twenty-four of the Manuscript:

> Are not the joys of morning sweeter
> Than the joys of night?
> And are the vig'rous joys of youth
> Ashamed of the light?
>
> Let age & sickness silent rob
> The vineyards in the night;
> But those who burn with vig'rous youth
> Pluck fruits before the light.          [K.172]

The eighteen poems that Blake culled from the Rossetti Manuscript and etched for the *Songs of Experience* express precisely the same naturalistic values as the other poems of the Manuscript. Five of the poems he culled are parodies of individual poems in the *Songs of Innocence*, but these parodic poems display precisely the same values as all the others, and if I omit to mention these parodic poems now, it is only because I want to discuss them separately in a moment. The unity of outlook of these eighteen poems is a unity that was imposed on them by Blake's powerfully optimistic mood in 1793, the mood in which he composed *Visions of the Daughters of Albion* and *America.*

Now the *Songs of Experience* are generally thought to be bitter poems, and in a sense they are, but their bitterness is that of indignation. They protest against and satirize a state of affairs which need not exist. The voice behind the poems is the voice of a reformer whose indignation is roused by the confrontation of unnecessary barriers to a state of life in which man could be joyful, titanic, and free instead of unhappy, restricted, and downtrodden. The bitterness is not against life but entirely against kings, priests, and the marriage hearse. Take, for example, one of the best poems of *Experience,* and one of the bitterest:

> London
> I wander thro' each charter'd street,
> Near where the charter'd Thames does flow,
> And mark in every face I meet
> Marks of weakness, marks of woe.
>
> In every cry of every Man,
> In every Infant's cry of fear,
> In every voice, in every ban,
> The mind-forg'd manacles I hear.
>
> How the Chimney-sweeper's cry
> Every black'ning Church appalls;
> And the hapless Soldier's sigh
> Runs in blood down Palace walls.
>
> But most thro' midnight streets I hear
> How the youthful Harlot's curse
> Blasts the new born Infant's tear,
> And blights with plagues the Marriage hearse.

The woes that the poet sees and hears are entirely owing to manacles that are mind-forged, and thus to artificial constrictions by Your Reason.[1] It is the isolated human reason that has created the repressive institutions of church, monarchy, and marriage; and all the woes of "London" are owing to these artificial institutions. The cry of the chimney sweep affronts the church that is responsible for it; the soldier's sigh affronts the palace, and the harlot's curse the marriage hearse. Without a church which sustains social injustice by promises of Heaven, there would be no chimney sweeps. Without kings who wage war for their private interest, empire would be no more and the lion and wolf would cease. Without marriage there would be no "unacted desires" and therefore no harlotry. The obverse of the poem's bitterness is a powerful faith in the rightness and perfection of the liberated natural world.

"London" is a poem of social satire, directed against social institutions. It implicitly advocates political and social revolution. This is true also of "Holy Thursday" and "The Chimney Sweeper," which like "London" are set in the city and are directed against the manifest evils of the social order. The majority of the *Songs of Experience,* however, are poems of psychological satire which implicitly advocate a psychological revolution. But the distinction between social and psychological satire in these poems is really a false one that pertains to their emphases rather than their substance.

The fundamental satire is always psychological because the source of all human ills is false metaphysics. The causes of social injustice and of individual spiritual disease are always the same mind-forged manacles. The Rose is sick for the same reason London is sick, and the revolution that will make London healthy is a political

1. I venture to transliterate "Urizen" here because I believe "Your Reason" to be the primary significance of the name during the early 90s. Later on, the name takes on a rich life of its own.

manifestation of the psychological revolution that will cure the rose. The revolution will result in man's return to his unfallen state as part of the natural order, because his Fall was, in the first place, his spiritual separation from the natural order. This separation of man from nature is entirely owing to Your Reason's isolation from the primal unity. The mind-forged manacles are entirely owing to Your Reason.

Thus the central poem of the *Songs of Experience* is "The Human Abstract." While it shows the origin of only one invention of Your Reason—institutional Christianity—and while it singles out for satire Mercy, Pity, Peace, and Love, it describes the typical origin of all the mind-forged manacles. They are in every case "human abstracts," ideas artificially constructed in abstraction from the natural reality. Only man is capable of making such abstracts, and within man only one of his faculties—the isolated reason. Thus the tree of mystery, like all the other fallen institutions, is simply a misguided human invention:

> The Gods of the earth and sea
> Sought thro' Nature to find this tree.
> But their search was all in vain:
> There grows one in the Human Brain.     [K.217]

The *Songs of Experience* are generally called poems of disillusionment, and the word "Experience" supports this conception, since "Experience" as Blake conceived it when he wrote these poems implies a repudiation of former illusions. Now, the *Songs of Experience* are poems that express disillusionment in the prevailing social and religious order that had been accepted in the *Songs of Innocence*; they express no disillusionment whatever in the infinite possibilities of life. I have already mentioned that one of Blake's favored words in these poems is "delight," a word that implies happiness and fulfillment in actual life. With respect to actual life there is no disillusionment in these lines:

> While the Lilly white shall in Love delight
> Nor a thorn, nor a threat stain her beauty bright.

["The Lilly"]

nor in:

> Because I was happy upon the heath.

["The Chimney Sweeper"]

nor in:

> But if at the Church they would give us some Ale,
> And a pleasant fire our souls to regale
> We'd sing and we'd pray all the live-long day,
> Nor ever once wish from the Church to stray.

["The Little Vagabond"]

The three passages just quoted, besides showing that Experience does not imply disillusionment in life, also show that it does not imply a loss of innocence. Like Oothoon in the *Visions,* the Lilly white is an innocent. She remains unstained by thorn or threat. The speakers of the other two passages, the Chimney Sweeper and the Little Vagabond, are innocents. It has rarely been noticed that there are, oddly enough, several innocent children in *Experience.* The child in "A Little Boy Lost," like the other children of *Experience,* speaks a divine truth that is authenticated by his total absence of hypocrisy and subterfuge, in short, by his innocence. These children, like the children of *Innocence,* are close to God. That is to say, they are close to Nature. Like the children of *Innocence,* they exist spiritually in an unfallen world that is an image of man's redemption; their naturalistic

Eden is the counterpart to the heavenly Eden envisioned in the *Songs of Innocence*. To enter the kingdom of God it is still necessary to become like a little child—like a child of *Experience,* who is free from the adult impositions of Your Reason.

I shall now, in what follows, give an account of the way the *Songs of Experience* came to be composed. Part of the account must necessarily be conjectural, but it will be an attempt to accommodate all known relevant facts—an attempt that has not hitherto been made. Blake apparently first conceived of *Experience* as a penitential work that would cancel out the sins he had committed in *Innocence*. His first recorded idea was to issue the *Songs of Experience* as a separate, companion volume to *Innocence,* as promised in the *Prospectus* of October, 1793:

7. Songs of Innocence, in Illuminated Printing,
   Octavo, with 25 designs, price 5s.
8. Songs of Experience, in Illuminated Printing,
   Octavo, with 25 designs, price 5s.       [K.208]

The point in time when Blake decided to bind the two works together as a single work is uncertain, but it may have been after he had issued copy A, which lacks a general title page and numbers the pages of each work separately.[2] The importance of the evidence in the *Prospectus* is that it suggests that Blake's original conception of *Experience* was primarily satirical rather than systematic. Each work was to have twenty-five designs, and it is highly probable that when he issued the *Prospectus,* Blake intended to provide poem-for-poem parodies of the *Songs of Innocence*.

2. The copies are identified by capital letters in Keynes and Wolf, where the alphabetical sequence is meant to correspond with the chronological sequence.

The satirical intention was still paramount after he had composed all the poems that would be used in the first issue of the work. This is certain because all of these poems within the Rossetti Manuscript precede number fifty-six, which Blake entitled "Motto to the Songs of Innocence & of Experience." By this time, then, Blake had decided to bind the two series together, but the "Motto" shows that Blake's primary aim was still to satirize *Innocence*:

> The Good are attracted by Men's perceptions,
> And Think not for themselves;
> Till Experience teaches them to catch
> And to cage the Fairies & Elves.
>
> And then the Knave begins to snarl
> And the Hypocrite to howl;
> And all his good Friends shew their private ends,
> And the Eagle is known from the Owl.          [K.183]

The first stanza describes the progress of "The Good" from Innocence to Experience. In Innocence, the Good accept "men's perceptions"—the standard and customary attitudes of society. But then they move from Innocence by beginning to think for themselves. At this point they cage the "Fairies and Elves"—by which Blake means childish superstitions such as Mercy, Pity, Peace, and Heaven. What Blake has traced in this stanza is a movement from illusion to truth, illusion being entirely on the side of Innocence and truth on the side of Experience. Furthermore he has, according to his own interpretation of the matter in the 90s, traced his own movement from Innocence to Experience. He has rejected traditional pieties, has begun to think for himself, and has caged the fairies and elves by satirizing them in *Experience*.

The autobiographical character of the "Motto" is

certified in the second stanza, which describes the consequences of rejecting "men's perceptions" and thinking for oneself. The plural of the first stanza ("The Good") becomes the autobiobraphical singular in the second. As soon as a man begins to speak an unacceptable truth, all his supposed good friends show their colors. Thus to speak an unacceptable truth (like the child in "A Little Boy Lost") does at least serve to separate true friends from false. They either become revolutionary Eagles or prudent Owls—prudence being "a rich ugly old maid courted by Incapacity" (K.151). When he wrote the "Motto," then, Blake's primary intention in etching the *Songs of Experience* was to satirize and repudiate the *Songs of Innocence,* and the application of the "Motto" to his own spiritual history shows the degree to which the satire of *Innocence* was also an act of penitential self-satire.

Since the "Motto" was written after the *Songs of Experience* had been composed, it is reasonable to assume that the satirical intention implied by the *Prospectus* had continued to be Blake's primary intention when he wrote the poems. It is, in fact, altogether likely that Blake was still intending to compose a set of poem-for-poem parodies. If one deletes from *Innocence* those poems which Blake at one time or other removed from that work, it would contain exactly twenty-five designs—the number allotted in the *Prospectus* to each series. Certainly the idea of a set of parodies had come early in the course of composing the poems in the Rossetti Manuscript. The first of these—a parody of "The Divine Image"—is number eight in the Manuscript. It ends:

> And Miseries increase
> Is Mercy, Pity, Peace.                    [K.164]

This was immediately followed by an attempt to parody "A Cradle Song":

> O the cunning wiles that creep
> In thy little heart asleep.
>
> [lines 14–15, K.165]

The very inferior quality of these two attempts apparently discourage Blake, since he did not write another parody before number twenty-three, "Nurse's Song." Then he composed his masterpiece, "The Tyger" (no. 25), a poem that does full justice to the grandeur of his naturalistic faith, but which begins as a parody of the childish questions in "The Lamb." The success of this poem was heartening enough to induce another attempt to parody "The Divine Image." The parody (no. 28) was first entitled "The Human Image" and then "The Human Abstract." That, too, was a success, but Blake's confidence waned when he managed to write only a truncated parody of "Night," which he called "Day" (no. 37):

| Night | Day |
| --- | --- |
| The sun descending in the west, | The Sun arises in the East |
| The evening star does shine | Cloth'd in robes of blood and gold; |
| The birds are silent in their nest | Swords & spears & wrath increast |
| And I must seek for mine. | All around his bosom roll'd |
| | Crown'd with warlike fires |
| | & raging desires. |

But confidence waxed again in numbers 47, 51, and 56, "The Chimney Sweeper," "Holy Thursday," and the "Motto."

At this point Blake had composed a total of nine parodies of *Innocence,* only five of which were suitable for etching. The prospect of achieving successful parodies of the other poems of *Innocence* had greatly diminished. Aside from "The Tyger," which was far more than a mere parody, Blake's most successful attempts had been those which could make capital of the social evils fostered by Mercy, Pity, Peace, and Love. It had been easy enough to satirize the complacent attitude of *Innocence* toward the poor and miserable, toward chimney sweeps, and charity school children, but it had been considerably harder to parody "A Cradle Song" and "Night." Blake now, wisely, gave up the attempt.

He did not, however, give up the idea of a satirical countervolume to *Innocence*. It is impossible to determine the precise sequence of events, but apparently Blake's next step was to go over the poems he had already composed to choose those suitable for such a countervolume. In doing so, he discovered that the first two stanzas of a nine-stanza poem (no. 13) could be used as a nonce parody of "Infant Joy," and he appended, with different ink, the title "Infant Sorrow." By the same inspired opportunism he later gave the poem beginning "Nought loves another as itself" (no. 35) the nonce title "A Little Boy Lost." But these nonce parodies could not fill the required twenty-five plates. Blake concluded that the *Songs of Experience* would have to be culled from the best poems, parodic or not, in the Manuscript.

This decision did not, however, change Blake's satirical and self-satirical conception of the proposed countervolume. As late as his actual etching of the plates this was still his fundamental conception, as can be seen in the frontispiece he etched for the *Songs of Experience*. This visual introduction to *Experience* is a brilliant little parody of the frontispiece to *Innocence*. The earlier design had shown a shepherd gazing upward at a child on a cloud. Behind the shepherd Blake had depicted a flock of quietly grazing sheep. Here were several primary themes of *Innocence*: the divine inspiration of the child and the adult; the Christlike joy in the child and the Christlike guardianship exercised by the shepherd;

the peace of the sheep who know when their shepherd is nigh. In the new design the sheep are still grazing and the shepherd wears the same skin-tight garment, but the winged child is now sitting squarely on the shepherd's head and seems to be enjoying a bouncy ride. The shepherd no longer gazes upward, but looks straight ahead at the reader. There is no bitterness in the new design, but there is a vigorous and brilliantly ironic translocation of values. Instead of looking upward to Heaven, the poet looks outward to an actual world having infinite value and infinite possibility, and the cherub that inspires him is squarely in that world. Blake pokes fun at *Innocence* for its trust in "an allegorical abode" and its failure to look at the world as it is, but he also affirms the great vitality of the new perspective.

The satirical and parodic conception of the *Songs* gave way to a broader, philosophical conception sometime between the production of copy A and copy B, the copy in which Blake appended the general title page *Songs of Innocence and of Experience, Shewing the Two Contrary States of the Human Soul.* This imposition of a more systematic relationship between the two volumes was induced by two considerations. The first was a practical one. While the *Songs of Experience* had originally been conceived as a separate volume of parodies, it had turned out to be a volume of poems of which the majority bore no direct satirical relationship to the individual poems of *Innocence.* If it were issued as a separate volume, its satirical point would be missed, since in most of its poems the reader would (quite correctly) fail to perceive any direct relationship to the poems of *Innocence.* Blake's first attempt to solve this problem was to compose the "Motto," but this attempt failed, both because the "Motto" lacked distinction as a poem and because it preserved the satirical emphasis that, as Blake came to realize, could not really unify the two works. The only conception that could unify them was one in which the two volumes were viewed as expressions (which indeed they were) of two distinct outlooks or states of the soul.

The second consideration that induced Blake to add his general title page was his recognition that the ruthless rejection of Innocence was not altogether consistent with his new philosophical ideas. In *The Marriage of Heaven and Hell* he had insisted that the Angelic and Heavenly were as necessary to human existence as the Satanic and Hellish. Thus Innocence is not a mere state of illusion on the pathway to truth but a necessary contrary to Experience. This is the dialectical relationship Blake suggested in the new title page. But the new title has precisely the same problematical character that numerous readers have observed in the similarly systematic title *The Marriage of Heaven and Hell*. The new title to the *Songs* pays lip service to a dialectical unity in which Innocence is just as important as Experience, but it fails to describe the fact that Innocence is in general satirized and Experience celebrated. Blake *says* in *The Marriage* that the Devourer is necessary to the Prolific, but the work is primarily a celebration of the Prolific. In the systematic unity which the new title imposed on the *Songs,* he *implies* that Innocence is as permanent and as necessary to human existence as Experience, but the addition of the countervolume is more a repudiation than a marriage. On the other hand, it is only fair to add that the vigorous opposition between the two works does conform to the vital strife of opposites to which Blake gave a high religious value in the 90s. In that sense the title is genuinely descriptive.

It is descriptive in still another way. There are two exceptions to the outright repudiations of Innocence among the etched Rossetti Manuscript poems, and these two poems show quite certainly the kind of dialectical necessity Blake meant to give Innocence when he added the general title page. The first is "The Clod and the Pebble":

> "Love seeketh not Itself to please,
> "Nor for itself hath any care,
> "But for another gives its ease,
> "And builds a Heaven in Hell's despair."
>
> So sung a little Clod of Clay
> Trodden with the cattle's feet,
> But a Pebble of the brook
> Warbled out these metres meet:
>
> "Love seeketh only Self to please,
> "To bind another to Its delight,
> "Joys in another's loss of ease,
> "And builds a Hell in Heaven's despite."

This confrontation of Heaven and Hell is a more convincing version of the necessary contraries than any of Blake's abstract statements in *The Marriage of Heaven and Hell*. The clod of clay is an innocent whose selfless love is just as necessary to existence as the female sex is. The pebble of the brook, on the other hand, is aware that "nought loves another as itself" and he may even be aware that his ruthless male mastery is just what the clod of clay wants.[3] She would hardly be able to cope with another clod of clay. We should not be misled by the verb "bind" which Blake associates with the pebble. That is one kind of binding he does not object to; it is, in fact, the kind of binding Orc, the great liberator, engaged in when he seized the nameless Female in the "Preludium" to *America*. The natural order requires both soft love and hard love, selflessness and selfishness, passivity and activity, female and male. The poem gives equal value to Innocence and Experience in a world

3. The phrase is quoted from "A Little Boy Lost."

whose richness and diversity has room for both the lion and the ox and a different law for each.

The other poem which allots value to both Innocence and Experience is "The Tyger," the one poem in which Blake combines parody with philosophical and tonal comprehensiveness. He who made the Lamb also made the Tiger, but he who made the Tiger made the Lamb. "Every thing that lives is holy," the gentle and selfless, as well as the ruthless and cruel. The poem acknowledges the value of the Lamb, but reserves its implicit satire for those who believe that only lambs, angels, and clods of clay are holy. This implicit satire, however, remains secondary to the affirmation which the poem makes in its brilliant and complex way of the divinity of both the Tiger and the Lamb. In this poem both are necessary to the richest of possible worlds.

But it is significant that these two genuinely comprehensive and dialectical poems are poems of *Experience*. The insight implied by the general title page into the value of both Innocence and Experience is an insight that Experience alone possesses. To Innocence, pebbles, tigers, cruelty, and pain have no ultimate truth or value in themselves because they are to be ultimately overcome. To Experience, on the other hand, they are just as fundamental as lambs, clods, selflessness, and joy because they are necessary components of a world which, the doors of perception being cleansed, is infinitely holy. Thus while Blake's systematic conception of the *Songs*, his endorsement of the two contrary states of the soul, assents to the necessity of each state, it entirely rejects the exclusiveness of Innocence and the "allegorical abode" to which it turns for consolation. The dialectical or systematic viewpoint implied in the title page belongs entirely to Experience, and Experience has the last word. This conception of the *Songs* was to change.

# 7. Return to Innocence

Blake's long public silence after 1795, a silence that veiled an immense spiritual turmoil, ended with the publication in about 1805 of a single lyric poem, "To Tirzah." [1] Blake relief-etched this poem and added it to the *Songs of Innocence and of Experience.* He thought it fitting that the *Songs,* the work that embodied more of his spiritual history than any other, should be chosen to record the latest chapter of that history. Blake's characteristic procedure when he changed his views had been to correct his past errors by altering the text in which they were embedded. This he had done in 1794 when he corrected *Innocence* by adding *Experience,* and again in 1795 when he added four lines of bitter disillusionment to *America.* He fundamentally revised the text of *The Four Zoas* twice. Later, he added several plates to *Milton* in order to bring its doctrines into harmony with those of *Jerusalem.* Still later he erased confessional matter from *Jerusalem* in order to annihilate all vestiges of

1. The dating is discussed in the commentary on that poem.

earlier mistakes.[2] The last addition which Blake made to
the *Songs*—"To Tirzah"—was a poem that not only
repudiated the naturalism of *Experience* but marked a
return (though Blake's beliefs were never to be exactly
as they had been) to the Christian pieties of *Innocence*.
The vigor of his repudiation and the ardor of his coun-
ter-affirmation are best shown in the words of the poem.
(The figure Tirzah represents the physical, natural aspect
of the world and man):

> Whate'er is Born of Mortal Birth
> Must be consumed with the Earth
> To rise from Generation free:
> Then what have I to do with thee?
>
> The Sexes sprung from Shame & Pride,
> Blow'd in the morn; in evening died;
> But Mercy chang'd Death into Sleep;
> The Sexes rose to work & weep.
>
> Thou, Mother of my Mortal part,
> With cruelty didst mould my Heart,
> And with false self-decieving tears
> Didst bind my Nostrils, Eyes, & Ears:
>
> Didst close my Tongue in senseless clay,
> And me to Mortal Life betray.
> The Death of Jesus set me free:
> Then what have I to do with thee?

To trace the path of Blake's development from *The
Book of Los* (1795) to "To Tirzah," it will be necessary

2. The number of plates Blake added to *Milton* varied from copy
to copy. The latest plates are, as numbered in K.: 4, 10, 18, and 32.
See Keynes and Wolf, and also the discussion of *Milton* in *The
Prophetic Writings of William Blake,* ed. D. J. Sloss and J. P. R.
Wallis (2 vols. Oxford, Clarendon, 1926), *1,* 342–52. The most tan-
talizing of the erasures in *Jerusalem* are those on plate 3. They occur within an explicitly autobiographical address "To the Public"
and apparently refer penitentially to past errors. See Keynes, pp.
620–21.

to examine some of the obscurest passageways in his literary remains, and disentangle some of its knotted chronological strands.

The course of Blake's monumental struggle can be partly charted in his extant letters, over three-fourths of which belong to the period 1800–05. (The letters from all the other periods of Blake's life are rather sparse, and fill only eleven pages in Keynes' edition.) But by far the most important sources of insights into this crucial period of Blake's development are the extant poetic manuscripts from that period, and particularly the manuscript of the long, abandoned poem, *The Four Zoas*. The reader confronts in this manuscript the mutilated remnants of at least three different poems or, rather, of a single poem that underwent at least two fundamental revisions. These revisions, like all the others in Blake's works, were undertaken in order to convert "incorrect" earlier ideas into "correct" new ones. The first draft of the poem, composed between 1797 and about 1800, was partly erased and partly destroyed by Blake. Of this purely early material, only two short fragments remain. However, Blake used a great deal of this earlier matter in the second version (ca. 1800–03) which he continued to write down on proof sheets to his illustrations of Young's *Night Thoughts*. This is the base manuscript of the poem as it now exists. To this stratum of the poem he then, about 1804–05, interpolated still other matter, and one entire section of the poem (Night VIII) belongs to this period.[3]

The first version of *The Four Zoas* (*Vala*) may have

3. See the discussions of the poem in Sloss and Wallis, *1*, 136–43, and especially in *Blake's "Vala,"* ed. H. M. Margoliouth (Oxford, Clarendon Press, 1956), pp. xi–xxvii, 97–181. These views are confirmed in Erdman, *Blake, Prophet against Empire*, pp. 369–74. Erdman also divides the composition of the poem into three stages (pp. 268–71).

been undertaken as early as 1795, since the first line
(deleted) of the manuscript begins:

> This is the Song of Eno,

which recalls the opening line of *The Book of Los* (1795):

> Eno, aged Mother.

On the other hand, Blake certainly did not begin working in earnest on the poem before 1797, the year of his
intensive work on the illustrations to the formal model
for this poem, Young's *Night Thoughts*. The kind of
poem he planned to write in 1797 is suggested by the
title page of that year: *Vala Or The Death and Judgement of the Ancient Man a DREAM of Nine Nights by
William Blake 1797*. The change in Blake's name for
Nature from "Eno" to "Vala" is significant. Eno had
been, in *The Book of Los,* a homely and rather friendly
Ossianic matriarch. Now she is a delusive female. This is
confirmed by one of the early fragments of the poem
that have been preserved:

> Beneath the veil of Vala rose Tharmas from dewy tears.
>
> [frag. K.380]

Vala is both a veil and a vale, a covering of expanded
perceptions and a vale of tears. The change of name suggests a change in Blake's evaluation of the natural world.
Tharmas (man's physical aspect) is born out of a covering
and a sorrow. This disvaluation of the natural world had
been foreshadowed in 1795 in Blake's manifesto of his
disillusionment in the Revolution—*The Book of Ahania*.

On the other hand, the last Lambeth Book of 1795,
*The Book of Los,* had foreshadowed a more positive
aspect of that disillusionment. The figure of redemption
was no longer the liberator of natural energy, Orc, but

the agent of imaginative perception, Los. The earliest extant passages from *Vala* suggest that Blake's original plan was to show man's separation from Vala as the collapse into disunity of his four aspects or "Zoas." This was to be followed by man's final Resurrection (after a "Death and Judgement") in a reconstituted unity. Vala would be transformed by man's now fused and imaginative perceptions. The poem was not to be an affirmation of Blake's earlier faith in the natural order but, like *The Book of Los*, was to affirm man's power to find fulfillment in Vala by transforming her within his own imaginative vision. Thus, imaginative perception was not to be merely a "melting apparent surfaces away and displaying the infinite which was hid" (*Marriage*, K.154). It was to be man's independent creation of a paradise within, that would be happier far than the violent and vital natural paradise that Blake had celebrated in *The Marriage, America* and the Rossetti Manuscript.

This movement in Blake's thought shows once again that he is no isolated figure in his time. The myth in which he clothed his new, post-revolutionary ideal may be fragmentary and obscure, but the movement of spirit it represents is precisely the same as that of his poetic contemporaries Wordsworth and Coleridge. Wordsworth traced this post-revolutionary crisis in *The Prelude*, and Coleridge recorded it at about the time Blake was writing *Vala*, in "France, an Ode" (1798):

> The Sensual and the Dark rebel in vain,
>     Slaves by their own compulsion! In mad game
>     They burst their manacles and wear the name
>         Of Freedom, graven on a heavier chain!
>     O Liberty! with profitless endeavor
> Have I pursued thee, many a weary hour:
>     But thou nor swell'st the victor's strain, nor ever
> Didst breathe thy soul in forms of human power.
>     Alike from all, howe'er they praise thee,

## Return to Innocence

(Nor prayer nor boastful name delays thee)
Alike from Priestcraft's harpy minions,
And factious Blasphemy's obscene slaves,
Thou speedest on thy subtle pinions,
The guide of homeless winds, and playmate
of the waves!
And there I felt thee!—on that sea-cliff's verge,
Whose pines, scarce travelled by the breeze above,
Had made one murmur with the distant surge!
Yes; while I stood and gazed, my temples bare,
And shot my being through earth, sea, and air,
Possessing all things with intensest love,
O Liberty! my spirit felt thee there.

The word "Liberty" is Coleridge's bridge between his earlier faith in the perfect transformation of all human institutions, and his later individual solace in the perfection and divinity of the nonhuman world. The restitution of natural holiness in the social order was to have been accomplished by the Revolution. That revolution having failed, the divine perfection of actual life could still be achieved by individual men through an imaginative fusion with Vala.

This inward yet still naturalistic ideal Blake later called "Beulah," or threefold vision. It is a paradise that hovers between the glorious world of natural strife celebrated in the poetry of the early 90s and the transcendent realm which was to be Blake's ultimate spiritual lodging. It is threefold by this logic: Single vision perceives the dead and spiritless world of Locke's philosophy and Newton's physics. It is the world of Your Reason. Twofold vision perceives the vitality and divinity which infuses that world by melting away apparent surfaces and disclosing infinite life and holiness. Threefold vision, by contrast, retains all the genuine fulfillment of natural holiness—the beauty and sexual bliss of natural life, but transcends all strife and conflict by an inward, spiritual transformation of Nature. Though Blake, of course, later satirized this half-way house, he himself resided in it when he began *Vala*. To confirm this, it is useful to look at two fragments from the earliest stratum of *Vala* that have survived Blake's ruthless destruction.[4] These on the whole incommunicative fragments show the character of Blake's first plan, and since Blake used two lines from these fragments in his second version, we are justified in concluding that other lines in the present Ms. probably had an early provenance. The first striking feature of these fragments is Blake's continued celebration of sexuality and vitality. Beauty is "all blushing with desire," and

> fiery flames of love
> Inwrap the immortal limbs struggling in
> terrific joy. [K.381]

But sexuality now has a new meaning. The sexual act is still a religious fulfillment, but the division of man into male and female is not a symptom of his participation in the natural order but rather a symptom of his self-division and Fall. The sexual act is redemptive not because it gratifies natural desire but because it restores the fallen unity and removes desire. That is why Blake consistently associates Beulah with sexual fulfillment. It is a fulfillment that transports man beyond the vital strife of opposites in the natural order to a threefold personal transcendence of nature's unending dialectic. It is a condition which in these early fragments Blake called "Eternity"—an indication that "Beulah" was his later, pejorative term for threefold harmony with Nature:

> "Glory, delight & sweet enjoyment born
> "To mild Eternity, shut in a threefold shape delightful,
> "To wander in sweet solitude, enraptur'd at every wind."

> [K.381]

4. These fragments are discussed in Sloss and Wallis, *1*, 338–41.

Once it is perceived that Beulah was Blake's visionary ideal when he began *Vala,* a central idea in the poem as it now stands becomes clear: The self-division and Fall of man is a lover's quarrel between the male and female components of each Zoa. Thus the second title of the poem, probably added around 1798–99 when Blake was still working on the first version: *The Four Zoas. The Torments of Love & Jealousy in the Death and Judgment of Albion the Ancient Man.* Vala is soon seen to be secondary because the real Fall is a separation from Beulah, not from Nature. Each Zoa has a quarrel of jealousy with his feminine counterpart and therefore no longer exists with her in the sexual union associated with Beulah. This conception is the one that informs the early fragments, as may be seen in Blake's presentation of Tharmas (the body) and his female counterpart Enion. Thus Tharmas:

> Male form'd the demon mild athletic force his shoulders
> spread,
> And his bright feet firm as a brazen altar; but the parts
> To love devoted, female.                    [K.380]

Enion, on the other hand:

> Female her form, bright as summer, but the parts of love
> Male.                    [K.381]

This translocation of "the parts of love" attempts to suggest a sexual fusion that is no longer a dialectical clash of opposites, but a return to unity of being in Beulah. When Blake, still about 1798, simplified his scheme by making the Zoas altogether male and their Emanations female, he did not thereby alter the ideal represented by their fusion or the general point of his myth.

Its point was simply this: to describe man's fallen state

and his ultimate Resurrection. Now if the perfection of
being is the harmony of man's faculties in the tranquil
state of Beulah—far from all turmoil on a moony bank
in the arms of his beloved—then the Fall must be the
disharmony of man's faculties, separated from his beloved and thrown upon the turmoil of the world. Thus
the Fall is the separation of male and female, and that
is the way the Fall is described in Night VII (a), which
according to internal clues contains some of the earliest
composed verses in the Ms.:[5]

> "Among the Flowers of Beulah walk'd the Eternal Man &
> saw
> "Vala, the lily of the desart melting in high noon;
> "Upon her bosom in sweet bliss he fainted. Wonder siez'd
> "All heaven; they saw him dark; they built a golden wall
> "Round Beulah. There he revel'd in delight among the
> Flowers.
> "Vala was pregnant & brought forth Urizen, Prince of
> Light,
> "First born of Generation. Then behold a wonder to the
> Eyes
> "Of the now fallen Man; a double form Vala appear'd, a
> Male
> "And female; shudd'ring pale the Fallen Man recoil'd
> "From the Enormity & call'd them Luvah & Vala, turning
> down
> "The vales to find his way back into Heaven, but found
> none,
> "For his frail eyes were faded & his ears heavy & dull.
>
> [VII (a), lines 239–50, K.326]

This bears numerous resemblances to Blake's earlier
versions of the Fall in the 90s. The Fall occurs when man
is divided from Nature through the separation of Urizen
from the primal unity. But now the form of the myth is

5. Another clue is the conflict in this Night between Urizen and
Orc. Orc appears very rarely in the work as a whole.

changed to one which involves a division into male and
female in order to make the myth coincide with the new
version of the ideal unity—Beulah. Thus the earliest
materials in the Manuscript as it stands are probably
those which deal with the lovers' quarrels between the
Zoas and their Emmanations, and the woes and lamentations that ensue from those divisions.[6]

In the second, far more complex, stage of the poem's
composition (1800–03), Blake, having once again changed
his conception of the Fall and Resurrection, launched
on a new and different plan into which he attempted to
integrate his earlier materials. The principal story was
no longer the torments of love and jealousy in man's
Zoas, but rather the conflict between the Zoas themselves.
Blake's reasons for introducing this complication into
the story involved his changing evaluation of Vala and
Beulah as well as his insight, in the early 1800s into his
own spiritual history. From this point on, Albion was
to have an ever greater kinship with Blake, and Albion's

6. There are only three certainly dated documents from the period
of Blake's first version (1797–99). These are two letters and a set
of marginal annotations to Bishop Watson's attack on Paine called
*An Apology for the Bible.* In the annotations Blake mentions the
year in which he writes: 1798 (K.383). The two letters are dated
August 1799. All of these show Blake in a mood that attempts to
conciliate between naturalism and revealed religion. "Tom Paine
is a better Christian than the Bishop" (K.396). Paine's attack
on "State Religion" is the Holy Ghost striving in him (K.387).
"Natural Religion is the voice of God!" (K.388). This defense of
Paine in 1798 should be compared with Blake's viewpoint after the
first version of the *Zoas.* In *A Vision of the Last Judgment* (1810),
he attacks Paine's ideas (K.615). The letters, particularly the letter
to Trusler, express the doctrine of Beulah or threefold vision quite
precisely: "I feel that a Man may be happy in This World. And I
know that This World Is a World of imagination & Vision. . . .
To the Eyes of the Man of Imagination, Nature is Imagination itself" (K.793). Blake is advocating the transformation of Nature by
"Spiritual Sensation" (K.794). When he rejected threefold vision,
he rejected even a transformed Nature or anything pertaining to
Nature. See, for example, *"A Vision of the Last Judgment,* K.609,
617, and passim.

Fall was to follow the path of what Blake was coming to regard as his own spiritual errors in the 90s. The universal implications of *The Four Zoas* were to be derived from Blake's own spiritual struggles.

In the letters Blake wrote at this period, he explicitly acknowledged both his spiritual struggles and the auto-biographical character of his poem:

> None can know the spiritual Acts of my three years' Slumber on the banks of the Ocean [1800–03], Unless he has seen them in the Spirit, or unless he should read My long Poem descriptive of those Acts; for I have in these three years composed an immense number of verses on One Grand Theme, Similar to Homer's Iliad or Milton's Paradise Lost. [25 April 1803, K.823]

On 6 July 1803 he again wrote to Butts that his "three years' trouble" will be forgotten by his affections and remembered only by his understanding in the form of a "Grand Poem" and "Sublime Allegory" (K.824–25). As late as December 1805 he was still planning to publish *The Four Zoas,* and wrote: "It will not be long before I shall be able to present the full history of my Spiritual Sufferings to the Dwellers upon Earth" (K.862). Thus the "spiritual acts" which Blake describes in the second stratum of *The Four Zoas* take us to the heart of the turmoil veiled by the years of silence before the publication of "To Tirzah."

Blake described this period as one of "trouble" and "spiritual suffering." For a mind whose spiritual nourishment had been in the revolutionary early 90s as well as in the pious 80s a powerful religious faith, "spiritual suffering" and "trouble" suggest religious doubt. In the years between 1799 and 1803 Blake was closer to complete despair than at any other period of his life. It had become intense just before July 1800 (a date that ap-

proximates Blake's decision to abandon the first plan
of the *Zoas*) when Blake wrote with unwarranted confidence: "I begin to emerge from a Deep pit of Melancholy, Melancholy without any real reason for it, a Disease which God keep you from & all good men" (K.798).
The year 1800 is also the time when Blake's letters began
to mention "Jesus," "Heaven," and "Eternity." The removal to Felpham apparently represented to Blake a
spiritual as well as a physical new start, and his second
letter to Butts from his new home, began: "Friend of
Religion & Order," and announced: "In future I am
the determined advocate of Religion and Humility, the
two bands of Society. . . . Now I have commenced a new
life of industry." This was also the letter in which Blake
enclosed a poem that very ambiguously mingled the
now departing ideal of Beulah with the new ideal of
Eternity:

> To my Friend Butts I write
> My first Vision of Light,
> On the yellow sands sitting.
> The Sun was Emitting
> His Glorious beams
> From Heaven's high Streams.
> Over Sea, over Land
> My Eyes did Expand
> Into regions of air
> Away from all Care,
> Into regions of fire
> Remote from Desire;
> The Light of the Morning
> Heaven's Mountains adorning.     [lines 1–14]

Yet this heavenly region of fire remote from desire is a
transformed version of the visible scene, and is given the
"soft female charms" Blake later always associated with
Beulah:

117

I stood in the Streams
Of Heaven's bright beams,
And saw Felpham sweet
Beneath my bright feet
In soft Female charms.          [lines 33–38]

Like dross purg'd away
All my mire & my clay.
Soft consum'd in delight
In his bosom Sun bright
I remain'd.

[lines 55–59. Letter to Butts, 2 Oct. 1800, K.804–05]

By October 1800 Blake had given up the purely secular ideal of Beulah, which was the type of redemption in the first version of *The Four Zoas,* but he had
not yet won his way to a realm that fully transcended the
soft female charms of transformed Nature and threefold
vision. By late 1801 he had done so, and by 1803 he had
completed the second, revised version of *The Four Zoas*
containing the history of his spiritual struggles from
1800 to 1803.

The best introduction to the account in *The Four Zoas*
of what Blake had gone through between 1800 and
1803 is found in the poems of the Pickering Manuscript,
which were, according to Sampson, composed around
1803. The Manuscript is a fair copy, and the ten poems
it contains evidently belong to the period 1799–1803. It
appears that Blake copied out these poems in their order
of composition, since, of the six important autobiographical ones, the first four relate to his period of
spiritual turmoil and the last two to his confident return
to Innocence about 1803. The date of the Manuscript
itself may be about 1804. The first four are, in their
Manuscript order, "The Golden Net," "The Mental
Traveller," "The Land of Dreams," and "The Crystal
Cabinet."

Significantly, the basic structure of all four poems is

the same. They all describe an optimistic search for a special kind of spiritual fulfillment (Beulah) which is actually attained in the course of the poem, but which, being attained, turns out to be a delusion and no fulfillment at all. As a result, the poet is in a worse state of dissatisfaction, or despair, than he was at first. The earlier failure of the natural apocalypse, described in *The Book of Ahania,* had left Blake, like Wordsworth and Coleridge, the consolations of the private, spiritual apocalypse in Nature, but when this last resort of naturalism failed, it left Blake to write his "Dejection" and his Peele Castle Stanzas. Only for Blake the shock was, if anything, greater and longer lasting. He was an older man than his two great contemporaries, and he found himself more totally deprived of faith, confidence, and vision.

"The Golden Net" is a despairing poem that emphasizes one of the root flaws in the ideal of Beulah—its failure to provide any positive renewal of actual life. A young man, the "I" of the poem, sees three virgins whose tears, like the "self-deceiving tears" of Tirzah, represent the built-in frustrations of actual life:

> "Alas for woe! alas for woe!"
> They cry, & tears for ever flow.
> The one was Cloth'd in flames of fire,
> The other Cloth'd in iron wire,
> The other Cloth'd in tears and sighs.

Their different garments symbolize the inevitable defeats of man's natural life. He is born with passionate desires ("flames of fire") which are bound down with the inherent repressions of nature and society ("iron wire"), and the only possible consequences of his natural life are therefore "tears & sighs." It follows, then, that man's inevitable condition in natural life is to be trapped under a net from which he cannot extricate himself:

Dazling bright before my Eyes.
They bore a Net of golden twine
To hang upon the Branches fine.
Pitying I wept to see the woe
That Love & Beauty undergo,
To be consum'd in burning Fires
And in ungratified desires,
And in tears cloth'd Night & day
Melted all my Soul away.

The pity felt by the young man for the tragic bafflements of life leads him to discover an escape—here symbolized by the raising, though not the removal, of the
net:

When they saw my Tears, a Smile
That did Heaven itself beguile,
Bore the Golden Net aloft
As on downy Pinions soft
Over the Morning of my day.

This is the smile of Beulah—that state in which one
escapes the bafflements of life by ignoring them. It is the
very smile that Blake had described in the first poem of
the Pickering Manuscript, the poem which immediately
precedes this one—not only physically in the Manuscript
but also chronologically in Blake's development. The
last lines are:

And no Smile that ever was smil'd,
But only one Smile alone,
That betwixt the Cradle & Grave
It only once Smil'd can be;
But, when it once is Smil'd,
There's an end to all Misery.

But in "The Golden Net" the smile does not work, since
no matter how effectively threefold vision makes dis-

agreeables evaporate, a man still exists in the actual world:

> Underneath the Net I stray,
> Now intreating Burning Fire,
> Now intreating Iron Wire,
> Now intreating Tears & Sighs.
> O when will the morning rise?

The "break of day" with which the poem began was a false dawn (one of Blake's favorite images of disillusionment), and the poet is left without fulfillment either in Beulah or the world.

The next poem in the Manuscript, "The Mental Traveller" is one of Blake's greatest and takes us closer to the substance of the revised *Four Zoas* than any other poem. It is the fullest presentation in the lyric mode of his pathway to despair. As the title suggests, the theme is a spiritual journey, but the poem is far more than autobiography. Like *The Four Zoas* it is an account of Blake's spiritual history universalized to represent the tragic spiritual history of mankind. It differs very strikingly from all Blake's previous epic phenomenologies of mind in that it deliberately omits to prophesy any apocalypse at the end of the journey. Instead, there is only the meaningless repetition of the cycle over and over again. In a brief summary of the poem such as I shall now give, it is difficult to do justice to its brilliance and intellectual control. A stanza-by-stanza analysis will be found in Appendix III.

The first stage on this journey is the naturalistic ideal Blake had embraced in the early 90s. Therefore, the first ideological biography he will trace will be that of a boy— an Orc figure. When this boy is born, he comes, like Christ and all other putative messiahs, to save the world —here represented by the "Woman Old." Instead of welcoming the savior, the world, as it always does with a new religious idea such as Christianity, persecutes him. But the parallels with Christianity are combined with references to Prometheus. Christ is the *type* of the savior, not the only one. Blake had already used the figure of Christ in this way in *America* and *Europe,* where he identified him with Orc, and also in *The Book of Ahania,* where he identified him with Fuzon. The boy is fundamentally a new, naturalistic religion that promises to renew the world just as the religion of the Revolution had promised. When the enthusiastic spirit of this new religion catches hold, the boy reaches maturity. He breaks his fetters and embraces earth (who, being renewed, is now a "Virgin bright") in a revivifying sexual union like that between Orc and the "Nameless Female" in *America.* This is the high point of the naturalistic ideal. Earth seems a paradise, a "Garden fruitful seventy fold."

The paradise is very short-lived (it was, after all, anticipatory rather than actual), and Blake does not bother to explain why it collapsed. His somber point is that it always does collapse—one reason being as good as another. By this time the boy figure (who is now also the mental traveler, Blake—the poet who celebrated the religious ideal represented by the boy) has grown into an "Aged Shadow." He wanders around a dismal "Earthly Cot" until, suddenly, out of the ruins of this earthly creed, a "little Female babe does spring." She is the new girl-ideology, the alternative to the boy-ideology and the reaction to its failure. The fiery female babe cannot be touched by anything earthly. She comes, like grace, to whomever she pleases, and her first task is to drive out the old ideal, which is sent to wander "weeping, far away."

From this point to the end of the poem, Blake bases his history of the girl-ideology on his own spiritual history from about 1796 to about 1801. First the older

ideal must be abandoned. The "Garden and its lovely
Charms" "fades before his sight." He now finds himself
in the situation described at the beginning of "The
Golden Net." Natural life is an array of frustrations and
bafflements capable of bringing only tears and sighs:

> The stars, sun, Moon, all shrink away
> A desart vast without a bound,
> And nothing left to eat or drink,
> And a dark desart all around.

The lack of spiritual nourishment corresponds to the
melting away of the young man's soul in the previous
poem, while the gradual renewal of the mental traveler
as he pursues the girl ideal corresponds to the lifting
of the golden net. Blake describes the pursuit as one of
"fear" and "wayward Love" in anticipation of the insufficiency that this new ideal, like the old one, will
betray. The tears of the girl, now grown to a "weeping
Woman Old" disclose, like the tears of the three virgins,
the same insufficiency. But this ideal, too, reaches its
high point. The mental traveler is renewed as a "wayward Babe." The sun and stars no longer seem distant.
The new ideal, we notice, is one that, like Beulah, remains friendly to the pastoral aspects of the natural
world, though it consists of a spiritual, threefold vision
that transcends Nature. It is a "City" that man himself
must create from the "desart." Yet it is a comfortable
place for "many a lover"; its "trees bring forth sweet
Extacy," and it harbors "many a pleasant Shepherd's
home."

The repudiation of Beulah that now follows is far
more sinister than it was in the previous poem. Beulah
collapses not because it fails to renew actual life, but because it turns into something altogether terrifying. Here
Blake gives us an insight into what must have been
around 1798–99 his most fundamental reason for being

wary of Beulah. When the mental traveler embraces Beulah, he is beguiled to "infancy," but while this implies renewal, the term "wayward Babe" also implies something disastrous—a return to Innocence, to that illusioned, Urizenic piety that had been repudiated once and for all. The pastoral state of Beulah with its "shepherd's home" was all too close to the pastoral state of Innocence with its stage props of "allegorical abodes" and "lands unknown." Instead of proving a haven, the shepherd's home turns out to be a trick to seduce the mind back to that false delusion from which it had escaped. Suddenly, as in a nightmare, the babe which the traveler has become turns into the Christ-child of pharisaic Christianity:

> They cry "The Babe! the Babe is Born!"
> And flee away on Every side.
>
> For who dare touch the frowning form,
> His arm's wither'd to its root;
> Lions, Boars, Wolves, all howling flee,
> And every Tree does shed its fruit.

Blake has come to a total impasse. Out of its denial of life, the Christ-child of Innocence will make the world old and will then have to turn into the Orc of Experience. For Blake or mankind to return to the pieties of traditional Christianity would mean the certainty of repeating the whole cycle over again. And this, in a prophetic and despairing flash is exactly what happens:

> And all is done as I have told.

The two poems which immediately follow "The Mental Traveller" show Blake's first errant steps out of this despair. While "The Land of Dreams" appears to be a celebration of the earlier Beulah, it really celebrates an

ideal like the vision Blake communicated to Thomas
Butts in October 1800. The land of dreams is a pastoral
land with "Lillies by Waters fair" and "Lambs clothed
in white" yet this visionary world is now no longer a
delusion or a dead end. The land "by pleasant Streams"
is "better far" than this world. Its only limitation is that
while one is in it, one can "not get to the other side":

> Dear Child, I also by pleasant Streams
> Have wander'd all Night in the Land of Dreams
> But tho' calm & warm the waters wide,
> I could not get to the other side.

The similarity of Blake's imagery to Bunyan's must be
more than coincidental:

> Now I saw in my Dream, that by this time the Pilgrims
> were got over the Inchanted Ground, and entering in the
> Country of *Beulah,* whose air was very sweet and pleas-
> ant. . . . Now I further saw that betwixt them and the
> Gate was a River, but there was no bridge to go over, the
> River was very deep.

> [*The Pilgrim's Progress,* Oxford University Press,
> N.Y., 1904, pp. 183, 186]

It is very probable that "The Land of Dreams" was composed at the time when Blake began to call his earlier
ideal of threefold vision, "Beulah," which, in Bunyan,
lies on the direct path to the Heavenly City. The "other
side" that the speaker cannot get to adumbrates a higher
ideal than the land of dreams, but Blake's acknowledgment of the insufficiency of Beulah also gives threefold
vision a higher and more hopeful value than it had in
"The Golden Net" or "The Mental Traveller."

This is likewise true of "The Crystal Cabinet."

> This cabinet is form'd of Gold
> And Pearl & Crystal shining bright,

> And within it opens into a World
> And a little lovely Moony Night.

But this will not suffice when one tries to get to the other side:

> O, what a smile! a threefold Smile
> Fill'd me that like a flame I burn'd.
> I bent to kiss the lovely Maid,
> And found a Threefold Kiss return'd.
>
> I strove to sieze the inmost Form
> With ardor fierce & hands of flame,
> But burst the Crystal Cabinet,
> And like a Weeping Babe became.

Beulah and threefold vision have turned out to be second-best ideals, but neither this poem nor "The Land of Dreams" falls into the futile cyclicity of "The Mental Traveller." Blake is apparently uncertain about the nature of "the other side" and "the inmost form," but he is at last certain that they represent the ideal he seeks. The despair of "The Mental Traveller" implies a total abandonment of hope in the natural world, or in any visionary and pastoralized version of it. But this loss of hope in Beulah is, in these last two poems of the first group, a herald of a new faith in which the very assumptions on which the earlier hope and its collapse had been based will be denied.

The last poems of the Pickering Manuscript, composed about 1803–04, are poems of Blake's return to Innocence. They vigorously express the faith of his earlier days. The desperate, private paradise of Beulah has entirely given way in "The Grey Monk" and "Auguries of Innocence" to faith in a Providence which overcomes all natural bafflements through Mercy, Pity, Peace, and Love:

> But vain the Sword & vain the Bow
> They never can work War's overthrow.
> The Hermit's Prayer & the Widow's tear
> Alone can free the World from fear.
>
> For a Tear is an Intellectual Thing,
> And a Sigh is the Sword of an Angel King,
> And the bitter groan of the Martyr's woe
> Is an Arrow from the Almightie's Bow.
>
> ["The Grey Monk," lines 25–32]

The title of the more famous of these two poems, "Auguries of Innocence," openly suggests a return to an earlier truth that Blake no longer has any desire to resist:

> For now! O Glory! and O Delight! I have entirely reduced that spectrous Fiend to his station, whose annoyance has been the ruin of my labours for the last passed twenty years of my life. . . . Suddenly, on the day after visiting the Truchessian Gallery of pictures I was again enlightened with the light I enjoyed in my youth. . . . I thank God that I courageously pursued my course through darkness. In a short time I shall make my assertion good that I am become suddenly as I was at first.
>
> [Letter to Hayley, 23 Oct. 1804, K.851–52]

A little over a month later, again writing to Hayley, Blake is even more explicit with respect to his recent spiritual history:

> I have indeed fought thro' a Hell of terrors and horrors (which none could know but myself) in a divided existence; now, no longer divided nor at war with myself, I shall travel on in the strength of the Lord God, as Poor Pilgrim says. [4 Dec. 1804, K.853]

The famous first four lines, which may be the only lines referred to by the title, "Auguries of Innocence," is a total surrender to the old truth and a total victory over the "spectrous Fiend":

> To see a World in a Grain of Sand
> And a Heaven in a Wild Flower,
> Hold Infinity in the palm of your hand
> And Eternity in an hour.

The auguries seen *by* Innocence are auguries *of* Eternity. They reaffirm the sacramental sense of life that had informed the *Songs of Innocence*.

I have interposed the poems of the Pickering Manuscripts between my account of the first and of the second version of *The Four Zoas* because these poems, contemporary with the second stratum of the longer epic, illuminate its fundamental story. I have already pointed out that the first version—particularly in the uninterpolated early fragments—had threefold vision or Beulah as its ideal of the Resurrection. Each Zoa, separated from his female counterpart, was to be reunited with her in a spiritually transformed natural world that corresponded to the visionary natural paradise of Wordsworth and Coleridge. For Blake it was a garden that, threefold as it was, also implied a calm sexual fulfillment. The reunion of man's "sexual" aspects was to be a transcendence of natural strife. However, when Blake around 1801 repudiated Beulah as an ideal, he shifted the emphases of the story and grafted a new version of Fall and Resurrection on the earlier matter. This attempt to intertwine a new story with the old accounts for much of the incoherence of the manuscript as it stands.

In this second version man has gone astray not because his faculties are self-divided but because he has permitted his lower functions—Tharmas (the body), Luvah (the emotions), and Los (the false prophet of natural apocalypse)—to gain mastery over his higher faculties—Urizen intellect) and Urthona the true prophet of the Divine Vision). Urizen is, miraculously, transformed into one of man's highest faculties. The ideal of the Resurrection implied here is man's redemption through the Divine Vision. This revised conception of the Fall and Resurrection is the most important unifying thread in the work as it now stands. And this new story is also an account of Blake's own Fall and Resurrection from 1789 to 1803 and, more particularly, an account of his "passage thro' these Three Years [1800–03] that has brought me into my Present State. . . . Those Dangers are now Passed & I can see them beneath my feet. It will not be long before I shall be able to present the full history of my Spiritual Sufferings to the Dwellers upon Earth" (11 Dec. 1805, K.862).

The best way to perceive the new pattern of the poem is to examine briefly the way Blake traces the histories of the individual Zoas. Taken together, these present the "full history" of the return to Innocence that culminated in the publication of "To Tirzah." The first of the Zoas, Tharmas, represents, among other things, man's body: "The Body of Man is given to me" (VI, 60, K.313). Now in the Fallen state of man—which is to say, Blake in the fervor of his naturalistic period—Tharmas is "God & Los his adopted son" (VI, 43, K.313). Tharmas is god in the way that physical nature and sexuality had been god, at the time Blake had denied the distinction between soul and body and had called Energy the only life (*Marriage,* plate 4). Los, the prophet of this Tharmic doctrine is thus his adopted son. Now, the whole pleasure of Tharmas in this fallen state is to make war—a fact that makes no sense if Tharmas is simply man's body, but a great deal of sense if Tharmas here also represents a naturalism which not only advocated Revolution but celebrated the vital strife of nature, with its clashes between selves and dialectical principles. Thus Tharmas to Los:

Tharmas laugh'd furious among the Banners cloth'd in
    blood,
Crying: "As I will I rend the Nations all asunder, rending
"The People: vain their combinations, I will scatter them.
"But thou, O Son, whom I have crowned and inthroned,
    thee strong
"I will preserve tho' Enemies arise around thee number-
    less.
"I will command my winds & they shall scatter them, or
    call
"My Waters like a flood around thee; fear not, trust in
    me
"And I will give thee all the ends of heaven for thy pos-
    session.                [VII (b), 49–56, K.334]

Blake's identification with Los will be discussed in a
moment. Here he also identifies himself with Tharmas as
he does with each of the Zoas.

Tharmas, like the naturalistic Blake, has his moment of
triumph, but soon, providentially, this triumph collapses
into defeat. It is, significantly, an inner collapse, and its
best expression is the passage given to his Emanation,
Enion:

"It is an easy thing to laugh at wrathful elements,
"To hear the dog howl at the wintry door, the ox in the
    slaughter house moan;
"To see a god on every wind & a blessing on every blast;
"To hear sounds of love in the thunder storm that destroys
    our enemies' house;
"To rejoice in the blight that covers his field, & the sick-
    ness that cuts off his children,
"While our olive & vine sing & laugh round our door, &
    our children bring fruits & flowers.

"Then the groan & the dolor are quite forgotten, & the
    slave grinding at the mill,
"And the captive in chains, & the poor in the prison, &
    the soldier in the field

"When the shatter'd bone hath laid him groaning among
the happier dead.

"It is an easy thing to rejoice in the tents of prosperity:
"Thus could I sing & thus rejoice: but it is not so with
me." [II, 408–18, K.290–91]

The celebration of natural strife, and the seeing of a
god on every wind is possible in youth, hope, and good
fortune, but it cannot last. Things that once seemed
delight and victory have become "shadows of false hope"
(VII (b), 241, K.339). Of Blake's many descriptions of his
own turbulent despair, that given to Tharmas is among
the most vivid:

All my hope is gone! for me ever fled!
"Like a famish'd Eagle, Eyeless, raging in the vast expanse,
"Incessant tears are now my food, incessant rage & tears.
"Deathless for ever now I wander seeking oblivion
"In torrents of despair: in vain; for if I plunge beneath,
"Stifling I live: If dash'd in pieces from a rocky height,
"I reunite in endless torment; would I had never risen
"From death's cold sleep beneath the bottom of the raging
Ocean.
"And cannot those who once have lov'd ever forget their
Love?
"Are love & rage the same passion? they are the same in me.
"Are those who love like those who died, risen again from
death,
"Immortal in immortal torment, never to be deliver'd?
"Is it not possible that one risen again from death
"Can die? When dark despair comes over, can I not
"Flow down into the sea & slumber in oblivion?

[IV 9–23, K.297–98]

The subsequent resurrection of Tharmas-Blake presented Blake with a difficult though not insuperable
problem. Now that Tharmas' redemption was no longer

his reunion with Enion, in Beulah, he would have to be
given a slightly revised redemption:

> The Eternal Man also sat down upon the Couches of
> Beulah,
> Sorrowful that he could not put off his new risen body
> In mental flames; the flames refus'd, they drive him back
> to Beulah.
> His body was redeem'd to be permanent thro' Mercy
> Divine.                          [IX, 354–57, K.366]

The sense in which the body is now risen allows Blake's
original idea of Tharmas' redemption to be fused with
the new. The original ideal was Beulah, and since that
is, in the new conception, the limit of Tharmas' possibility, Blake can reunite Tharmas, as he had originally
planned, both with Enion and "the gardens of Vala."
But this later version of Beulah is not that of the first
conception, or that of "The Golden Net," and "The
Mental Traveller." It is Blake's and man's return to
what he "was at first":

> For Tharmas brought his flocks upon the hills & in the
> Vales.
> Around the Eternal Man's bright tent the little children
> play
> Among the woolly flocks.            [IX, 838–40, K.379]

The second Zoa, Luvah, represents the instinctual
and emotive aspect of man. The Fall and Resurrection
of Luvah-Blake repeats that of Tharmas-Blake. Being a
lower faculty (from Blake's new anti-naturalistic standpoint), he falls by rising, that is, by usurping the functions of man's higher faculties: "And Luvah strove to
gain dominion over the Ancient Man" (III, 78, K.293).
This usurpation, which corresponds to Blake's rejection
of Urizen and his elevation of instinct, life, and joy in the

90s, is caused when Luvah is deluded by Vala and
Enitharmon (I, 287, K.272). He leaves the place of seed
(or alternatively, the heart) where he belongs and enters
Albion's brain. Blake's most vivid version of Luvah's
usurpation, and one which he used again to good effect
in *Milton,* was patterned on the Phaethon myth. The
Fall began when Luvah (who is also, of course, Orc) took
the chariot of the sun from Urizen and attempted to
guide it himself:

> Why didst thou [Urizen] listen to the voice of Luvah that
>     dread morn
> To give the immortal steed of light to his deceitful hands?
>
> [III, 31–32, K.292; see also I, 264 ff.; IV, 113 ff.; VII, 147–57]

The result of this usurpation is the same revolutionary
era that resulted from the setting-up of Tharmas as god.
The two usurpations are, of course, the same: the celebration of instinctual emotions, particularly the sexual
ones, is the same as the celebration of the body. The
steeds of light are no longer obedient to the control of
Urizen:

> "No longer now obedient to thy will, thou art compell'd
> "To forge the curbs of iron & brass, to build the iron man-
>     gers,
> "To feed them with intoxication from the wine presses of
>     Luvah
> "Till the Divine Vision & Fruition is quite obliterated.
> "They call thy lions to the field of blood; they rouze thy
>     tygers
> "Out of the halls of justice, till these dens thy wisdom
>     fram'd
> "Golden & beautiful, but O how unlike those sweet fields
>     of bliss
> "Where liberty was justice, & eternal science was mercy."
>
> [II, 32–40, K.292]

Even though this usurpation is the origin of the Fall, Blake in 1803 does full ironic justice to Blake in 1793. Thus he preserves the description (probably composed early) of Orc's expansive vision (V, 121–33, K.308), and of all the other deluded victories of the naturalistic era. But these delusive hopes end in Orc-Luvah's being so bound to earth that his "young limbs had strucken root into the rock," never to be extricated (V, 155–56, K.309). This is but one of the numerous defeats suffered by the hopeful Luvah, perhaps the most memorable being the parody of the "Preludium" to *America* in which Luvah violently embraces the nameless Female only to discover that she is a nothingness, a "nameless shadowy Vortex" (VII (b), 125–28, K.336).

The Resurrection of Luvah is, of course, the same as that of Tharmas. Since the natural and instinctive aspect of man belongs to his corporeal and temporal existence, it cannot achieve Eternity and must remain in the lower paradise with Vala. But it is a version of Beulah which is once again the world of Innocence, a place which is sacramental and referential, not an end in itself:

Then Luvah passed by, & saw the sinless soul,
And said: "Let a pleasant house arise to be the dwelling
    place
"Of this immortal spirit growing in lower Paradise."
He spoke, & pillars were builded, & walls as white as ivory.
The grass she slept upon was pav'd with pavement as of
    pearl.
Beneath her rose a downy bed, & a cieling cover'd all.

Vala awoke. "When in the pleasant gates of sleep I enter'd,
"I saw my Luvah like a spirit stand in the bright air.
"Round him stood spirits like me, who rear'd me a bright
    house,
"And here I see thee, house, remain in my most pleasant
    world.

"My Luvah smil'd: I kneeled down: he laid his hand on
    my head,
"And when he laid his hand upon me, from the gates of
    sleep I came
"Into this bodily house to tend my flocks in my pleasant
    garden."

So saying, she arose & walked round her beautiful house,
And then from her white door she look'd to see her bleat-
    ing lambs,
But her flocks were gone up from beneath the trees into
    the hills.
"I see the hand that leadeth me doth also lead my flocks."

[IX, 458–74, K.369]

The third Zoa, Urizen, has, in Blake's revision of the
poem, undergone an astonishing transformation. I have
already quoted the apparently early passage of the epic
(VII (a), 239–50, K.326) in which the birth of Urizen is
still regarded as the origin of man's Fall. In the revised
version of the story, however, Blake not only equates his
own better self with the better side of his former arch-
villain, but also regards the Fall as Urizen's failure to
retain mastery over man. Urizen's mistake was not his
attempt to achieve dominion, for intellect with imagination (Urthona) ought to have dominion. His mistake
was to give his reins over to Luvah. Consequently, the
earlier account of his Fall—the separation from his Emanation, Ahania (III, 113–30, K.295)—is no longer
integrated into the revised story. Urizen now regrets a
past world remarkably like the world of *Innocence*:

A Rock, a Cloud, A Mountain,
Were now not Vocal as in Climes of happy Eternity
Where the lamb replies to the infant voice, & the lion
                      to the man of years
Giving them sweet instructions.      [VI, 133–37, K.315]

The Fall from this Innocence is described in limpid verses that brilliantly equate the Blakean collapse into the wrath and drunkenness of naturalism with the fall of Lucifer and the disastrous chariot-ride of Phaethon:

"Then in my ivory pavilions I slumber'd in the noon
"And walked in the silent night among sweet smelling flowers,
"Till on my silver bed I slept & sweet dreams round me hover'd,
"But now my land is darken'd & my wise men are departed.

"My songs are turned into cries of Lamentation
"Heard on my Mountains, & deep sighs under my palace roofs,
"Because the Steeds of Urizen, once swifter than the light,
"Were kept back from my Lord & from his chariot of mercies.

"O did I keep the horses of the day in silver pastures!
"O I refus'd the lord of day the horses of his prince!
"O did I close my treasuries with roofs of solid stone
"And darken all my Palace walls with envyings & hate!

"O Fool! to think that I could hide from his all piercing eyes
"The gold & silver & costly stones, his holy workmanship!
"O Fool! could I forget the light that filled my bright spheres
"Was a reflection of his face who call'd me from the deep!

"I well remember, for I heard the mild & holy voice
"Saying, 'O light, spring up & shine,' & I sprang up from the deep.
"He gave to me a silver scepter, & crown'd me with a golden crown,
"& said, 'Go forth & guide my Son who wanders on the ocean.'

"I went not forth: I hid myself in black clouds of my wrath;

136

"I call'd the stars around my feet in the night of councils
dark;
"The stars threw down their spears & fled naked away.
"We fell. I siez'd thee, dark Urthona. In my left hand
falling

"I siez'd thee, beauteous Luvah; thou art faded like a
flower
"And like a lilly is thy wife Vala wither'd by winds.
"When thou didst bear the golden cup at the immortal
tables
"Thy children smote their fiery wings, crown'd with the
gold of heaven.

"Thy pure feet step'd on the steps divine, too pure for
other feet,
"And thy fair locks shadow'd thine eyes from the divine
effulgence,
"Then thou didst keep with Strong Urthona the living
gates of heaven,
"But now thou art bow'd down with him, even to the
gates of hell.

"Because thou gavest Urizen the wine of the Almighty
"For Steeds of Light, that they might run in thy golden
chariot of pride,
"I gave to thee the Steeds, I pour'd the stolen wine
"And drunken with the immortal draught fell from my
throne sublime.                    [VI, 202–37, K.310–11]

In spite of his identification of Urizen with his earlier,
better self, Blake reserves his severest moral judgments
in the poem for that side of Urizen which was always
antipathetic to Blake—the abstract and pharisaic perversion of true worship. Blake preserves this earlier conception of Urizen alongside the new, autobiographical
conception, and does not attempt to unify Urizen's Fall
into abstraction and pharisaism with his Fall into naturalism. On the other hand, Blake makes it quite clear
that the truly pious Urizen-Blake would never have

given the steeds of light to the revolutionist Luvah-Blake, had not the pharisaic Urizen, who was never Blake, planted the seeds of revolution:

"Compell the poor to live upon a Crust of bread, by soft
  mild arts.
"Smile when they frown, frown when they smile; & when
  a man looks pale
"With labour & abstinence, say he looks healthy & happy;
"And when his children sicken, let them die; there are
  enough
"Born, even too many, & our Earth will be overrun
"Without these arts. If you would make the poor live with
  temper,
"With pomp give every crust of bread you give; with gra-
  cious cunning
"Magnify small gifts; reduce the man to want a gift, &
  then give with pomp.
"Say he smiles if you hear him sigh. If pale, say he is ruddy.

[VII (a), 117–25, K.323]

That is why Urizen, even more than Tharmas or Luvah, is the aboriginal cause of bloody strife. "Enquire of my sons," says the pharisaic Urizen to Luvah, "& they shall teach thee how to War" (VII (a), 91, K.322). That is also why, in the final part of the poem, man says to Urizen:

"My anger against thee is greater than against Luvah,
"For war is energy Enslav'd, but thy religion,
"The first author of this war & the distracting of honest
  minds
"Into confused perturbation & strife & honour & pride,
"Is a deceit so detestable that I will cast thee out
"If thou repentest not.          [IX, 151–56, K.361]

Yet when Urizen is restored to his original glory and man is redeemed, it is not simply because Urizen has given up the perversions of priestcraft but also because

he has regained his proper mastery over man. It is
Urizen who inaugurates the apocalypse of Night IX, and
it is he who sows the seed and gathers in the harvest:

> Then Urizen arose & took his sickle in his hand.
> There is a brazen sickle, & a scythe of iron hid
> Deep in the South, guarded by a few solitary stars.
> This sickle Urizen took; the scythe his sons embrac'd
> And went forth & began to reap; & all his joyful sons
> Reap'd the wide Universe & bound in sheaves a wondrous
>   harvest.
> They took them into the wide barns with loud rejoicings
>   & triumph
> Of flute & harp & drum & trumpet, horn & clarion.
>
> [IX, 579–86, K.372]

And it is also Urizen to whom the risen Albion first
speaks:

> "Hear my words, O Prince of Light
> "Behold Jerusalem in whose bosom the Lamb of God
> "Is seen; tho' slain before her Gates, he self-renew'd re-
>   mains
> "Eternal, & thro' him awake from death's dark vale.
>
> [IX, 204–07, K.362]

Urizen attains, as Tharmas and Luvah cannot, Eternity.

The fourth Zoa, Los, is easily the most interesting
figure in the epic, and also the most thoroughly autobiographical. Why did Blake give this Zoa a double name,
in fact a triple name: "Los," "Urthona," "The Spectre
of Urthona"? The second Zoa had two names—Luvah
and Orc, and the preponderance of Luvah over Orc reflected Blake's loss of interest in his earlier symbol of
energy and revolt. But the three distinct names given to
man's imaginative faculty have an even more personal
meaning. Blake had invented the name "Los" at the
height of his ardent naturalism (Los first appears in *The*

*Book of Urizen*) to represent the imaginative fusion of intellect and emotion. Los was the primal unity of the soul as well as the fiery energy of the sun (sol). He was also, because of his imaginative vision, the eternal prophet of apocalypse, and therefore Blake himself. Now, from Blake's standpoint after about 1800, this prophet of the natural apocalypse represented not simply the fallen spirit of prophecy whose god was Tharmas, but also an entirely different Blake, a spectrous self so totally discrete from the "true" Blake as to require a discrete name.

In the Notebook poems that Blake composed around 1803, it is this spectrous Los who is the anti-self that torments the poet:

> My Spectre around me night & day
> Like a Wild beast guards my way.    [K.415]

And it is the "true" Blake, Urthona, who arises from the annihilation of Los:

> And, to end thy cruel mocks,
> Annihilate thee on the rocks,
> And another form create
> To be subservient to my Fate.

This repudiation of Los-Blake can, fortunately, be fairly precisely dated from a poem Blake composed "above a twelvemonth" before he quoted it in a letter to Butts on 22 Nov. 1802:

> Then Los appear'd in all his power:
> In the Sun he appear'd, descending before
> My face in fierce flames; in my double sight
> 'Twas outward a Sun, inward Los in his might.

To this twofold image, corresponding to the twofold vision beyond which the naturalistic Los cannot progress, Blake gives his defiance in this wise:

## Return to Innocence

> This Earth breeds not our happiness.
> Another Sun feeds our life's streams,
> We are not warmed with thy beams;
> Thou measurest not the Time to me
> Nor yet the Space that I do see;
> My Mind is not with thy light array'd.
> Thy terrors shall not make me afraid.

In these same verses Blake announces for the first time not only his transcendence of the natural infinite through Beulah but his transcendence of Beulah as well. Thus in spite of the turbulence of his three years on the banks of the ocean, Blake had glimpsed his final haven. The "Now" of the triumphant lines marks late 1801 as the beginning of that victory which was finally confirmed in the letter to Hayley of late 1804:

> Now I a fourfold vision see,
> And a fourfold vision is given to me;
> 'Tis fourfold in my supreme delight
> And threefold in soft Beulah's night
> And twofold always. May God us keep
> From single vision & Newton's sleep!

These memorable lines explain Blake's triple name for the eternal prophet. Los, the prophet of the natural infinite, has now given way to Urthona, the prophet of Divine fourfold Vision. The Spectre of Urthona, who in the epic is sometimes identified with Los, sometimes with Urthona, represents the intermediate Blake of 1797–1800, the Blake of threefold vision and the celebrant of Beulah.

From this superior vantage point, Blake revises the Fall of Los as he revised the Fall of the other Zoas. Instead of being separated from Enitharmon as before, he has taken on a new, fallen selfhood:

141

> I know I was Urthona, keeper of the gates of heaven,
> But now I am all powerful Los, & Urthona is but my
> shadow. [IV, 42–43, K.298]

The change from Urthona-Blake to Los-Blake is, of course, the change from the poet of *Innocence* to the poet of *Experience*. "Night or Day Los follows War" (VII (6), 75, K.335). Having immersed himself in the fallen strife of the world, the eternal prophet becomes part of that fallen world:

> Terrified at the shapes
> Enslave'd humanity put on, he became what he beheld:
> He became what he was doing: he was himself transform'd.
>
> [IV, 285–87, K.305]

Los's first step toward redemption was, like Blake's, his faltering return to Innocence, through the intermediate stage of Beulah, here associated with the Spectre of Urthona:

> Los embrac'd the Spectre, first as a brother,
> Then as another Self, astonish'd, humanizing & in tears,
> In Self abasement Giving up his Domineering lust.
>
> [VII (a), 339–41, K.328]

To which the Spectre responds:

> Be assur'd I am thy real self,
> Tho' thus divided from thee & the slave of Every passion
> Of thy fierce Soul. Unbar the Gates of Memory: look upon
> me
> Not as another, but as thy real Self.
>
> [VII (a), 345–48, K.328]

What the Spectre has to offer are the temptations of Beulah:

> If we unite in one, another better world will be
> Open'd within your heart & loins & wondrous brain,
> Threefold as it was in Eternity. [VII (a), 353–55, K.329]

## Return to Innocence

It only remains now for Los-Blake to become fully what he was—Urthona, the prophet of *Innocence*. After this decisive transformation occurs, Blake and mankind are no longer haunted by false hopes and delusive ideals. This highly personal apocalypse is the triumphant ending of the poem:

> The Sun arises from his dewy bed, & the fresh airs
> Play in his smiling beams giving the seeds of life to grow,
> And the fresh Earth beams forth ten thousand thousand
> springs of life.
> Urthona is arisen in his strength, no longer now
> Divided from Enitharmon, no longer the spectre Los.
> Where is the Spectre of Prophecy? where the delusive
> Phantom?
> Departed: & Urthona rises from the ruinous Walls
> In all his ancient strength to form the golden armour of
> science
> For intellectual War. The war of swords departed now,
> The dark Religions are departed & sweet Science reigns.

[IX, 846–55, K.379]

This triumphant ending is written in the spirit of the last poems in the Pickering Manuscript—particularly in the spirit of "Auguries of Innocence." The prophet is once more as he was at first, and his self-renewal seems impregnable. But, in fact, the momentum of the change that had led Blake to repudiate Los and everything connected with the naturalism of the early 90s was too great to be halted at this point. So long as Blake-Urthona was content, as in Night IX of *The Four Zoas,* to lodge Tharmas and Luvah in a "lower paradise" corresponding to the sacramental pastoral world of *Innocence,* there was still hope that the poem could be unified by a final revision and published. As I have noted, this was Blake's intention as late as December 1805 (K.862). All that was needed was that Blake should remove the disparities between the first and second versions by further

143

subordinating the lovers' quarrels between the Zoas and
their Emanations, or by removing them altogether.
But when Blake did undertake his second and final
major revision of the poem in about 1805, his antipathy
to everything connected with the natural world—that
is, to Tharmas—Luvah and Vala, had become so powerful that successful revision was impossible. The poem
was about the four Zoas, but Blake was no longer in-
terested in two of them.

Blake's first expedient in this last, desperate attempt
to salvage the poem was to identify Luvah with *caritas*
and thus make him a prefiguration of Christ. All the
identifications of Luvah with Christ, it may be noted,
belong to passages that were interpolated into the second
version.[7] But even if that expedient had succeeded,
Tharmas, the body, had still to be dealt with, and the
ruins of Blake's attempt to do so lie strewn among the
late additions to Night I, most strikingly in the revised
version of Enion's lament over Tharmas:[8]

> "Once thou wast to Me the loveliest son of heaven—But
> now
> "Why art thou Terrible? and yet I love thee in thy terror
> till
> "I am almost Extinct & soon shall be a shadow in Ob-
> livion,
> "Unless some way can be found that I may look upon thee
> & live.
> "Hide me some shadowy semblance, secret whisp'ring in
> my Ear,
> "In secret of soft wings, in mazes of delusive beauty.

7. Anyone who wishes to isolate Blake's last interpolations can do
so by comparing Margoliouth's text (*Blake's "Vala"*) with Keynes'
full text. The verses in K. that are not found in Margoliouth are
the last interpolations.
8. Blake is still trying here to salvage the original plan. But the
"Sin" Enion finds in Tharmas' secret soul is the unexpungeable sin
of corporeality.

"I have look'd into the secret soul of him I lov'd,
"And in the Dark recesses found Sin & cannot return."

[I, 38–45, K.265]

The flavor of Blake's last additions to *The Four Zoas* is altogether that of *A Vision of the Last Judgment* and *Jerusalem*. They are written by the Blake who said "this world of dross is beneath my Notice and beneath the Notice of the Public" (K.600), and who thought of the physical world as a "hindrance" and "as the Dirt upon my feet, No part of Me" (K.617). It is in these last additions that the figure Tirzah first appears as Blake's disdainful symbol of the natural world. What is common to both the last stratum of *The Four Zoas* and "To Tirzah" is a violent repudiation not merely of naturalism but of Nature. Like "To Tirzah," the last stratum of the epic equates the creation of the natural world with the Fall.

This is a new conception which raised the final, insuperable barrier to the completion of *The Four Zoas*. In both the first and the second versions and in all his previous myths, Blake's descriptions of the Fall had referred to man's spiritual history. The natural world in which that history was acted out was a fundamental given that played no decisive role in the story. The crucial element in man's Fall and Resurrection had been his attitude to the natural world, his fusion with it or his transcendence of it. But in these last additions, as in "To Tirzah" and *Jerusalem*, the myth of the Fall has become a genuinely cosmological myth of the creation.[9] Thus in the midst of the lamentations of Enion and Tharmas, Blake feels impelled, even though it confuses the narrative, to shift the perspective away from their natural strife to the realm beyond the created world:

9. See below, the commentary on "To Tirzah."

> But those in Great Eternity Met in the Council of God
> As One Man, hovering over Gilead & Hermon.
> He is the Good Shepherd, He is the Lord & Master
> To Create Man Morning by Morning, to give gifts at Noon
> day.                                    [I, 198–201, K.269]

The earlier, psychological account of the Urizenic creation becomes a cosmological account by the addition of one line:

> Thus was the Mundane shell builded by
> Urizen's strong Power.
>
> [II, 248, K.286]

More to the point, Blake intersperses his earlier account of the forging of Urizen by Los with a new account of the creation that corresponds to the one in "To Tirzah":

> The Saviour mild & gentle bent over the corse of Death,
> Saying, "If ye will Believe, your Brother shall rise again."
> And first he found the Limit of Opacity, & nam'd it Satan,
> In Albion's bosom, for in every human bosom these limits
> stand.
> And next he found the Limit of Contraction, & nam'd it
> Adam,
> While yet those beings were not born nor knew of good
> or Evil.
>
> Then wondrously the Starry Wheels felt the divine hand.
> Limit
> Was put to Eternal Death.          [IV, 269–76, K.304]

Blake's new myth has become genuinely cosmological for a fundamental, compelling reason. Blake now regards the physical, natural world as *inherently* fallen—as the dirt upon his feet and the barrier to all spiritual activity. His statements on this point in "To Tirzah," *Milton, Public Address, A Vision of the Last Judgment,*

*Jerusalem,* the Annotations to Berkeley and Words-worth, and *The Laocoön* are unambiguous. The natural world can no longer be assumed as the given in terms of which man's spiritual life, his Fall and Resurrection, are enacted. The physical world is so antithetical to man's spiritual life and so inherently debased that its creation must be explained as part of the Fall, in fact, as the central event of the Fall.

"To Tirzah," a poem that equates the Creation with the Fall, is, then, the first poem of Blake's last phase. It is a repudiation of Experience, but it is more than a return to Innocence. It does mark a return to Blake's primordial faith in the Atonement, in the saving agen-cies of Mercy, Pity, Peace, and Love, but it goes far beyond *Innocence* or *The Book of Thel* in its total repudiation of natural life. Blake's return to Innocence was the brief period around 1803–04, the period when he wrote that he had become as he was at first. It was the period in which he composed the victorious final lines of *The Four Zoas* and the last poems of the Picker-ing Manuscript. The "Auguries of Innocence," like the *Songs of Innocence,* had given a Swedenborgian, sacra-mental value to the actual world. Both works had seen "Heaven in a Wild Flower." But after about 1805, and certainly after the composition of "To Tirzah," Blake had no inclination to seek for Swedenborgian corre-spondences in the natural world. He was to find Eternity entirely in the realm of "Imagination" which is "the real & eternal World of which this Vegetable Universe is but a faint shadow" (*Jerusalem,* plate 77, K.717). This movement of Blake's spirit beyond the happy pieties of *Innocence* with its sacramental conception of natural life is poignantly shown in the last of Blake's several highly significant comments on Swedenborg. It was writ-ten down the year before Blake died and marks the

antipodes to his rejection of Swedenborg's Angels in
*The Marriage of Heaven and Hell:*

> Poor Churchill said: "Nature thou art my Goddess." . . .
> Swedenborg does the same in saying that this World is
> the Ultimate of Heaven. This is the most damnable False-
> hood of Satan & his Antichrist.                    [K.785]

# 8. Innocence and Experience
## 1794 - 1827

While I began this essay with a caveat against systematic interpretations of the *Songs,* I shall end it with a discussion of the kinds of systematization that may validly be applied to them. Now, the individual poems of the work are independent poems that, as poems, mean what they mean regardless of the larger systematic context in which they are placed. They were composed as independent poems and at least seventeen of them were not originally written for the *Songs.*[1] Therefore, in discussing the work as a whole, a great deal of trouble can be avoided by separating two questions that are often confused: "What does this or that poem mean?" and "What does this or that arrangement of the poems mean?" These questions, being separate, should not be confused, but neither should the second one be slighted, since

1. The seventeen are the three poems of *Innocence* that first appeared in *An Island in the Moon* and the fourteen poems of *Experience* that bear no direct satirical relationship to the *Songs of Innocence.*

Blake attached importance to the larger implications of the collection as a whole.

I propose in this section to trace the history of Blake's larger conception of the *Songs* in order to determine the most valid and authoritative systematic conception implied by the work as it now stands. I propose, also, to explain the alterations that Blake made in the order and classification of the *Songs,* since these alterations have an intimate connection with the larger meanings he intended the *Songs* to convey. This constellation of interrelated problems can be solved by examining the history of Blake's five distinct editions of the *Songs.*

By an "edition" I mean a particular arrangement of the *Songs* that characterized the copies Blake issued at a particular period. Before discussing the significance of these different arrangements, I shall lay out their succession in the form of a table which will, I hope, make clear to the reader the general pattern of the history to be described. The letters by which the extant copies are designated are those of the Keynes and Wolf *Census* which lists them alphabetically in chronological order.[2]

2. Although I have preserved the relative chronology of Keynes and Wolf, I have ventured to differ with them on the question of actual dates. Their conclusion that copies L and M were etched about 1799 causes them to date copies E and I earlier than I do. But L and M, like E and I, contain "To Tirzah," which Sir Geoffrey was still dating: ca. 1801–03, in 1957, four years after the publication of the *Census* by Keynes and Wolf. The Keynes and Wolf dating of L and M is based on a penciled inscription on the flyleaf of L: "J. S. 1799." This puzzling conflict between the probable date of "To Tirzah" and the inscription caused me to make inquiries of Mr. Willis Van Devanter, librarian for Mr. Paul Mellon, the present owner of copy L. Mr. Van Devanter writes: "There is an inscription, "J. S. 1799" in pencil, but I doubt very much whether it is contemporary. I also wonder whether it is even a date at all." Since the inscription conflicts so emphatically with the evidence that "To Tirzah" is of late composition, I must share Mr. Van Devanter's doubts. The inking and coloring of all the leaves of copy L are the same, and they are numbered in sequence. "To

## Innocence and Experience

| Edition | Extant Copies Displaying Similar Arrangements | Approximate Dates |
|---|---|---|
| I | A | 1794 (watermark 1794) |
| II | C, D * | 1794–1795 (no watermark dates) |
| III | E, I ** | ca. 1805 (no watermark dates) |
| IV | L, M | ca. 1808 (no watermark dates) |
| V | U, V, W, X, Y, Z, AA | 1815–1827 (watermark dates in various copies: 1815, 1818, 1825) |

\* B has been rebound. Its arrangement is not authoritative and is not given in Keynes-Wolf.

\*\* F, G, H, and K are incomplete. J has been rebound and re-arranged.

*Explanation of the Table:* Copies N through T are left out of account because their arrangements are not authoritative: N and T are incomplete copies; O through S are copies in which the plates of *Innocence* and *Experience* are numbered separately. This separate numeration is Keynes' ground for grouping them together, although the watermarks vary from 1794 to 1808. Their arrangements are not significant because these volumes were formed by adding a copy of *Experience* to an already existing copy of *Innocence,* so that no alteration of the previously bound volume was possible. Thus, in

---

Tirzah" was not therefore subsequently added. The inscription could possibly be a catalogue number or some other form of red herring. It is interesting to note that Sir Geoffrey's earlier conjecture about copy M in his *Bibliography* accords with my own. It is also gratifying to note that his ordering, based on physical evidence, accords with my ordering, based on the arrangements of the poems.

O, Q, R, and S the two series are printed in two different inks. In copy P the ink color is approximately the same in both series, but the copy was probably formed as the others were. The lack of copies between 1795 and 1805 is most significant. Copy E must belong to ca. 1805 because it is the first copy that contains "To Tirzah," composed ca. 1805. Apparently, Blake not only failed to etch any new works during this decade of turmoil but failed to re-issue those he had already etched. His diminished confidence in his earlier ideas is reflected in the gradual decline in the number of extant copies of his works as they approach the year 1795. Thus, of the *Visions* (1793) there remain seventeen extant copies, of *America* (1793) eighteen, of *Europe* (1794) twelve, of *Urizen* (1794) seven, of *The Song of Los* (1795) five, of *The Book of Los* (1795) one, of *The Book of Ahania* (1795) one.

*Editions I and II, 1794–95.* These two editions, comprising copies A, B, and C, have already been discussed in Section 6, above, and the implications of their arrangements may be recapitulated very briefly.

The great interest of the first edition, copy A (1794) lies in what it does not contain. The sequence of poems does not lend itself to any larger, systematic interpretation, and this is not surprising, since the absence of the general title page indicates that no larger systematic conception was intended. The final plate is the one that contains "My Pretty Rose Tree," "Ah! Sun-Flower," and "The Lilly," a group of poems so heterogeneous as to defy conclusive generalizations about the implications of Blake's final statement. Furthermore, this is the only early edition having any numeration at all, and in this case the fact that the two series are numbered separately indicates that Blake is still following the conception implied in the *Prospectus* of October 1793 that they are separate works. In this edition, therefore, *Experience* stands as a satire and a partial parody of *Innocence*. This is further confirmed by Blake's choice of "Infant Joy" as the last poem of *Innocence,* a rather tendentious choice which suggests that the joys of Innocence are infantile and need to be replaced by the mature insight of Experience. That is the view of Innocence implied by the contemporaneous "Motto to the Songs of Innocence & of Experience" (q.v. K.183). Besides the general title page and, of course, "To Tirzah," the edition lacks "A Little Girl Lost" and "A Little Boy Lost." This strongly indicates that Blake's contrary titles for these poems were afterthoughts made possible by his less parodic and more systematic conception of the two works in the subsequent edition.

The second edition, copies C and D (1794–95), is the first systematic edition of the work, and the only edition that adequately corresponds to the systematic implications of the general title page (*Shewing the Two Contrary States of the Human Soul*), now added for the first time. The purely satirical purpose of the first edition is now subordinated to a comprehensive philosophical statement about the human soul. The most remarkable feature of the new arrangement is the transfer of "A Dream" from *Innocence* to *Experience.* This change discloses the same broad conception of the two states which permitted Blake to add "A Little Girl Lost" and "A Little Boy Lost" to the canon. By removing "A Dream" from *Innocence,* Blake purified that work of a poem that might be construed as having some of the naturalistic implications of *Experience:* the way that ants, beetles, and glowworms perform their different functions in the poem could be taken as an instance of the way the different kinds of creatures in the world interact to form the vital, natural order. This is a root idea in *The Marriage of Heaven and Hell* as well as "The Tyger" and "The Clod and the Pebble." The speaker of "A Dream" leaves his angel-guarded bed not to see Eternity but to lie on the grass and watch the providential interactions of the natural world. That was not, of course, Blake's point when he wrote the poem, but it was his point when he transferred it to *Experience*.

In this and all subsequent editions of the *Songs*, Blake indicated his systematic intentions by his choice of terminal poems for the two series. The first poem of each series could not be shifted, and while Blake had since 1789 consistently grouped two and sometimes three poems of *Innocence* together, the poems in the middle of each series were too heterogeneous to permit an obviously significant sequence in each group as a whole. The sequence of the middle poems changed from issue to issue up to 1815, and Blake's different orderings of them were apparently governed by formal concerns. A rationale for each sequence could, no doubt, be made, but since this rationale would involve formal and artistic as well as systematic considerations, the explanation would complicate rather than clarify Blake's systematic intentions. To determine these it is sufficient to note the terminal poems of each series. This procedure reflects Blake's inconsistencies in ordering the middle poems of the early copies, and his consistency in preserving the terminal poems.

In the second edition, the terminal poems of *Innocence* are "The Little Boy Lost" and "The Little Boy Found." To make this the last word of *Innocence* is less damaging than to make the work trail off in the infantilism of "Infant Joy," but the termination is satirical and damaging nevertheless. It implies the progress from illusion to truth that Blake had sketched in the "Motto." The little boy (Blake himself as well as the human soul) has been lost in the illusioned state of Innocence and is about to be found in the mature state of Experience.

Since this termination implies a movement of the soul from one state to another rather than a dialectical opposition between the two states, Blake hovers here between the conception implied by the "Motto" and the conception implied by the dialectical title page. But this thematic inconsistency is justified by the fact that the combination of satire with dialectic remains true to the original satirical flavor of the *Songs*.

The terminal poem of *Experience,* however, conforms entirely to the dialectical conception of the title page. It is "The Clod and the Pebble," a poem which, as I have already indicated, confronts, without passing judgment on either, the two contrary states of Innocence and Experience. Here the two states of the soul correspond to the two eternal forces or principles that govern all life: Reason and Energy, Devourer and Prolific, Feminine and Masculine. Neither state is to be preferred: "These two classes of men are always upon earth, & they should be enemies: whoever tries to reconcile them seeks to destroy existence" (*Marriage,* K.155). The new, systematic conception of the work grudgingly gives, then, an eternal dialectical validity to Innocence even though the dialectic itself is entirely a conception of Experience.

*Edition III. The Period of* Milton. The third edition of the *Songs* (ca. 1805) shatters Blake's public silence with a note of victorious self-repudiation. "A Dream" is wrenched from *Experience,* where it had been impiously placed, and returned to what it was at first. "The Clod and the Pebble" is ruthlessly banished from the *Songs* in copy E. (This is the only extant example of Blake's removing a plate from the *Songs* and is reminiscent of his removing the first plate of *Europe.*) The whole state of Experience is reduced to nullity by terminating the work with "To Tirzah." If this edition implies any system at all, it must be considered a precise

inversion of the earlier system, and if it implies any
satire at all, it must be considered a satire on the god-
less attempt to satirize *Innocence*. But, in fact, Blake's
primary intention is neither systematic nor, in the ordinary sense, satirical. His intention is to recant and
repudiate without even pausing to mock.

This interpretation of Edition III may be confirmed
by glancing at the long work Blake composed and etched
at about the time he issued this edition. *Milton* was
begun, according to the date on the title page, in 1804,
just before Blake composed "To Tirzah" and finally
abandoned *The Four Zoas*. The work is openly autobiographical. It is Blake's celebration of his return to
true prophecy and the Divine Vision, after having been
a victim

> of the False Tongue! vegetated
> Beneath your land of shadows, of its sacrifices and
> Its offerings: even till Jesus, the image of the Invisible God
> Became its prey, a curse.         [plate 2, K.481]

The return to genuine prophecy is symbolized by Milton's descent from Eternity to enter Blake. Milton is
viewed as another prophet who has made errors which
must be corrected, and Milton is made to rectify his
own mistakes through Blake's now invincible Divine
Vision.

In *Milton*, Blake again uses the Phaethon myth to
describe his spiritual Fall, but he gives new names to
the characters. Now it is a figure called Palamabron who
relinquishes the reins of the chariot (instead of Urizen)
and it is Satan, not Luvah, who takes the reins. Blake's
equating of his lapse into naturalism with his giving
over the reins to Satan is a good gloss on Blake's letter
to Hayley of October 1804. It is also a good gloss on
the ruthless rejection of his former self in "To Tirzah":
"Then what have I to do with thee?"

A good deal of *Milton* may have been composed in 1804, since it is on the whole more tolerant of the natural world than the writings which follow "To Tirzah." Several passages of *Milton* find the same kind of sacramental value in the natural world as the *Songs of Innocence* and the "Auguries of Innocence" (1803–04). On the other hand, the pastoral attractions of trilling larks, singing thrushes, White-Thorn, Jasmine, and Jonquil (plate 31, K.520–21) are associated with the state of Beulah, "a pleasant lovely Shadow Where no dispute can come" (plate 30, K.518) and a "beautiful House for the piteous sufferer" (plate 28, K.515). Now, immediately after the attractive vision of Beulah on plate 31, Blake (in the first edition of the poem) makes answer as the true prophet:

> And the Divine Voice was heard in the Songs of Beulah, saying:
> When I first Married you [i.e. Beulah] I gave you all my whole Soul.
> I thought that you would love my loves [i.e. Eternity] & joy in my delights,
> Seeking for pleasures in my pleasures, O Daughter of Babylon.
> Then thou wast lovely, mild & gentle; now thou art terrible
> In jealousy and unlovely in my sight.     [plate 33, K.522]

This is Blake in a slightly later and more intolerant mood. Beulah is less a pleasant rest than a "soft delusion," and because of her acceptance of the sacramental, pastoral aspects of Nature, a "Daughter of Babylon."

This same mild tension is again apparent in *Milton* when we compare Blake's sentimental return to his admiration of Swedenborg (the standpoint of "Auguries of Innocence") with his repudiation of everything in the material world (the standpoint of "To Tirzah"). Here is Blake's comment on Swedenborg as well as on the propagandists of the Revolution that he had supported four-teen years before:

Rahab created Voltaire, Tirzah created Rousseau,
Asserting the Self-righteousness against the Universal Saviour,
Mocking the Confessors & Martyrs, claiming Self-righteousness,
With cruel Virtue making War upon The Lamb's Redeemed
To perpetuate War & Glory, to perpetuate the Laws of Sin.
They perverted Swedenborg's Visions in Beulah & in Ulro
To destroy Jerusalem as a Harlot & her Sons as Reprobates,
To raise up Mystery the Virgin Harlot, Mother of War,
Babylon the Great, the Abomination of Desolation.
O Swedenborg! strongest of men, the Samson shorn by the
    Churches.                      [plate 22, K.506]

But far more like "To Tirzah" are the passages in *Milton* which show Blake's disgust with the physical aspects of the world. As in "To Tirzah," the sense of touch is "Death Eternal" and must be obliterated. It is:

Ulro, Seat of Satan
Which is the False Tongue beneath Beulah: it is the Sense of
    Touch.                      [plate 27, K.514]

Even more like "To Tirzah" is the antepenultimate plate of the poem:

These are the Sexual Garments, the Abomination of
    Desolation,
Hiding the Human Lineaments as with an Ark & Curtains
Which Jesus rent & now shall wholly purge away with Fire
Till Generation is swallow'd up in Regeneration.

                     [plate 41, K.533]

*Edition IV. Between* MILTON *and* JERUSALEM. The fourth edition of the *Songs,* copies L and M (ca. 1808), was published between the first issue of *Milton* and the composition of the greater part of *Jerusalem.* The arrangement of the poems implies an outlook that is much less violently self-repudiating than the previous one, and much more contemplative and mellow. "The Clod and the Pebble" is now back in the canon, as it is in all the extant copies except E. By far the most significant change Blake has made is to place "To Tirzah" in the middle of *Experience* instead of, vindictively, at the end. And, among the poems which follow "To Tirzah" in *Experience,* Blake has placed a poem that previously had always been a poem of *Innocence*—"The Schoolboy." Now, the purpose Blake accomplished by placing "To Tirzah" in the middle was to avoid placing it at the end. This does not imply a softer attitude to the natural world but rather Blake's softer attitude toward his former self. The Blake of *Experience* is not to be totally rejected: "Then what have I to do with Thee?" He is to be forgiven. His moment of waywardness was perhaps even a necessary way station on the path to the Divine Vision. The same forgiving attitude is reflected in the transfer of "The Schoolboy" to *Experience.* It was a poem that Blake had written in late 1789 along with the other poems that hover between Innocence and Experience. While "The Schoolboy" expresses some of the naturalism of *Experience,* it also expresses an ideal to which Blake remained true all his life—the ideal of freedom, whether political or spiritual. To place "The Schoolboy" in *Experience* does not palliate the grievous errors of Experience, but it does express forgiveness of those errors because of the good intentions that shine through them. Like "The Schoolboy," *Experience* in its misguided way was devoted to spiritual freedom.

This interpretation of Blake's alterations in the *Songs* can be corroborated by referring to the alterations he made in *Milton* about this time. Most of the matter in the five plates which Blake added to *Milton* involved doctrinal corrections that brought the poem into harmony with the evolving scheme of *Jerusalem.* Of these five plates, the most significant is the one numbered 32 in Keynes' edition. Blake placed it directly between the plate which celebrated the innocent pleasures of Beulah and the plate which rejected Beulah as being a daughter of Babylon. The insertion interrupts the narrative, but softens the force of the repudiation. Blake's newly found self-forgiveness required the inclusion of the plate:

Distinguish therefore States from Individuals in those States.
States change, but Individual Identities never change nor cease.
You cannot go to Eternal Death [i.e. fall into spiritual error]
  in that which can never Die.        [K.521]

It is a charitable and humane conception that was to be Blake's central tenet in *Jerusalem* and all the last writings:

> Mutual Forgiveness of each Vice,
> Such are the Gates of Paradise.

["The Gates of Paradise," K.761]

It is a charitable conception that extends even to one's own former errors which were not part of the true man, but merely a state through which the true man had passed. This is the reason that the central autobiographical figure in *Jerusalem* is called Los instead of Urthona. The Los that Blake had seen in *The Four Zoas* as a totally different self requiring a different name was really only a State into which Los-Blake had fallen.

*Edition V. The Period of* JERUSALEM. The final and definitive form of the *Songs* has all the mellowness of the fourth edition and more. Blake's small but gratifying circle of admirers in his last years, his peace with himself and his former states, caused him to regard the history of those spiritual struggles with Olympian calm and self-forgiving charity, and in this last period of his life he issued far more copies of the *Songs* than in any other. His labor on *Jerusalem*, for which he did not expect to find a customer, was a devotional "Use of that Talent which it is Death to Bury, & Of that Spirit to which we are called." [3] But the *Songs of Innocence and of Experience* was his favorite work. In the year he died he was engaged in printing a set of the *Songs,* and estimated that it would take him six months to complete the coloring.[4]

The final form of the work is briefly this: "The Schoolboy" still remains in *Experience.* "To Tirzah" remains apart from the end. The final poem of *Innocence* is "On Another's Sorrow," the poem of *Innocence* that most closely approximated the tone of Blake's final attitudes: Actual life is a vale of sorrow, and man's central moral duty, besides his duty to follow "that Spirit to which we are called," is the exercise of pity and forgiveness toward other men. The final statement of the whole work is to be found in the three poems which terminate the *Songs.* As we might expect, none of them is a poem of *Experience.* That series of poems is terminated by "To Tirzah," which repudiates their errors but does not have the last word. Then comes "The Schoolboy," a poem that hovers between Innocence and Experience and, in its affirmation of spiritual freedom, shows the true man "which can never die" shining through an incipient state of error.

The final poem of the work is a poem of *Innocence* that Blake had never before transferred—"The Voice of the Ancient Bard." This act of Blake's deepens the

3. Letter to Hayley, 11 December 1805 (K.863). Blake's conviction that no one would buy *Jerusalem* is recorded in his letter to Cumberland, 12 April 1827 (K.878): "The Last Work I produced is a Poem Entitled Jerusalem the Emanation of the Giant Albion, but find that to print it will Cost my Time the amount of Twenty Guineas. One I have Finished. It contains 100 Plates but it is not likely that I shall get a Customer for it."
4. Letter to Cumberland, K.878.

point he made in shifting "The Schoolboy" to the coda of the work. Like "The Schoolboy," it was composed at a moment of spiritual balance between Innocence and Experience, and, like it, belongs to the State of neither work. But it is a poem that belongs very much to Blake, the true man who transcends all states. The new dawn that is prophesied in "The Voice of the Ancient Bard" is, as I have pointed out, ambiguous and unspecific. Nevertheless, placed at the end of this final edition, it surely prophesies the dawn of an entirely spiritual and inward Jerusalem which prefigures the final, spiritual Eternity that will end time and death forever. While this is not what Blake thought he meant when he wrote the poem, he saw later that it was really what he had always meant. Even when he fell into Error, he had preserved the true man which was, for him, the spirit of prophecy. Like Los, in *Jerusalem,* he had always, even when he was unaware of it, "kept the Divine Vision in time of trouble" (*Jer.* plate 95, K.74). Blake's final voice is what it had always been—the voice of the ancient bard who throughout human history has pronounced God's word.[5]

In the *Songs* this spiritual triumph can be expressed only by the indirect device of giving them a special arrangement. In *Jerusalem,* Blake traces his past travails and their conclusion with calm good humor and biting accuracy. As in the self-satirical passages of *The Four Zoas,* he catches the enthusiastic fervor of his wrongheaded naturalism:

5. The order of this final edition, which is also the order in which I have arranged my commentaries, is that of all seven final copies except copy V, which bears a watermark of 1818. The poems of this copy occur in a sequence which Blake once (apparently in 1818) wrote down on two leaves that have been preserved. See *The Letters of William Blake,* ed. G. Keynes (New York, Macmillan, 1956), pp. 179–81. I have not been able to perceive the rationale of this list, but it lacks, in any case, the authority of Blake's final issues, which bear watermarks as late as 1825.

Cast ye, Cast ye Jerusalem forth! The Shadow of delusions!
The Harlot daughter! Mother of pity and dishonorable
    forgiveness! [plate 18, K.640]

In place of Jerusalem we shall have "War and deadly
contention":

That the Perfect
May live in glory, redeem'd by Sacrifice of the Lamb
And of his children before sinful Jerusalem, To build
Babylon the city of Vala, the Goddess Virgin-Mother.
She is our Mother! Natuie! Jerusalem is our Harlot-Sister.

[plate 18, K.640]

The most significant corroboration of the interpretation I have given the final edition of the *Songs* is the
section of the epic where Innocence and Experience confront one another as Jerusalem and Vala. This confrontation corresponds to the larger meaning Blake imposed on the *Songs* in their final form. The scene occurs
in the midst of the Fall. Innocence has been rejected
and closed off, and Jerusalem, in tears, asks Vala:

Wherefore hast thou shut me into the winter of human life,
And clos'd up the sweet regions of youth and virgin innocence
Where we live forgetting error, not pondering on evil,
Among my lambs & brooks of water, among my warbling birds:
Where we delight in innocence before the face of the Lamb?

[plate 20, K.642]

Vala's answer is by no means an unwitting satire on
herself and on the state of Experience. Blake's judicious
self-evaluation and self-forgiveness permits Vala an answer which quite justly represents the valid objections
of Experience to the social complacency of Innocence:

When winter rends the hungry family and the snow falls
Upon the ways of men hiding the paths of man and beast,

Then mourns the wanderer: then he repents his wander-
   ings & eyes
The distant forest: then the slave groans in the dungeon of
   stone,
The captive in the mill of the stranger, sold for scanty
   hire.
They view their former life: they number moments over
   and over,
Stringing them on their remembrance as on a thread of
   sorrow.
Thou art my sister and my daughter: thy shame is mine
   also:
Ask me not of my griefs! thou knowest all my griefs.

[plate 20, K.642]

Vala has become a version of Experience in which the
true man shines through. Vala's reason for rejecting
pity is that she pities too much the stranger sold for
scanty hire to be satisfied with pity alone. Jerusalem,
though wiser than Vala, cannot defend herself against
what was true in Experience. Instead she gives an answer that reflects Blake's forgiveness of all his spiritual
errors both as the poet of *Innocence* and of *Experience:*

O Vala, what is Sin, that thou shudderest and weepest
At sight of thy once lov'd Jerusalem? What is Sin but a
   little
Error & Fault that is soon forgiven? but mercy is not a Sin,
Nor pity nor love nor kind forgiveness. O, if I have Sinned
Forgive and pity me! O unfold thy Veil in mercy & love!

[plate 20, K.643]

Blake's last act of forgiveness was one that even went
beyond this merciful reconciliation with the Blake of
Experience. In the great, final apocalypse of the poem
(plate 98), Blake depicts the redemption of his peren-
nial spiritual enemies, Bacon, Newton, and Locke. They,

too, are saved by his now invincible Mercy and Pity, along with Milton, Shakespeare, and Chaucer. The reader familiar with Blake's comments on Bacon, Newton, and Locke will regard this final act of magnanimity with awe.

Blake's last, conciliatory conception of the *Songs,* like any poet's final recension of his work, must stand as the authoritative version. It is very fortunate that this should be so, since it means that we are obliged to read the *Songs* not as an elaborate dialectical system but as expressions of two distinct moments of Blake's spiritual history, two contrary states of his soul. It also means that we are obliged to read each group of poems with the same comprehensive sympathy with which Blake finally regarded all his works regardless of the state in which he existed at their composition. Under this conception the work is not an intellectual game played with bloodless counters, but a rich and various collection of lyric poems, and also, like each of Blake's major works, a moving personal document.

# PART TWO

*Commentaries*

## Note

*Sequence of the Poems.* I present my commentaries in the sequence that Blake gave the *Songs* in his final issues of the work. This is the authoritative sequence, and it is the one modern editions should use. However, since this is not the sequence in which the poems were composed, the comments on the poems will appear to move backward and forward in time. The reader should therefore be aware of the following facts: "The Little Girl Lost," "The Little Girl Found," "The Schoolboy," and "The Voice of the Ancient Bard" were all originally poems of *Innocence* in the editions before 1794. These poems belong to late 1789–early 1790, a time of transition in Blake's thinking. To this transitional period belong also the "Introduction" to *Experience* and "Ah! Sun-Flower." I have discussed the implications of these chronological facts in Sections 4 and 8, above.

*The Designs.* Although it has been said that Blake's designs are an integral and indispensable part of his poems, this was not the conception under which Blake produced the *Songs*. He considered the designs not as integral to his poetry but as integral to a beautiful book. He was fortunate, he thought, that as a painter and a poet he could *present* his poems in the most beautiful and at the same time the cheapest possible way:

> Even Milton and Shakespeare could not publish their own works. This difficulty has been obviated by the Author of the following productions now presented to the Public; who has invented a method of Printing both Letter-press and Engraving in a style more ornamental, uniform, and grand, than any before discovered, while it produces works at less than one fourth of the expense.
>
> [*Prospectus* of 1793, K.207]

This *Prospectus*—the only such statement made in the period of the *Songs*—says nothing about a special kind of illuminated *poetry;* it describes a unique method of "Illuminated Printing":

> If a method of *Printing* which combines the Painter and the Poet is a phenomenon worthy of public attention, provided that it exceeds in elegance all former methods, the Author is sure of his reward.
>
> [*Prospectus,* K.207. My emphasis]

Blake would not have seen a metaphysical distinction between his "elegant" method of printing his own works and his laborious adornments of Young's *Night Thoughts*.

Blake's designs, then, have their own value in the work of art which is Blake's book; to the commentator on his poems their chief value is heuristic and corroborative. Except for those that are purely decorative, Blake's designs can provide clues to his poetic meaning and can corroborate a particular interpretation. While the poems are independent as poems and do not require the designs, the critic should use all significant aids to interpretation—not because he must have them but

## Note

because by using them he is more likely to be right. My remarks on them are not meant to be adequately descriptive, but rather to show how they reinforce the poems.

The copies I have used in commenting on the designs are *Songs of Innocence,* copy P, and *Songs of Innocence and of Experience,* copy M, both in the Beinecke Library of Yale University.

## 9. Songs of Innocence

### INTRODUCTION

This graceful poem introduces the realm of Innocence by telling how these poems came to be written, what they are to be about, and to whom they are to bring joy. That is all very clear, and the dramatic form of the poem, characteristic of most of the poems that follow, relates these things in a way that unites the adult poet with the child. The simplicity of the words, the repetitions of phrasing, and the directness of feeling belong to the speech of children; the intellectual control and the symbolic implications are adult. This fusion of the childlike and the adult presents the child's unfallen world as being penetrated by religious insight but given form and explicitness by the wise innocence of a more comprehensive intelligence. The idea of Christ, who is both child and man, is the underlying idea that unifies, indeed identifies, the piper and the child in this and all the poems of *Innocence*. This identification of naive and wise innocence is symbolized also in the Lamb, who is at once the helpless and vulnerable child and also the Lamb of God—the watchful and shepherding adult. This special realm of child, adult, and lamb, all ultimately one, as implied by the word atonement, is imaged as a special pastoral world, that must be written about with a "rural pen."

I have mentioned already (above, pp. 27–28) that the poem is also a symbolic account of the way Blake was inspired to compose this unique series of poems. The secular and Panlike occupation of the unthinking piper at the beginning presents a contrast with his serious and dedicated occupation at the end, a contrast which also applies to the difference between Blake's earlier secular pastorals and the religious poems of *Innocence*. But the poem is not just about the moment of joyful religious and artistic inspiration; it is also about the process of making poetry out of such inspiration, and here the controlling force of adult intelligence is both represented and shown in operation. At first the inspiration is wordless, a feeling, a melody without lyrics. But the melody is so beautiful it must not be lost:

> "Piper pipe that song again."
> So I piped: he wept to hear.

It must be given words:

> "Drop thy pipe, thy happy pipe;
> "Sing thy songs of happy chear:"
> So I sung the same again,
> While he wept with joy to hear.

And, finally these words must be preserved "In a book that all may read." The poem, graceful and modest in its form, implies no false modesty as to its origin and intent. The form is simple and lyrical, but the purpose is in the line of prophecy—a direct statement of that which is divinely inspired. The "joy" that "every child" who hears these songs will feel, like the joy which filled the child on a cloud, is a divine and prophetic joy.

*The Design.* The intertwined stems on the right and left margins form symmetrical oval enclosures, four on each side. These frame various tiny scenes, not etched in detail. They are as follows: Left margin, from top to bottom: A child stands before a seated adult. A naked youth stretches his arms outward in joy. An adult stands pensively beside a bed, possibly a sickbed. A mother looks lovingly into a cradle. Right side, top to bottom: A bird flies upward. An adult sits pensively. A girl sows seed. An old couple sit under a bough. The bird may represent the upward flight of the soul. The other scenes represent various stages of life from birth to old age. Thus, while the design does not illustrate the poem, it does introduce some of the main themes of *Innocence:* joy, sorrow, guardianship, and the cycle of life.


## THE SHEPHERD

As a figure who represents the sacramental relationship between an adult and the children nurtured by him, that is, the relationship between God and Man, the Shepherd is also a symbol of the poet who concerns himself with the spiritual nurture of children. *His* lot is sweet because he fulfills the divine care; *his* tongue shall be filled with praise. Blake usually placed this poem immediately after the "Introduction," probably because it so perfectly expressed the interchangeable identities of God and Man, Shepherd and Lamb, Guardian and Child. It is one of the most direct expressions of the meaning to Innocence of life in its worldly dimension, the dimension which pertains to human interrelationships. The central theme of Innocence with respect to this side of life is guardianship (Mercy, Pity, Peace, and Love) and that is probably why Blake immediately after "The Shepherd" often placed "Infant Joy," a poem which pertains to the first expression of the inborn "Divine Vision." The two poems taken together comprehend the two main themes of *Innocence,* and I have, accordingly, discussed them in some detail in the introductory essay. Comments on "The Shepherd" are to be found above, pp. 28–30.

To these comments it may be added that "The Shepherd" emphasizes the terrestrial meaning of "Peace," which is primarily, "Trust":

> He is watchful while they are in peace.

The trust which brings peace is that of the sheep *and* the shepherd the guardian *and* the child. He follows his sheep, and he, too, knows when his shepherd is nigh. When he "hears the lamb's innocent call" and the "ewes tender reply," his heart is at rest within his breast, just as the nurse's is when she hears the voices of children on the green and laughter on the hill. One reason, of course, that the feeling of trust becomes the paramount feeling is that the poem deliberately recalls the most famous poem of trust ever written. In doing so, it effectively fuses the Old Testament symbol of the Shepherd with the New Testament symbol of the Lamb; it fuses them by identifying them.

*The Design.* While the shepherd, crook in hand, watches, his sheep peacefully graze. One lamb is looking up at him. This is a pattern that recurs in "The Lamb" and "Spring." By distinguishing one lamb from the rest of the flock, Blake preserves the symbolic value of *the* Lamb, and at the same time preserves the sacramental meaning of all sheep and shepherds.

## THE ECCHOING GREEN

For an extended discussion of this poem the reader is referred to pp. 39–41, above.

It is of small consequence to an interpretation of the poem, but still helpful in understanding Blake's poetic development, to compare his use of pastoral imagery in *Poetical Sketches* with his use of it in this poem. The following is from "I love the jocund dance":

> I love the oaken seat
> Beneath the oaken tree
> Where all the old villagers meet
> And laugh our sports to see.

Taken out of their context, the similar lines from "The Ecchoing Green" do not seem a great advance:

> Old John, with white hair,
> Does laugh away care
> Sitting under the oak
> Among the old folk.
> They laugh at our play.

The later lines would be no more worthy of preservation than the earlier if they had not been transformed into a symbol of the larger cycle of life instead of pastoral pleasures like jocund dances, innocent bowers, and "Kitty." In "The Ecchoing Green" (the earlier poem has an "echoing hill") Old John and the young folk are alike children of God, and represent the full spectrum of earthly existence, which is, looking at its happier aspects, only a brief period of "play" before the sun goes down. Blake managed to deepen his unpromising early use of the pastoral mode only by bringing it to the service of a religious vision; and in helping Blake discover the sacramental implications of the pastoral mode, the much-dismissed Swedenborg deserves the principal credit.

*The Design.* First plate: The upper half of the plate is entirely filled with a carefully etched scene of the village green. Under a great tree in the center sit three mothers who caress their weary children. A father sits with them. Older children are playing on the green. To the left of the text a boy stands holding a bat; to the right another boy rolls a hoop. Second plate: The bottom half shows a family on their way home from their sports. A mother and father are surrounded by seven children. The father points homeward. In both of these illustrations the themes of parenthood and guardianship are stronger than in the text. But the image of the father who gently guides his weary children home strongly reinforces the sacramental implications of the poem. Like most of the poems having two plates, the first refers to actual life, the second points to Eternity.

## THE LAMB

This is a question and answer poem like "On Another's Sorrow." The child who questions the lamb is like the adult who catechizes the child, and one important idea of the poem is, of course, that the questioner and questioned are in a deep sense identical. As in the other poems of Innocence, the higher and lower in consciousness are identified through their mutual identity with God, who himself combines all levels of conscious life: as a helpless animal (the lamb), as an infant (the Christ child), and as a suffering man. Here, of course, Christ the man is deliberately omitted, along with all idea of an adult percipience that includes tears and pity. The poem emphasizes the joy of the immanent God, his mildness, and his tenderness, while the adult reader implicitly knows that this joy is owing to an atonement neither the child nor the lamb are aware of.

The viewpoint is similar to that of "Infant Joy" and "Nurse's Song." Life itself is joyous and mild, and un-fallen nature echoes the lamb's tender voice just as the hills and valleys in other poems echo the voices of chil-dren. Bateson points out that the phrase "clothing of delight" is not a personification, but a characteristic way of saying "delightful clothing." [1] Surely, though, the lamb both has delightful clothing and is clothed by God with delight; the phrase tries to identify the actual and the sacramental just as the poem identifies the child and the lamb.

The construction of the poem is artful. The couplets which open and close each stanza are three-stress with feminine endings, the central couplets four-stress with masculine endings. This rhythmical contrast is effective in presenting the child's playful delight while asking the question, and then his more thoughtful enumeration of the question's implications. In this enumeration the child takes up one idea in each couplet, on the principle of one rhyme—one thought, as is proper in the poetry of Innocence. The child is equally delighted in asking the question, in announcing that he will give the answer, and then finally, in giving his blessing. The force of the poem is cumulative, and the sensitive reader will feel the victory of the child's mind over its superficially tame matter as it works its way to a conclusion which goes beyond its original thought. The new idea comes in at the line:

He became a little child.

And from that point the movement is crescendo.

1. *Selected Poems of William Blake,* ed. F. W. Bateson (London, Heinemann, 1957), p. 117.

# The Little Black Boy

*The Design.* This is an illustration of the poem. Below the text a child stretches his arms towards a lamb. Sheep graze behind them and to the right stands a thatched cottage. Since the poem is about the delight of actual life as well as its sacramental meaning, the realistic touch lent by the cottage is quite appropriate.


## THE LITTLE BLACK BOY

Blake did not attempt to parody this poem in the *Songs of Experience.* From the standpoint of the social reformer the poem would have been a pointless object of satire, since it was already an implicit indictment of slavery. The little Black boy and the little English boy have the same father, and ultimately the same color:

> And I am black, but O! my soul is white.

The final lines of the poem are meant as an admonition that refers to life in the world as well as to Heaven:

> And *then* I'll stand and stroke his silver hair,
> And be like him, and he will *then* love me.

But since the poem shows that the little black boy is *already* like the "English child," the point of the poem vanishes unless the reader responds to its gentle didacticism. The lack of moral indignation in handling these explosive materials does not imply a lack of moral fervor. Men are cruel to each other just as they had been cruel to Christ, but the true meaning of that cruelty resides in the love with which it is answered by Christ and by the little Black boy, who in this poem quite explicitly has Christ's role as intermediary between the little English boy and God.

The bad luck of his having a dark skin "as if bereav'd of light" is compensated for by his being able to bear the rays of the sun—"the beams of love." This is the Christian paradox on which not just this poem but all of the *Songs of Innocence* center. "We are put on earth a little space" to experience sorrow and to feel Mercy, Pity, and Love. That is how we gain what Blake in his marginalia to Swedenborg called "Understanding." The greater our sorrow, the greater our understanding of the "beams of love." It is the little Black boy who at first stands closest to God in his Golden Tent, for he has already "learn'd" what the little English boy must still discover.

The color of the little Black boy is therefore not just an occasion for Mercy, Pity, and Love, but also a symbol of human life. All men are like the little Black boy in that their souls are purer and better than the clouds they inhabit. The built-in ills of life are symbolized by the built-in bad luck of the little Black boy. Not all have black skins, but all have what that darkness symbolizes—ineluctable suffering and sorrow. Ultimately his bad luck will change and so will everyone's, but without suffering we cannot learn to bear the beams of love. The little heathen myth of the mother is thus an explanation of the nature of life and of evil. The Negro mother expresses the universal poetic-prophetic genius: All religions are one, and they are all versions of Blake's kind of Christianity.

This poem, as I suggested in the introductory essay, is a central and typical poem of Innocence. The primary themes of sacramental guardianship and prophetic vision have equal weight and are perfectly integrated. The mother is the guardian-Christ who lovingly explains both the meaning of suffering and of Eternity:

Comfort in morning, joy in the noonday.

# The Blossom

(Since God dwells in the Sun, the noonday, the time when his beams are strongest, is the symbol of Eternity.) Similarly, the little Black boy is the guardian-Christ of the English child, shading him from the heat until he too can bear the beams of Love. And, finally, of course, God is the ultimate guardian who comforts us through life and then mercifully releases us from it:

> Saying: "Come out from the grove, my love & care
> And round my golden tent like lambs rejoice."

*The Design.* The poem is presented on two plates. First plate: The upper third is entirely filled with a picture of the little Black boy being lovingly instructed by his mother. The sun has just risen, and symbolizes the beginning of the little boy's earthly life. Second plate: A very fine design. God as Christ is seated beneath a tree, on the far bank of the river of life. Under his arm, a shepherd's crook rests against his shoulder. He caresses the little English boy while the little Black boy strokes the English boy's hair. Needless to say, the first plate is a scene from earthly life showing the guardianship of the little boy's earthly parent. In the second scene the children are in Eternity with their heavenly parent.

## THE BLOSSOM

This is the most difficult poem in the *Songs of Innocence.* The only full-dress explication I know of is by Wicksteed, whose theory that the poem symbolizes love and sexual intercourse I cannot accept. The difficulty of the poem is not that it is elliptic and compressed, for that is true of all the songs, but that it does not point very clearly to a literal context. We are puzzled in trying to visualize the scene and in trying to make out who is speaking. We are puzzled, too, by the shift from third to first person in each stanza and from sparrow to robin between the stanzas. Oddly enough, the seen sparrow is "merry" while the heard robin is "pretty." These difficulties in making out the literal context of the poem suggest that an analogue to the symbolic meaning is not easily found in direct experience. Thus our very difficulty in visualizing the scene suggests that the symbolic implications lie outside ordinary experience.

In the separate issues of *Innocence* Blake always placed the poem before or after "The Lamb," another poem involving animals and the pastoral scene. In "The Lamb" the speaker is a child; in "The Blossom" the speaker is not identified, and this presents a great difficulty, for there must be some significance in the fact that the scene is viewed not from the speaker's perspective, but from the blossom's. Perhaps this double perspective is required because Blake did not want the blossom to commit the absurdity of speaking. Another problem is that Blake calls the poem "The Blossom" even though it is about a sparrow and a robin.

The blossom is happy, unchangeably happy, just as it is unchangeably rooted to one place. The sparrow is merry and in flight, the robin sad and for the moment apparently stationary. The scene is set under leaves so green —in a kind of Arcadian bower. And, quite remarkably, everything apparently happens near the speaker's bosom. Except for the fact that it treats both joy and sadness, this poem is unlike any other of *Innocence*.

The design, however, bears striking resemblance to the design of "Infant Joy," except that the flamelike structure in "Infant Joy" represents a blossom, while that in "The Blossom" does not. In both designs a female figure lovingly holds an infant, and in "The Blossom" that figure is an angel surrounded by cherubs.

## The Blossom

In "Infant Joy," however, an angel has just handed the babe to the mother. Another fact that may be of significance is that Mrs. Barbauld, from whom Blake gleaned many of his images and themes, associates blossoms with the bosom of a personified nature and also frames her scene with green leaves (*Hymns in Prose for Children,* Hymn VII).

At least two reasonably plausible interpretations of the symbolic sense present themselves. The first is supported by the images from Mrs. Barbauld. The speaker is earth, and therefore everything happens near her bosom. In earth's realm—"under leaves so green"—there is a contrast between the insentient and unconscious creatures, represented by the blossom, and the more human dimension of life, represented by the birds. Unconscious life is mutely happy and unchanging; conscious life feels intenser joy and intenser sorrow. While this more human existence is no more divine than the other (both belong to God's creation), it is more like the Godhood itself, more like the divine humanity. "We," says Mrs. Barbauld, "are better than they and can praise Him better" (Hymn II).

While this interpretation does fit the poem, and explains better than any other why everything occurs near the speaker's bosom, it is troublesome because it is so disjunctive both with Blake's design and with the characteristic themes of *Innocence.* An interpretation that is more in conformity with these would be that the blossom is itself a symbol of birth—as in the design to "Infant Joy." The merry sparrow on its way to its narrow cradle is the soul, still free of corporeality, on its way to be born into life. The sad robin would be the soul imprisoned in the body at birth, sobbing because of its imprisonment. The speaker, in that case, could still be earth.

A third interpretation that has been suggested is that

the speaker is a mother who is disposed to call her baby
a sparrow when it is happy and a robin when it is sad,
though one wonders why, in that case, the blossom need
be alluded to.

*The Design*. Tongues of flame dart into the spaces
of the text from a stem of flame on the right. On the
flames above the text six cherubs are happily playing.
Among them an older, female angel bends over a baby
which she holds in her lap. This figure lends support
to the idea that this is a poem about birth.


## THE CHIMNEY SWEEPER

This is the poem of Innocence that most directly confronts what is elsewhere called "distress," "sorrow,"
"grief," and "care." But just because the misery of life
is so concretely realized, the affirmation of visionary joy
is more triumphant than in any other poem of the series.
The moving contrast between the squalor, soot, and
hopelessness of the sweepers' actual existence and the
joy, freedom, and brightness of their visionary existence
is one of the most memorable effects in Blake's poetry.
This contrast, too, evokes more forcefully than any
other poem by Blake the interwoven sacramental experiences of sorrow and joy.

One hardly notices the virtuosity with which Blake
accomplishes the feat. In the first stanza he consciously
exploits explosive materials, and his offhand way of
presenting a Dickensian situation is dangerously double-
edged, quite as congenial to Swiftian irony as to the complex quite unironic effect Blake actually achieves. The
speaker recounts his Christlike sufferings with an acceptance like Christ's own. His mother's death he puts
into a dependent clause, and his being sold by his father

like a piece of merchandise he emphasizes less than the fact that he was very young. The words "died" and "sold" fall at the same relatively unemphatic point:

> When my mother died I was very young,
> And my father sold me while yet my tongue
> Could scarcely cry " 'weep! 'weep! 'weep! 'weep!"

The third line compels our response in the direction of pity, not savage indignation. The appeal to the sacramental emotion of pity is direct; the child, in the next line, offers to sweep *our* chimneys. This element of social protest is neither explicit nor angry. We must act as the child's guardian and relieve his suffering, just as he acts as guardian to little Tom Dacre. But there is no protest against the system. The poor you have always with you, and suffering—the memory of Christ's story—will exist in another form if not in this one. The didactic element in the poem is directed to individual acts of Mercy, Pity, and Love, not to acts of Parliament.

Having introduced the reader to the squalor that elicits pity, Blake in the second stanza moves closer to the spiritual triumph that elicits joy. The chief personage becomes Tom Dacre, who now stands to the speaker as the speaker ought to stand to us. We are not reassured to know why Tom is lucky to have his hair shaved, but Tom is reassured. And while Blake again skirts the domain of Swiftian irony, the more fundamental irony is that this is the only kind of comfort men can provide each other for the built-in ills of life. This comfort, so incapable of changing the fact of those ills, nevertheless works. The triumphant effectiveness of the pathetically ineffectual is the most inspiriting idea of Christianity, and this poem catches the flavor of the New Testament, as Blake meant it to do.

The sweep is Tom's guardian and comforter, and

brings him peace: "And so he was quiet." Then Tom has his dream of Eternity—a bright summer's day, a green plain, and a pleasant, liberating swim. This vision which keeps Tom warm in the cold winter morning is something that has descended on him like grace, but it is also something he has borne within himself ever since he was an infant like the one in "Infant Joy." It is the memory of his source and the prophetic vision of his destination. It is the vision that warms every man in this life—not just chimney sweepers. The last line:

> So if all do their duty they need not fear harm.

is a misfortune that has already been discussed above (pp. 26–27), but a sympathetic reader will feel that the tone of the poem requires "duty" to be taken in a wider religious sense than "doing what one is told." It is not only Tom's duty that is spoken of but the duty of "all," and this involves *our* duty to Tom and to the speaker of the poem. It is the duty of Mercy, Pity, and Love, and the "harm" is spiritual harm—callousness and loss of hope. The harms of the world cannot be escaped.

*The Design.* Below the text, children are leaping and laughing in the sun. One child is being helped out of his coffin of black by God.

## THE LITTLE BOY LOST
### and
## THE LITTLE BOY FOUND

Though the two poems almost always appear together in Blake's issues of the *Songs,* "The Little Boy Lost" was evidently composed as an independent poem, and appears as such in *An Island in the Moon.* (In his final version Blake made a few very minor changes.) The main crux of the first poem is in the last words:

> the child did weep,
> And away the vapour flew.

This is radically ambiguous. Is there a causal connection between the child's weeping and the flying away of the vapor? If so, the flying away of the vapor would then be a positive event, a lifting of the mist. On the other hand, Blake in the sequel speaks of "the wandring light," and this implies that the vapor was an *ignis fatuus,* a delusion. And this, in turn, suggests that there is no causal connection between the little boy's weeping and the flying away of the vapor. On the whole, it seems probable that this was intended to be a poignantly sad little poem, rather than an affirmation that tears can miraculously lift fogs:

> Think not thou canst weep a tear
> And thy maker is not near.    ["On Another's Sorrow"]

This is the affirmation that is reserved for the sequel. The poem ends as it began, with the child still lost and following an illusion.

It is only in the sequel that the child's tears become efficacious. God appears "like his father in white" and leads the little boy back to his mother. Erdman has suggested rather plausibly that in its final form the pair of poems "implies that the will-o-the-wisp that has misled the boy is an impersonal god, for only a god in human form—or only a human father—can kiss and save the child." [1] This is the best symbolic interpretation that has been put forward, but the implicit satire against an impersonal God, though Blakean, is not characteristic of the *Songs of Innocence.* It is possible that the two poems affirm the humanity of God without satirizing anything at all. The poems may simply be another ex-

---

1. Erdman, *Prophet against Empire*, p. 115.

pression of the Divine Care in which the father (now dead) is replaced by God, and in which both God and the mother express the parenthood of God and the sacramental nature of guardianship. My own feeling is that the child began wandering in the dale to look for his father because he could not understand the fact of his father's death ("No father was there"). If so, the boy is in the position of poor Tom Dacre, an orphan who like everyone else has "God for his father."

*The Design.* "The Little Boy Lost": Above the text, a little boy in a dark forest follows a wandering light which is about to disappear off the left-hand edge of the picture. Blake's use of line emphasizes the threatening aspect of the place and the isolation of the little boy. The branch of the tree seems about to strike and the arched lines of the background appear to enclose the child in darkness. "The Little Boy Found": Above the text, God as Christ holds the child's hand and leads him out of the forest. The halo surrounding God's head contrasts with the treacherous *ignis fatuus* of the previous plate.


## LAUGHING SONG


This little poem was evidently composed earlier than any other song of *Innocence*. A variant version is found written (not in Blake's hand) in a copy of *Poetical Sketches* inscribed "From Mrs. Flaxman May 15, 1784." Just as the later, transferred poems fall between the contrary attitudes of Innocence and Experience, this poem falls between the secular pastorals of *Poetical Sketches* and the religious pastorals of the *Songs of Innocence*. At least once (in copy "E" of the combined *Songs*) Blake transferred the poem to the more secular world of *Ex-*

*perience,* though he showed his indecisiveness by keeping it in the *Songs of Innocence* as well.

Blake apparently decided to etch it as a song of Innocence because it was a pastoral poem about children and joy. Just as in "Nurse's Song" and "The Ecchoing Green," the landscape gaily echoes the laughter of children, and the atmosphere is one of complete harmony and joy. The speaker himself, if not a child, is a person who invites us to join in this thoughtless and unclouded happiness. Although the repetitions of "When" do throw the scene into an envisioned future moment, it is stretching matters to discover religious or prophetic reverberations. Essentially the poem is a combination of traditional pastoral and traditional children's poetry, with the key element of religious vision left out. It shows Blake just before he encounters the laughing child on a cloud, and is on the whole more interesting as a document showing the direction of his development than as a poem. The absence of symbolic associations is less impoverishing than the verbal tameness. In the green woods the stream is "dimpling," the birds are "painted," and the table "spread" with cherries and nuts. Nevertheless, the poem has its charm, and one can understand why Blake might have been fond of it, especially in its illustrated form. The etched version (with its illustration of dressed maidens and naked youths) is made more vigorous than the earlier manuscript version by the rearrangement of verses and the substitution of "Mary" and "Susan" for "Edessa" and "Lyca." But these are not substantial changes, and the poem belongs to the end of Blake's literary apprenticeship rather than to his poetical majority.

*The Design.* Above the text is a totally secular scene that fits the secular quality of the text. A table surrounded by elegant chairs is spread in a bower. The hands of the seated figures reach for wine goblets, and one figure stands to give a toast.


## A CRADLE SONG

I have discussed this poem in some detail in the introductory essay (pp. 30–31). The dream landscape which the mother invokes in the first stanza is a pastoral one that augurs Eternity, and in the second stanza the phrase "infant crown" suggests the Christ child even before the mother explicitly identifies her baby with Jesus in stanza five. It should be pointed out that the verbs of the first three stanzas, "form," "weave," and "hover" are imperatives, making the tone of the stanzas that of a prayer, not a description. The fourth stanza, for all its verbal infelicity is not altogether cloying:

> Sweet moans, dovelike sighs,
> Chase not slumber from thy eyes.
> Sweet moans, sweeter smiles,
> All the dovelike moans beguiles.

Moans are made by doves, sighs are not, but the line makes sense as a reference to the divinity of the infant, whose sighs do pertain to the dove as a symbol of the Holy Ghost. While smiles beguile (not "beguiles"), it is of more importance to notice that they are ultimately victorious over moans, just as the joy symbolized by Christ is victorious over his meaning as the man of sorrows. The victory is won by beguilement, by the charming away of suffering, cruelty, and sorrow through Mercy, Pity, Peace, and Love. In stanza three the mother smiles; in stanza five she weeps. She does both because her infant is the Christ, just as every man is. She weeps over the infant as Christ wept over her, but that weeping is overcome by the same Christ who "smiles on thee, on me, on all." Finally, in the poem as a whole just as in the stanza quoted above, holy joy gains the victory over a sorrow which is no less holy. This poem is the clearest instance of the way the *Songs of Innocence* sanctify the sorrow, love, and joy of ordinary life—not by making the human figures into anagogical symbols but by showing them to be the thing itself, the human form divine.

*The Design.* First plate: The text is decorated with vegetation. Second plate: Below the text Blake has etched a very detailed picture of a mother watching over her sleeping infant.

## THE DIVINE IMAGE

From the standpoint of theme and doctrine this is the central poem of the *Songs of Innocence.* The unabashed and unambiguous identification of the divinity of man and the humanity of God is, as I have pointed out, the foundation for the sacramental vision of life that is the theme and motivation of the *Songs of Innocence.* The true attributes of man are those of Christ, and the divine attributes of Christ are those of "the true Man." (*All Religions Are One.*)

Why does Blake choose the attributes of Mercy, Pity, Peace and Love? Why not Justice or Power or Glory? The current of Blake's religious feeling is toward God the Son, not Jehovah the Father, and the idea to which he is most fervently attached is the sense derived from the Christ story of the holiness of man's ethical being. When, therefore, Blake satirizes in *Experience* the "selfish father of men" ("Earth's Answer"), he turns his irony on a religious concept which had no place in *Innocence* even though, in his titanic rebellion and self-repudiation he attempted to find it there. The rejection of a separate, lawgiving Father (as opposed to a Christ-like Father) was implicit in his religious sentiment from the beginning, and when he later associated Innocence with the tyrannical repressions of such a Father, he committed an act of self-injustice that is as unfair to *Innocence* as it was convenient to the satirical purposes of *Experience*. In the one the feeling is ethical and sacramental, in the other naturalistic and direct. In the one the root ideas are "man" and "love," in the other "nature" and "life."

It is not very difficult to perceive that Mercy, Pity, and Peace are expressions of human, which is to say divine, Love. These attributes are what Love consists in because all men experience "distress." The world is a vale of tears because distress is necessary in teaching the soul the meaning of Love. Thel had failed to accept this necessary immersion in suffering life, and therefore remained in the twilight zone of the trimmer, neither damned nor redeemed. But Thel did recognize, even if she failed to gain "Understanding" (annotations to Swedenborg, K.89), that life is "A land of sorrow and of tears," and this is the fact that transforms human and divine Love into Mercy, Pity, and Peace. The Christ story is man's story and man's story Christ's. His Mercy and Pity is our Peace (which is also our joy: see pp. 33–34) and these compassionate virtues are therefore "virtues of delight." Our services of Mercy and Pity to others bring to them the Peace that Christ's Pity and Mercy bring to us.

Blake's poetic expression of this ardently sacramental Christianity is couched in a simplicity which is appropriate to the "delight and instruction of children" but which is no less complex for that. The childish simplicity of the verse expresses the New Testament paradoxes of wise innocence and complex simplicity:

## The Divine Image

> And all must love the human form
> In heathen, turk, or jew.

These are the traditional foes of the Christianity Blake advocates, but we love them ("must" implies both an admonition and a logical necessity) because they are Christians too—Christians in the real sense of the term:

> Where Mercy, Love & Pity dwell
> There God is dwelling too.

All religions are one because all men are one as Christ and in Christ.

Another complexity of the poem (overlooking the imaginative complexity of Love's being "the human form" and Peace "the human dress") is the identification of man and God in terms of father and child:

> For Mercy, Pity, Peace, and Love
> In God our father dear,
> And Mercy, Pity, Peace and Love
> In Man, his child and care.

This father is, of course, Christlike, not Jehovah-like, and man, his son, is the same as Christ, his son, while Christ is the same as the Father. Blake's view of God as a Christlike father (important in "The Chimney Sweeper," and "The Little Boy Found") is his way of expressing at once the identity of God and man and their loving separateness. God is both transcendent and immanent, but the relationship of the transcendent God (Father-Christ) to the immanent God (Man-Christ) is the feeling of sameness in difference which is the essence and meaning of love. It is the same loving relationship that subsists sacramentally between man and man. It is ourselves—"the human form"—that we love in "heathen, turk or jew" and it is at the same time God. Blake's equation of divine and human love implies a genuine love of God, for love is ultimately the sense of identity we feel with others, whether men or gods.

*The Design.* A flame, similar to that of "The Blossom," darts about the text. At the base of the flame God stands with arm outstretched in blessing. Below him, Adam reaches to touch his hand, and Eve lies close by. At the top of the flame angelic figures—without wings—are playing. One holds a loaf of bread and a pitcher of wine. The divine figures are human figures, and the flame a symbol of holiness.


## HOLY THURSDAY


Blake's two London poems in the *Songs of Innocence,* this and "The Chimney Sweeper," are among the best in the series. The verbal infelicity of "Seated in companies they sit," and the palpable design upon us of "Then cherish pity" are easily absorbed in the larger movement, so that Blake's lack of concern for elegant variation and his unabashed willingness to address the reader are both part of the strong simplicity of the poem. It is a relatively early piece, one of the three that appear in *An Island in the Moon.*

Blake is describing an actual scene. Bateson points out that in Blake's time the average attendance of charity school children on Holy Thursday was between four and five thousand.[1] No matter how dirty they might have been on other days, they were scrubbed for this occasion—a fact that gives point to Blake's appreciative first line: " 'Twas on a Holy Thursday, their innocent faces clean." They were also dressed in their best clothes. Their parade into St. Paul's must have been an impressive and moving sight. Blake is certainly delighted by the visual splendor of the scene: the children in red, blue,

1. *Selected Poems,* p. 121.

and green, the beadles with gray hair and snow white wands. What stirs Blake is the re-enactment before his eyes, and in an overtly religious context, of Christ's guardianship of man. It is re-enacted on an overwhelming scale. The beadles are shepherds: "wise guardians of the poor"; the children are "lambs." But once inside the cathedral, the aged men sit "beneath" the children, so that the roles of sheep and shepherd are interchanged just as in "The Shepherd."

Blake's imagination being stirred, the words that present themselves to him are inevitably biblical:

> O what a multitude they seem'd, these flowers of London town.

When he describes them "seated in companies," he is paralleling the occasion with the gathering of another multitude:

> And Jesus when he came out saw much people, and was moved with compassion toward them, because they were as sheep not having a shepherd . . . And he commanded them to make all sit down by companies.   [Mark 6:34, 39]

This biblical context explains Blake's use of the word "but" in the next line:

> The hum of multitudes was there but multitudes of lambs.

He is distinguishing between this peaceful sound and the sound his own words call to mind:

> The noise of a multitude in the mountains like as of a great people; a tumultuous noise of the kingdoms of nations gathered together: the Lord of hosts mustereth the host of the battle.   [Isaiah 13:4]

The song of the children is also a biblical re-enactment:

> Now like a mighty wind they raise to heaven the voice of song.

"The voice of song" is a majestic phrase that is quite commensurate with the imaginative impulse of the line:

> And when the day of Pentecost was fully come they were all with one accord in one place. And suddenly there came a sound from heaven as of a rushing mighty wind, and it filled all the house where they were sitting.
>
> [Acts 2:1–2]

The song is also like another sound:

Or like harmonious thunderings the seats of heaven among.

Blake's imagination has moved from the miracle of the loaves and fishes through the mighty wind that brings the gift of tongues and now lodges firmly in the Book of Revelation, where not only the song and the children, but also the "aged men" are transfigured:

> And round about the throne were four and twenty seats: and upon the seats I saw four and twenty elders sitting, clothed in white raiment; and they had on their heads crowns of gold. And out of the throne proceeded lightnings and thunderings and voices.   [Revelation 4:4–5]

In this poem one need not press the point that Blake's sacramental imagination typically moves from the idea of guardianship in the suffering world to the idea of joy in Eternity. The final scene is in Heaven as much as in St. Paul's and the child or beggar you drive from your door—cf. Revelation 3:20—is an angel of the Lord.

*The Design.* Above the text a straight line of boys march across the plate to the right, two by two, behind gray-headed beadles. Below the text a similar line of girls march two by two across the plate to the left, following a gray-headed matron. The effect of this is to suggest an immense line of children moving in a clockwise direction beyond the limits of the plate. Blake was obviously greatly impressed by the "multitude" of the innocents.

## NIGHT

This is a poem neither spoken by a child nor contrived to bring a child joy, but it is emphatically a poem of Innocence, for *Innocence* unlike *Experience* is much concerned with the fact of death. Death is a fact that *Experience* is not disposed to face, though it does come to grips with it in one poem, "The Fly." Individual death, on any naturalistic view, is individual extinction, and the best *Experience* can do is to affirm that the extinction of the individual is not the extinction of its life principle. Another individual will take its place. Plow over the bones of the dead; pluck the flower: "Another flower shall spring because the soul of sweet delight Can never pass away" (*Visions,* plate 1). Innocence fronts fearlessly "the cloud of mortal destiny"; Experience must "put it by." That is why Innocence can afford to admit that guardians can only "pitying stand and weep," when the tigers take their prey.

"Night" is an ambitious and visionary poem, but not one of Blake's most memorable. It has some fine touches. The setting, as in all the poems of Innocence, does not abandon the literal for the symbolic, but even so, the speaker who is seeking for *his* nest does make his symbolic point a little tendentiously. On the other hand, the poem effectively shows night to be a sorrowful and "dreadful" experience as well as a peaceful and fulfilling one.

Some verbal cruxes require comment. "Flocks have took," is normal usage, as may be confirmed by consulting Milton's "Nativity Ode." "Silent moves" disagrees with "feet of angels." The "thoughtless nest" where each bird is "cover'd warm" implies not just that birds cannot think, but that they are trusting.

The vision of Eternity in the final stanzas is based on Isaiah 11:6: "The wolf shall dwell with the lamb, and the leopard shall lie down with the kid; and the calf and the young lion and the fatling together; and a little child shall lead them," and also on Isaiah 65:25: "The wolf and the lamb shall feed together, and the lion shall eat straw like the bullock." Of course, Blake's lion is more Christian than Isaiah's; he not only lies down, but becomes a weeping guardian. "Life's river" is part of the landscape of Heaven in Revelation 22:1, and from the same chapter Blake takes the idea of contrasting earthly night with the "immortal day" of Eternity: "And there shall be no light there; and they shall need no candle, neither light of the sun; for the Lord giveth them light."

*The Design.* First plate: The design is primarily decorative. The branches of the tree in the right margin follow the contours of the text. But below the tree a lion sleeps. Since he is neither guarding the fold nor washing in life's river, he must be a real, predatory lion who might "rush dreadful." Second plate: A large, detailed design fills the lower part. Five figures are strolling in a bright garden. In some copies the figures have halos. As in most of the two-part designs, the second is an image of Eternity.

## SPRING

Since I have already commented on this little anagogical pastoral, I refer the reader to pp. 38–39 above, and here will merely try to startle him into looking at my comments and at the poem by quoting the relevant analogue to "Sound the Flute! Now it's mute":

## Nurse's Song

We shall not all sleep, but we shall all be changed, in a
moment, in the twinkling of an eye, at the last trump;
for the trumpet shall sound, and the dead shall be raised
incorruptible, and we shall be changed.

[I Corinthians, 15:51–2]

*The Design.* Another of the poems presented on two
plates, though this poem was obviously short enough to
fit on one. First plate: On the upper third of the plate
a mother gently supports an infant who stands on her
lap. He is reaching out toward a lamb who looks up
from among other peacefully grazing sheep. Second
plate: The infant is reclining on the grass and is gently
pulling the wool of the lamb who passes the infant. Like
most of the other two-part designs, this one moves from
actual life to Eternity. In the second plate the mother
has disappeared. Once the child has joined the Lamb, it
no longer needs its earthly parent or guardian.

### NURSE'S SONG

The nurse speaks to herself meditatively, then aloud to
the children. A little drama ensues, and finally the poet's
own voice speaking in the past tense, distances the scene
and gives it a significance that has already been discussed
above (pp. 32–33). These shifts of voice impose shifts of
perspective—from the adult world to the children's and
then to a "wise innocence" that embraces both. The emphatic image is of laughing children in a happy, echoing
landscape. It is the world of carefree childhood which
knows nothing of suffering. But the nurse's mood at the
beginning places this joy in the same adult perspective
in which the poet places it at the end. Her heart is at
rest,

## Songs of Innocence

When the voices of children are heard on the green.

Implicitly there are times when her heart is not at rest.

The center of the poem is the contrast between adult knowledge and childish ignorance. Each has a different way of interpreting the disappearance of the sun below the horizon. The nurse knows that this augurs night and unhealthy dews. The children know that it is still light, and so do the sheep and the birds. Both the nurse and the children are right; and in giving way to the children, the nurse expresses not only her love for them but also her understanding of their divine insight. Thus it turns out that the innocent children are just as wise as the experienced adult, and the full truth is one that encompasses both innocent joy and "the dews of night."

The nurse so perfectly re-enacts the role of the divine guardian that it is perhaps distracting to insist on the auguries of eternity in the poem. The reader should decide for himself the emphasis to be given phrases like "Till the morning appear in the skies," "And the hills are all covered with sheep," and

> play till the light fades away
> And then go home to bed.

Certainly, the laughing children are already in Eternity in an important Blakean sense, and I prefer not to stress the idea of that final Eternity which is so much more important in some of the other poems.

*The Design.* Below the text, across the width of the plate, Blake depicts a rather pretty nurse who peacefully sits reading. Before her on the green, boys and girls are dancing in a ring. The nurse does not have to watch the children. Their laughter has put her in peace.

## INFANT JOY

In the first stanza an infant and an adult address one another; in the second only the adult speaks, or rather, as we discover, sings. The singing adult is probably, then, the infant's mother, and the poem is a cradle song in which the mother ponders a name for her baby and finally, victoriously, discovers one. The happiness of the infant solves the mother's problem by suggesting the name "Joy," and the mother then sings a lullaby in which she confirms the name and prays for its continued appropriateness. This is the "realistic" account of what happens in the poem, and should be kept in mind in order to avoid the irrelevant question "How could a two-day-old speak?" On the other hand, the infant does speak, even carries on its share of a dialogue. Here Blake's reticence in employing inverted commas is functional, since it brings home to the reader the primary demands of the *Songs of Innocence*—adult empathy with the child. The poem expresses that empathy in its strongest form, motherly love. The absence of pointers like "the infant said," "the mother said," dramatizes the feeling of love and empathy. Neither the mother nor the child speaks separately; the child speaks the mother's joy, the mother the child's meaning. The dialogue is to be understood as occurring in the mother's singing as she listens to and watches her baby.

The refrain of the mother's cradle song is "Sweet joy *befall* thee." The infant's refrain is "I happy *am*," and we have therein the counterpoint between the child's knowledge of joy and the mother's foreknowledge of the sorrow in life. Yet the mother, through her empathy with the child knows both joy and sorrow, and the sacramental significance of both is implied here as in all the other poems of *Innocence*. All the Blakean sacramental themes are present—the idea of guardianship, the sense of peace which is also the sense of joy, and the feeling of love. The themes of Mercy and Pity are not, of course, emphasized, because there is no occasion for them, but they are implicit in the mother's solicitude for her child's future existence in a world that is inimical to joy.

The wider significance of building a little poem around the joy of a two-day-old is discussed in the introductory essay (pp. 41–43), but may be briefly alluded to here. The cycle of life as conceived in the poems of *Innocence* is a departure from Eternity, into a period of mixed joy and sorrow on Earth where man re-enacts the Christ story in order to learn "Love" and "Understanding," before he returns to Eternity. This is the cycle that Blake described on plate 99 of *Jerusalem* and alludes to in his earliest annotations of Swedenborg. It is also, I think, the idea underlying "The Blossom" and the other poems of *Innocence* that describe the unalloyed joy of children. A young child, having not yet fully entered the world, still retains the joy (Innocence *is* prophetic joy) of his heavenly origin. This primal joy, man's birthright and his truest being, is particularly pure in a two-day-old, and Blake daringly makes this very new infant the symbol of that inborn spark of divinity which preserves us through life.

The movement of the little poem is one of gradual distancing—from the pure identity of mother and child in the first stanza to their loving separateness in the second. The second stanza thus consolidates in a more conscious, meditative way what has happened in the first:

> Thou dost smile
> I sing the while
> Sweet joy befall thee.

The effect of this distancing is to suggest the larger cycle of life in which this is a significant moment.

*The Design.* Above the text of the poem, filling the upper third of the plate is a great opened blossom with petals of flame. Within the blossom a mother holds an infant on her lap while an angel stands close by with arms outstretched toward the infant. Below, on the right, is an unopened blossom that points downward. The opening of the blossom is probably a symbol of birth. The design supports the idea that the infant's joy is an inheritance from its divine source: the angel has, apparently, just given the infant to its earthly parent.

## A DREAM

This is, first of all, a poem that at every point celebrates the ideal of guardianship. The speaker's bed is guarded by angels as he sleeps:

> Once a dream did weave a shade
> O'er my Angel-guarded bed.

The ant, though lost, is herself a guardian, more concerned with the plight of her family than herself:

> O my children do they cry?
> Do they hear their father sigh?

Finally, the glow-worm and the beetles are guardians:

> I am set to light the ground
> While the beetle goes his round.

The dreamer's world is one in which everyone is both guarded and guardian, and even if he cannot help the ant in her trouble he does what every helpless guardian (cf. "Night") does:

> Pitying I dropt a tear.

The main idea of the poem is that of "The Divine Image," except that the divine lineaments are seen not just in the "human form divine" but in all life. God's care extends to the tiniest crannies of the creation.

Thus "A Dream" is an authentic poem of Mercy, Pity, Peace, and Love whose tone is that of unqualified trust in God's beneficence. The most interesting problem it presents, therefore, is that Blake in three early issues of the combined *Songs* transferred the poem to *Experience*. His probable reasons for doing so are highly suggestive because they give an insight into the latent naturalistic possibilities always existing in the outlook of *Innocence*. In this poem we witness, for instance, the ease with which Blake's faith in the immanental divinity of man can be extended to include the immanental divinity of the natural world as well. While this idea is merely latent in the original impulse of the poem (the insects are humanized not naturalized), it is not difficult to make the naturalistic side of the poem more prominent. Once we are inside the dream, there are no longer any angels. The speaker finds himself lying on the grass in the middle of the night, and in this trusting immersion in nature angels are apparently unnecessary. Furthermore, though the ant has lost her way, she has not been looking to providence but has been foraging like the ant in the adage who, "having no guide, overseer, or ruler, provideth her meat in the summer and gatherest her food in the harvest." And when the ant is "found," she is the beneficiary not of a special act of mercy, as in "The Little Boy Found," but only of the glow-worm and the beetle, who are following their appointed rounds. This lack of any special providence for this particular ant is just as suggestive of the divine autonomy of nature as of God's special care. No doubt it was God who set the "watchman of the night" to "light the ground." But once he is set there, "nature" will take care of the rest. It is notable that this is the only dream in *Innocence* which is about the natural world, and the only poem in which a nonhuman speaker is not in Eternity. It is, in other words, possible to read the poem as an illustration of the "Proverbs of Hell," and this is apparently what Blake in 1794 did.

Nevertheless, that is not the way the poem should now be read. Blake returned "A Dream" to *Innocence* because his exploitation of it in 1794 was not true to his original conception. On the other hand, it is a great mistake to take the poem too seriously. It is a fable that makes a serious and pious point about Divine care, but the subject is treated with a touch of Dr. Watt's "condescension," and there is also a touch of humor in the poet's sympathy with the insects. The glow-worm is not very Christlike or angelic but an appointed functionary who is slightly self-important:

> "What wailing wight
> Calls the watchman of the night?"

A "wight" is a person addressed by a gleaming knight, and in this case he is not the only watchman or knight in the forest. His way of handing over his charge is more constabulary than angelic.

*The Design.* The text is decorated with Blakean vegetation. In the lower right corner there is a tiny picture of a night watchman going his rounds.

## ON ANOTHER'S SORROW

Superficially this is the most vulnerable poem of the *Songs of Innocence*:

> Can I see another's woe,
> And not be in sorrow too?
> Can I see another's grief,
> And not seek for kind relief?

To this catechism the child is taught to answer

> "No, No! never can it be!"

but the adult knows perfectly well that there is something in the misfortune of his dearest friend that does not displease him. If Blake had not read La Rochefoucauld, he had read Swift. The poem is not written in forgetfulness of what is implied by the apparently sinister maxim of La Rochefoucauld; it is predicated upon it. Without a knowledge that men can be cruel, callous, and perverse, there would be no point in affirming that the "true man" is not these things. Can a parent remain unmoved by the sorrow of his child? The answer is "no" not because there are not callous, cruel, and perverse parents, but because such parents are not parents at all. The "true man," like the true guardian, is Christ in us, and this poem, like all the other *Songs of Innocence,* is built on the sacramental sense of life. In his last writings Blake turned the pietistic distinction between the "self" and the "true man" into an explicit principle that demanded the "annihilation of selfhood." In this poem— addressed to the child in the adult and to the "true man" in the child—the selfhood is "annihilate" to start with. Both the unknowing child and the poet-adult affirm a truth that empirical and palpable evidences of cruelty, callousness, and perversity cannot touch. The poem is, in fact, invulnerable.

It makes itself so by the simple assertion that we pity another's sorrow because Christ pities ours. This must be, since Christ is the Divine humanity and so are we:

## On Another's Sorrow

> He doth give his joy to all
> He becomes an infant small
> He becomes a man of woe
> He doth feel the sorrow too.

The present tense discloses the sacramental sense of life out of which the poem is written. Christ by becoming an infant gives joy, just as all infants give joy. The ambiguous identification of the Christ child with all infants is deliberate, and just as every infant is the Christ child, so is every man the man of woe. *That* is why every man pities another's sorrow. The poem could not be more impeccably logical. One need only set the first and the penultimate stanzas side by side to see the impossibility of a different answer to the questions of the poem:

| | |
|---|---|
| Can I see another's woe | Think not thou can'st sigh a sigh |
| And not be in sorrow too? | And thy maker is not by; |
| Can I see another's grief | Think not thou can'st weep a tear |
| And not seek for kind relief? | And thy maker is not near. |

While the poem is about guardianship and pity—like all the *Songs* that pertain to life in the world—the final stanza summarizes the entire sacramental cycle of life. The first two lines present the joy that is the inner vision of eternity:

> O! he gives to us his joy
> That our grief he may destroy.

Until we fully enter that envisioned Eternity all men, like Christ, must pity another's sorrow:

> Till our grief is fled & gone
> He doth sit by us and moan.

# Songs of Innocence

*The Design.* The text is decorated, not illustrated. On the left are stems and tendrils and outlines of human forms. On the right, the branches of a tree follow the contours of the text.

# 10. Songs of Experience

## INTRODUCTION

This was undoubtedly composed in late 1789 or early 1790 along with the quite similar "Voice of the Ancient Bard." Like the other transitional poems it combines something of the orthodox piety of *Innocence* with something of the naturalistic chiliasm of *Experience*. The only other poem in the original issue of *Experience* that does not appear in the Rossetti MS, "Ah! Sun-Flower," displays the same double emphasis on a fulfillment both in the natural world and in Eternity. Unlike any other poem of *Experience*, it pays serious homage to the "Holy Word" both as a concept and as part of the biblical tradition. (John was Blake's favorite Gospel.) The biblical allusions that fill the poems of *Innocence* are, excepting this one poem, notably absent in the poems of *Experience*. Blake quite clearly made this poem the "Introduction" to *Experience* by the same kind of cheerful opportunism by which he turned "Rintrah roars" into the

"Argument" of *The Marriage of Heaven and Hell*. But that is not to say that the poem is inappropriate as an introduction to *Experience*. It displays (in some of its lines) the same hopeful naturalism that is found in the poems that follow, and those elements in the "Introduction" which belong more to Innocence than Experience are immediately satirized in the parody that follows—"Earth's Answer." What could be more appropriate than to begin a self-satirical work with a piece of self-satire?

The plain sense of the words has eluded some readers. The first stanza presents—as always in the tradition of biblical prophecy—the prophet's credentials as one with divine authority:

> Hear the voice of the Bard!
> Who Present, Past, & Future, sees;
> Whose ears have heard
> The Holy Word
> That walk'd among the ancient trees,

The present Bard *was* there, because he *is* in the unbroken line of God-inspired men; he is but the latest vessel of the eternal voice of prophecy—"Thus saith the Lord." In that sense, this poem is as much the "Holy Word" as the voice that called out to Adam and Eve "among the ancient trees": "And they heard the voice of the Lord God walking in the garden in the cool of the day: and Adam and his wife hid themselves from the presence of the Lord God amongst the trees of the garden":

> Calling the lapsed Soul,
> And weeping in the evening dew;
> That might controll
> The starry pole,
> And fallen, fallen light renew!

## Introduction

The image of the Lord weeping in the evening dew
brings not only the authors of Genesis but also Milton
into the unbroken line of the Bard's predecessors, for it
was Milton who showed that God the Son called to the
lapsed soul. His Holy Word might (subjunctive of
"may") control the heavens ("pole") and bring redemption. The allusion here could be either to the renewal
of day after the night-time centuries of fallenness, or to
the restitution of that eternal Spring that was lost when,
according to Milton, the Fall turned askance the globe
of earth "twice ten degrees and more" to produce the
"change Of Seasons to each clime" (Bk. X, lines 668–79).
The first possibility is the more probable in view of lines
13–15. In either case, Blake's emphasis is not on a spiritual renewal in man alone, but in a total renewal of
Earth, which I take to mean a renewal of man's perception of and participation in the natural order:

> O Earth, O Earth, return!
> Arise from out the dewy grass;
> Night is worn,
> And the morn
> Rises from the slumberous mass.

In this stanza there has occurred an interesting shift of
perspective. The resurrection is no longer seen as the act
of a God who controls the heavens, but as the self-redemp-
tion of Earth. The image is of a sleeper under the night
stars who now rouses himself from the "dewy grass."
(The sequel-poem suggests in its use of "locks" that
Blake was thinking of Milton's "noble and puissant nation rousing herself like a strong man after sleep and
shaking her invincible locks," *Areopagitica*.) The autonomy and natural inevitability of Earth's resurrection is
suggested by its connection with the natural cycle of
night and day. Thus, while Blake has paid his homage in

the first two stanzas to the transcendent source of the redemption he prophesies, he affirms in this stanza his faith in the natural apocalypse as well.

But the poem is highly ambiguous on this immensely significant issue, and illustrates quite forcibly the ambivalence of Blake's attitude in the short period between the publication of *Innocence* and *The Marriage*. For he shows, in the last stanza, a certain mistrust or apprehension with respect to the natural or autonomous resurrection. Inevitably, as Shelley well realized, the natural apocalypse is sanctioned by natural processes—the cycle of the seasons, of night and day. These are the very cycles, we recall, that authenticate the "Proverbs of Hell." But these natural cycles are unceasing. If the renewal of Earth is the morn rising from the slumberous mass, then there is nothing to prevent Earth from going back to sleep, just as there is nothing to prevent the return of night in the natural world. The Bard therefore addresses the newly risen Earth with a plea (like Shelley's at the end of *Hellas*) for an end to cyclical lapses:

> Turn away no more;
> Why wilt thou turn away?

The coaxing tone is one that recognizes the cyclical possibility all too well. There is, after all, no reason to turn away:

> The starry floor,
> The wat'ry shore,
> Is giv'n thee to the break of day.

The Bard returns in the end to the idea of that greater daybreak of Eternity imaged in the *Songs of Innocence*. Until that daybreak, the beauty of the heavens and earth is sufficient fulfillment in the temporal world. The dome of earth is heaven's floor and the stars are earnests of the final dawn. One thinks of Novalis' address to Day in the first of the *Hymns to Night:*

> Do you sow
> In the expanse of space
> Those shining spheres
> To herald your omnipotence
> Your return,
> While you are far away?

*The Design.* The text appears in a luminous cloud that floats among the stars. Below, on another cloud, is a graceful couch on which a naked woman reclines. She is Earth at the moment of awakening. Like the poem, the design is idealized and optimistic.

## EARTH'S ANSWER

By asking "Does Spring hide its joy?" Earth satirizes Urizenic institutions; by copying the stanza form of the "Introduction" she parodies the preceding poem. Even within the *Songs of Experience* Blake combines social satire and self-satire. Earth ironically twists the Bard's own pious words in verbal echoes like "wat'ry shore," "Starry Jealousy," "Weeping," and "ancient men." One wonders how a systematic conception of the *Songs* could account for this parody within *Experience* of another poem of *Experience.* The poem is Blake's answer to the traces of his former pieties found in the "Introduction." "Earth's Answer" appears, of course, in the Rossetti Manuscript (#17) while the earlier "Introduction" does not, and most of the ironic verbal echoes found in the Manuscript are first thoughts, not later corrections. The main impulse of the poem is the impulse to self-satire.

Like the other parodic poems "Earth's Answer" is dependent for its meaning on another, independent poem that precedes it. Earth satirizes two elements in the Bard's prophecy: its docility before the "Holy Word," and its complacent optimism. The Bard had seen Earth actually arising; Earth quite properly answers: "Look, does this grey despair appear to be a resurrection?" The irony begins in the very first line, when Earth confronts the Bard's prophetic present tense with the actual present. She "arises," but only far enough to complain, and her night is far from being "worn":

> Earth raised up her head
> From darkness dread & drear.

The "fallen, fallen light" is *not* "renewed":

> Her light fled
> Stony dread!
> And her locks cover'd with grey despair.

"Fled" is adjectival (see canceled readings "eyes fled" and "orbs dead") and "Stony dread" is in apposition to "Her light fled." That is to say, Earth's lack of light is represented by her blind eyes, which look like stones. The eyes express "dread," and "dread" like a blind eye is as cold and lifeless as a stone. The compression is immense. The lines would have been less difficult if Blake had preserved "orbs dead," but, irony being more important than clarity in a parodic poem, he chose to echo the "light" of the previous poem. The locks that are covered with gray despair ironically echo the source of Blake's image of Earth's awakening—that is, Milton's awakening nation "shaking her invincible locks."

Earth is not consoled by being given the "starry floor" and "wat'ry shore" until some far-off Last Judgment. As the world is now constituted, the watery shore is a prison and the heavens the "allegorical abode" of "Starry Jealousy"—that is, of Nobodaddy, who is jealous of all natural delight. The liberation of natural instinct would, after all, dispose of the need for Nobodaddy and his heaven. Furthermore, Nobodaddy and the weakly cunning men who have invented him are incapable of releasing their natural energies. They have too little life to release, (They lack the divine substance, and are literally damned.) and they are therefore jealous of those in whom life surges. Just as the shore is now a prison, the garden is now a "den." The culmination of the parody is the allusion to the Bard's timid orthodoxy. The Bard was present when the "weeping" Christ had called to the fallen soul; he is one

> Whose ears have heard
> The holy word
> That walked among the ancient trees.

Earth has heard something else:

> Cold and hoar
> Weeping o'er
> I hear the father of the ancient men.

The counterfeit Christ is really a hoary old man (*he* is cold and hoar, not Earth), and his weeping if not counterfeit still sounds like death.

Here the parody, after a petulant outburst against the "cruel, jealous, and selfish" father, ends. The poem becomes a series of indignant rhetorical questions that contrast "delight," "joy," "youth," "morning," "spring," and "free Love" with "chains," "night," "hide (v.)," "darkness," "freeze," and "bondage." The plea of Earth, bitter as it is, implies that natural energies *can* arise apocalyptically to burst the bonds:

> Break this heavy chain
> That does freeze my bones around.
> Selfish! vain!
> Eternal bane
> That free Love with bondage bound.

*The Design.* The text is decorated with Blakean vegetation. Below, undulating across the width of the plate,
is a snake whose tongue darts out of his open jaws.
Like the poem, the design is a bitter comment on the
foregoing plate. Instead of the resurrection that was
promised, we are given an image of the continuing Fall.

## THE CLOD AND THE PEBBLE

This poem presents more clearly than any other song
the precise, metaphysical concept of the "Contrary States"
implied in Blake's general title page. It is therefore
highly significant that in the copies he etched immediately after adding the title page (copies C and D)
Blake placed this poem last as if to summarize the larger
dialectic. The poem is a brilliant example of the way
Blake combined the metaphysical idea of dialectical
oppositions (Prolific and Devourer, Hell and Heaven,
Male and Female) with satire. What the Clod of Clay
sings is not only a satirical representation of a feminine
or "Heavenly" view which, valid as it is, has false pretensions to exclusiveness, but also a self-satire of Blake's
own viewpoint in *The Book of Thel.* There the Clod
of Clay had sung to Thel:

> O beauty of the vales of Har! we live not for ourselves.
> Thou seest me the meanest thing, and so I am indeed.
> My bosom of itself is cold, and of itself is dark;
> But he, that loves the lowly, pours his oil upon my head.

> [plates 4–5, K.129]

The poem is very precisely structured and perfectly
symmetrical; six lines are devoted to each figure, and
each line in the last quatrain is the mirror opposite of
the corresponding line in the first. This precise balance

of the Clod by the Pebble implies an interpretation which gives them equal weight. The poem rejects neither of them as a valid form of love. It satirizes only the grandiose pretensions to exclusiveness in the view of the selfless Clod of Clay. That is why the Clod's view is presented first; the Pebble pronounces his views with equal exclusiveness, but his pronouncements have the positive effect of countering the views of the Clod. Like *The Marriage of Heaven and Hell* this poem gives equal philosophical validity to each of the contraries, but gives Hell the last word. In its reticence, however, the poem is a much less partisan presentation of the dialectic than *The Marriage*. It symbolizes the eternal opposition in a fearful symmetry, a terrible affirmation. Both sides are admired, and the whole cosmic principle which the poem so concretely presents is admired.

As I pointed out in discussing *The Marriage,* this cosmic principle is "life," and the aspect of the principle Blake treats here is "love." All life divides itself into opposing and conflicting principles and the same is true of love. Love is by its nature selfless, yet

> Nought loves another as itself
> Nor venerates another so
> Nor is it possible to thought
> A greater than itself to know.

> ["A Little Boy Lost"]

Love is both selfless and selfish, and must always be so. The contraries must always conflict. Moreover, the fundamental expression of life's polar oppositions, sexuality, is the foundation of the contrary aspects of love. The clod, selfless, passive, "devouring" is feminine; the pebble, selfish, active, "prolific" is masculine. Feminine love builds a gentle and passive Heaven in despite of Hell. Male love builds a violent and energetic Hell in despite of Heaven. The poem marries Heaven and Hell not by reconciling them (He who tries to do so "seeks to destroy existence") but by opposing them.

The opposition in the poem is, however, immensely affirmative, for the two kinds of love require each other and could not exist without each other. If the Clod seeks not "Itself to please" then it seeks to please another self. But what happens when two clods come together, neither of whom *can* be pleased by the passiveness of the other? The encounter of the two female principles would have the unfulfilling, even repelling effect of bringing two similarly oriented magnetic poles together or two poles of a battery both equally lacking in electrons. The vital spark occurs when the Clod and the Pebble come together, since the Pebble also requires the Clod. She whom he binds to his delight is surely no pebble! (The word "bind" in this context is not pejorative. The Clod *wants* to be bound in this way, just as the Nameless Female wants to be raped by Orc in the "Preludium" to *America*. This is another illustration of the danger of making facile generalizations about Blake's recurrent images.) Ultimately, then, the poem for all its uncompromising reticence and its element of satire, is a deeply affirmative representation of the holiness of life and the rightness of the natural order.

*The Design.* The upper third of the plate is entirely filled with a picture of six animals drinking from a stream. Together on the left are two ewes, a lamb, and a ram; on the right, a cow and a bull. Blake has used thematically two images from the poem: the cattle that trample the clod of clay, and the brook that holds the pebble. However, the design makes its point somewhat differently. It stresses the variety of created life in the contrast between sheep and cattle and also in the contrast of sexes. The idea of richness and variety is enforced by the figures below the text: two frogs, a snake, and a duck.

## HOLY THURSDAY

This is one of the four parodic poems of *Experience,*
and like them does not benefit on the whole by comparison with the poem it parodies. The "Holy Thursday" of *Innocence* is a finely imagined poem that traces
a majestic movement from a parade of London orphans
to the seats of Heaven. This poem is inspired by a partisan impulse of self-satire which makes it more vulnerable to satire than the poem it satirizes. The earlier poem
fastened on the actual scene to achieve its larger meaning; the parody presents the scene in images that belong
less to the poet's imagined perception of it than to his
determination to make a point. The actual sympathy
with the orphans of the earlier poem—sympathy with
their joy as well as their suffering—is transposed into
an abstract sympathy that makes the charity school
children appear merely as victims of social injustice:

> Is this a holy thing to see
> In a rich and fruitful land,
> Babes reduc'd to misery,
> Fed with cold and usurous hand?

Such an interpretation of the scene leaves out more of
the human complexity of the occasion than the highly
filtered interpretation of *Innocence.*

On the other hand, the lines that directly refer to the
singing of the children are the most effective ones in
the poem:

> Is that trembling cry a song?
> Can it be a song of joy?

That is telling, but one should be hard-headed with a
hard-headed poem and point out that several thousand

voices, even of deprived children, do not produce a trembling cry. This poem has a certain moral rightness, but it refuses to permit awkward complexities. Its partisanship falsifies by exaggeration what *was* true in the earlier conception.

This exaggeration is most apparent in the next stanzas:

> And their sun does never shine,
> And their fields are bleak & bare,
> And their ways are fill'd with thorns:
> It is eternal winter there.

Presumably, this must allude entirely to the physical plight of the children. As a description of their spiritual condition the lines fail to carry conviction. Is a charity school orphan always unhappy? Does he never see the sun? Are there no flowers among the thorns? In the earlier poem the suffering of the children was at least implicit; in this poem the children are disallowed even momentary joy.

It is, then, an overly partisan and overly simple poem which shows quite clearly the apocalyptic naturalism of the *Songs of Experience*. Blake's images imply that the social arrangement that has produced charity schools and usurous hands has gone wrong because it has gone against nature. It is unnatural for the sun never to shine and for winter to persist forever. But, on the other side, it is natural that babes should never hunger:

> For where-e'er the sun does shine,
> And where-e'er the rain does fall,
> Babe can never hunger there
> Nor poverty the mind appall.

Blake's images of the natural paradise are sanctioned by natural processes, and these are already in operation. Man could remake his world, by being only what he ought to be, that is, by cleansing the doors of perception. What makes this poem, quite apart from its exaggeration, more vulnerable than its predecessor is its failure to recognize that if "eternal winter" is unnatural, so is eternal spring. No poem in the series better illustrates what Blake later came to perceive: that the *Songs of Innocence* have a firmer grasp on actual experience than the *Songs of Experience*.

*The Design.* Above the text, Blake shows a woman looking in horror at a naked child stretched out on the ground, dead. To the right of the text, a mother sits with face averted from her two children. She holds one of them in her lap while the other stands, weeping. Below, on the right, another child lies dead. Like the text, the design strikes a melodramatic note of protest.


## THE LITTLE GIRL LOST
and
## THE LITTLE GIRL FOUND


As I indicated in Section 4 of the introductory essay, these were composed in late 1789 when the Revolution was beginning to exercise its immense effect on Blake's thinking. The pair of poems is similar in a number of ways to the other poems of the transitional period—"The Voice of the Ancient Bard," "The Schoolboy," the "Introduction" to *Experience,* and "Ah! Sun-Flower." "The Little Girl Lost" and "The Little Girl Found" are to be regarded as two parts of a single unit, since Blake printed the beginning of the second poem on the same plate with the end of the first. Even if he had not done so, the story related in the first poem would obviously be incomplete by itself; Lyca's parents are prominently mentioned there, and a sequel is clearly required to disclose what has happened to them. This is one of the strangest and most haunting of all the *Songs,* and it is in some ways unique. Though he originally issued the poem in the *Songs of Innocence,* Blake transferred it to the *Songs of Experience* in the earliest extant copy of the combined *Songs,* and he kept it there in all subsequent copies. It is, then, the only transferred poem which he consistently regarded as a song of Experience. Some of the major difficulties of interpretation involve the relationship of the Bardic introduction to the rest of the poem, and it seems best to reserve comment on the introduction until after the narrative has been discussed.

One striking aspect of the narrative is its fairy-tale quality. Its world is one where lions weep ruby tears and turn into human-like spirits armed in gold. Yet these things happen, as in many fairy stories, somewhere in the actual world. The setting is the "southern clime," where it is always summer—a perfectly accurate fact of equatorial climate. Nor is there anything strange about the depicted landscape. It is true that Blake pictures a "desert" which he calls "wild" and which contains trees, birds, and forest beasts, but this simply indicates that he is using "desert" in its root meaning: an uninhabited and uncultivated tract of country, a wilderness. Within this desert there are caves and a "lovely dell." When the lion turns into a "spirit armed in gold" his cave, to which he had taken Lyca, turns into a "palace." The fairy-tale quality of the poem resides in the fact that quite miraculous things occur in the real world. Lyca is lost in quite a different way from the child in "The Little Boy Lost." She is not pursuing a mirage. She is not even calling out to her parents, and she is far more concerned with their sorrow in losing her than with her own plight. Her most striking characteristic is her childlike trust. She has the child's trust, for example, in telepathic communication. She knows whether or not her mother is asleep, and decides to sleep only if her

mother does, attempting a kind of loving blackmail to
prevent her mother from crying:

> How can Lyca sleep
> If her mother weep?
> If her heart does ake
> Then let Lyca wake;
> If my mother sleep,
> Lyca shall not weep.

This same kind of trust extends to her own situation.
She is not afraid to lie down under a tree and go to
sleep. Though she regards the night as "frowning," she
is not afraid openly to ask him to send his moon to
shine over her. In her trust, she does not *feel* lost; she
feels at home in the "desert bright." Her lostness is her
separation from her parents.

How did she become separated? Certainly not because
she deliberately ran away. (This needs to be said only
because some commentators insist that Lyca is asserting
her independence at seven years of age!) Blake does not
tell us so explicitly, but he suggests that the separation
was quite accidental. Probably Lyca is like the schoolboy Blake wrote about at the same period:

> I love to rise on a summer morn
> When the birds sing on every tree.

For all that we know about the cause of Lyca's predica-
ment is that:

> She had wandered long
> Hearing wild birds song.

It is not until the "beasts of prey" appear that the
poem becomes fairy-tale-like, and it is at this point that
interpretation becomes problematical. The stanza which
introduces the beasts is rather ominous, since Blake does

not at first explain that these particular beasts of prey
are harmless:

> Sleeping Lyca lay;
> While the beasts of prey,
> Come from caverns deep
> View'd the maid asleep.

But if this is contrived to make the reader slightly ap-
prehensive, the next stanzas are contrived to reassure
him. Lions who "gambol" and tigers who "play" on
"hallowed ground," are not very frightening. Lyca has
evidently wandered to a special holy place, though we
are not sure whether the ground was already hallowed
or her presence made it so. (The latter seems more
strongly suggested by the verse.) Nor can we be sure
why the affectionate lion weeps "ruby tears" over the
sleeping maid. The problem is not why his tears are
red (Flaming eyes would produce ruby tears) but why
he weeps there at all. Since he gamboled happily at the
sight of Lyca, perhaps these are Blakean tears of joy.
But one feels also that they are tears of pity and love
like those golden tears wept by the lion in "Night" who
had been translated to Heaven. This lion's tears may
be for the girl's lostness, but (and this is the greatest
problem of all) they may be for her death. This startling
idea is suggested by the final stanza:

> While the lioness
> Loos'd her slender dress
> And naked they conveyed
> To caves the sleeping maid.

The removal of the dress, a far from self-evident thing
to do, is strongly reminiscent of the removal of the
cloud in "The Little Black Boy," and the divestment
of the coffins in "The Chimney Sweeper"—both symbols
of the soul's separation from the body after death. The

case is even stronger when we note that Lyca is still sleeping when, seven days later, she is "found" by her parents. On the other hand, the place to which Lyca has wandered is remarkably like the natural Eden prophesied in the introductory stanzas, a place where lions are not ferocious and the season is always the same. And in such a natural Eden one is supposed to be naked, as Blake carefully shows us in his illustration on the final plate.

With the desert weeping in sympathy, Lyca's parents wander mournfully for seven days and nights, following a "fancied image" of their starving child. The biblical number seven begins to appear significant. Lyca's age and the number of days the parents wander strongly suggest providential control of events, as though everything happens at a divinely appointed time. After seven days, the mother collapses from sorrow and exhaustion, and just at that point the parents encounter a "couching" lion, ("couchant," "ready to leap"). The lion's actions are, to say the least, inconsistent, but they do follow a discernible pattern by moving gradually from the bestial to the human. The lion pounces violently, sniffs, licks hands, stands silent, and, finally, turns into a princely spirit who leads the parents to Lyca. Although the lion insists that Lyca sleeps in his "palace," the parents actually find her sleeping "among tygers wild." And there, in a "lovely dell" they live happily ever after. But the reader is again beset by doubts as to what has happened, for in the transformations of the lion we suspect that we are being told that Lyca's parents have been killed; the transformation of the lion into a kindly spirit looks suspiciously like the heavenly transformation of the lion in "Night." Lyca's parents are evidently in Eternity. And yet this is surely a new kind of Eternity never before adumbrated in the *Songs of Innocence:* a lonely dell, with tigers wild, howling wolves, and growling lions. These ominous sounds are not to be feared, but they are quite unlike the harmonious thundering among the seats of heaven.

If we now turn back to the Bardic introduction, we discover that it underscores these ambiguities, for the prophetic Bard by no means foresees the "immortal day" of the earlier poems of Innocence. He sees instead a self-transformation of "the earth." The image of the earth arising from sleep is, of course, the central image in the "Introduction" to the *Songs of Experience,* and here Blake goes on to say exactly what the result of this self-transformation will be. Earth

> Shall arise and seek
> For her maker meek
> And the desert wild
> Become a garden mild.

Blake's explicit insistence that "earth" will transform herself leaves no doubt that he envisions quite literally a New Eden, a reversal of the biblical Fall. Furthermore, the way he begins Lyca's story leaves little doubt that it is to be viewed as an earnest of his prophecy, for the first thing we are told is that Lyca lives in a land of eternal summer. Clearly, we are meant to view the story as a prophecy, not of Eternity as in the earlier innocence poems, but of "futurity." This is perhaps the first of Blake's poems in which the apocalyptic and prophetic impulse is explicitly directed toward the actual world rather than heaven. But it is also the last of Blake's prophecies of Eternity, and shows more clearly than any transferred poem the kind of transition Blake's thought was undergoing.

This is especially clear in his symbolic use of wolves, lions, and tigers. In the earlier poem, "Night," these animals are dangerous and dreadful predators who symbolize life's cruelty and evil. When they rush dreadful, the spirits of their victims are ushered into the bright new world of Heaven. There they discover quite a different kind of lion, one who is washed in the river of life, who weeps with pity, and who lies down with the lamb. There is none of this double-existence in "The Tyger," composed in the 90s. The terror of the tiger is not compensated for in some realm beyond natural life. He is confronted in all his danger, power, and beauty, and he is just as real and inevitable as the lamb, with whom he shall *not* lie down, not here, nor in any brighter, better world. A world which contains such fearful symmetry is quite awesome enough to fill the speaker's entire imagination. It seems to me that the wolves, lions, and tigers of "The Little Girl Lost" and "The Little Girl Found" are neither merely terrible as in "Night" nor beautifully terrible as in "The Tyger." Yet they are considerably more ominous than the lion who lies down with the lamb. They seem to exist somewhere between Eternity and the forests of the night.

The same thing may be said of Lyca and her parents. They are certainly innocent in their selfless love and in their pitying sorrow, but they inhabit a world which is far removed from the idealized pastorals of *Innocence*. That is not to say that the desert wild is not idealized; it is a wilderness in which there is permanent summer, singing birds, and only vaguely ominous beasts. But it is, nevertheless, a wilderness. The naturalistic quality of the setting is emphasized in Blake's illustration. Two adult figures embrace in the first plate. On the last, two lions and four naked humans appear in an attitude of loving repose under a double tree-trunk mutually entwined like the strands of a rope. This is not unlike a vision of Eternity, but it is also very like a terrestrial paradise. The realm of the poem is, in short, ambiguous. What has happened is that Blake's pastoral prefigurations of Eternity have fused with the Revolutionary

prophecy of the terrestrial paradise. The divine visionary realm that resided in the innocent breast is beginning to be connected not just with Heaven but also
with a perfected natural world. In a quite remarkable
way the poem hovers hesitatingly between these two
realms. In spite of this hesitation, the *direction* of the
poem is given in the Bardic introduction that is so
very like the prophecy in "The Voice of the Ancient
Bard." The transformation of life that occurs in Heaven
after death is beginning to be sought and envisioned in
the actual world. That is why Blake leaves the reader
in uncertainty as to whether Lyca and her parents have
died. On the whole, Blake's "Paradisal" "lovely dell"
is more Earthly than Heavenly, and that is why he never
doubted that the poem belongs in the *Songs of Experience.*

*The Design.* First plate: The first two, prophetic
stanzas of the poem are separated from the rest of the
text by half an inch of vegetation. To the right of the
text, a youth and maiden embrace. Her left arm is extended upward. These figures are very similar to those
in the design of "The Voice of the Ancient Bard," and
Blake probably means that they should reinforce the
prophecy of the first two stanzas rather than the rest of
the narrative. The "garden mild" which earth shall become is one in which love will be exalted and unre-
stricted. Second plate: The top half contains the end of
the "Lost" poem and a picture of Lyca about to go to
sleep under the trees. Lyca is, however, more than seven
years old. This probably does not have significance for
the text. The beginning of the "Found" poem is on the
lower half of the plate. To the right of the text is an
animal that could be a tiger, a leopard, or a female lion.
Third plate: To the right of the text two very thick
tree trunks twine around one another. Below the text
there are four naked human figures and a male and

female lion. Three of the human beings are children. One caresses the male lion, one is perched on the female lion, while the third helps him to dismount. Stretched out on the grass in the foreground is a naked woman who resembles the reclining "Earth" of the "Introduction." This is the earthly paradise prophesied in the first two stanzas. Earth has become a garden mild, and, as in the garden of Eden, the animals are gentle. Just as Blake terminated his earlier multiple-plate designs with Eternity, he terminates this one with "Futurity."

## THE CHIMNEY SWEEPER

The adult who speaks to the chimney sweep in this poem sees him not as a bright spirit in the midst of poverty and soot—the triumphant achievement of the poem being satirized—but as a sooty *object* ("a little black thing") of socially caused misery amidst the brightness and purity of the natural order. The " 'weep 'weep" of this poem could be the cry of some forlorn domestic animal. Blake's purpose in making the sweep an object in the first lines of the poem is the reformer's purpose of pointing to a horrid example:

> "Where are thy father & mother? say?"
> "They are both gone up to the church to pray."

It is not convenient to make *this* sweep an orphan, because to do so would subvert the point that poverty and suffering are entirely owing to the Urizenic social order. On the other hand, the disinclination of the earlier poem explicitly to deplore the exploitation of children did leave it open to attack. Not all sweepers are orphans, but all are objects of exploitation.

It is the genuinely vulnerable side of the earlier poem

(Blake in *Jerusalem* was penitential about his social complacency in *Innocence*—see pp. 163–64) that permits him to make a better job of a satire on "The Chimney Sweep" than on "Holy Thursday." Since the sweep really is exploited, Blake can safely grant him that measure of childish happiness which he should also have granted to the children of "Holy Thursday." The happiness of the sweep in no way justifies his misery but simply makes the wickedness of his being exploited all the more apparent. Consequently the attack on *Innocence* is highly effective, because what makes the sweep happy in his misery is not that sinister delusion, Heaven, but the strength of life that is in him:

> Because I was happy upon the heath
> And smil'd among the winter's snow
> They clothed me in the clothes of death
> And taught me to sing the notes of woe.

It is the continuation of that heath-nurtured vitality even within the squalor of the city that accounts for his irrepressible joy:

> And because I am happy & dance & sing,
> They think they have done me no injury.

The two parallel uses of "because" show Blake at his satiric best. First, it was because the sweep was happy upon the heath that he had to be taught the notes of woe. The notes are " 'weep! 'weep!" and also hymns in church to the jealous god. The clothes of death and the notes of woe are the same, since without social misery there would be no point in laying up treasures in heaven. The parents therefore,

> are gone to praise God & his Priest & King,
> Who make up a heaven of our misery.

## The Chimney Sweeper

The first "because" implies that his happiness and freedom is the cause of his being made subservient to the "Father of Jealousy" and to his Priest and King. The parents are simply the willing agents of the order to which they are themselves enslaved. The second "because" is equally incisive. The parents have misunderstood the sweep's happiness and think they have done him no injury because they think his happiness is owing to his docile doing of his duty and his hope of Heaven. The poem, on the other hand, makes quite clear that the sweep is happy in spite of these mournful and repressive "clothes of death." Nor do the parents understand that the heaven which supposedly cheers up the sweeper is really made up of his misery. Without that misery it would not exist.

The savage indignation of the poem is conveyed with great compactness and telling irony. Blake's favorite kind of phrase—"clothes of death," "notes of woe"—is used with great effectiveness. It should be pointed out, too, that the generating source of this passionate satire is a religious faith that is quite as fervid as the faith that inspired the earlier poem. The image of the chimney sweep on the heath represents a possible fulfillment that in being naturalistic is no less piously believed in than the heavenly fulfillment represented in Tom Dacre's wonderful dream of washing in the river and shining in the sun.

*The Design.* Below the text, a winter scene in London. Snow is falling. In the center "a little black thing among the snow" wearily trudges with his bag on his back. The scene is made as dismal as possible by Blake's use of black to represent footprints and falling snow.

*Songs of Experience*

## NURSE'S SONG

This satire of "Nurse's Song" is the most thoroughly parodic poem of *Experience*. Three of the eight lines precisely repeat lines of the earlier version, and the five remaining lines echo its wording and approximate its rhymes. The original is called "Nurse's Song," which is to say a song sung by Nurse. The parody is etched as "NURSE'S Song" which implies a song that is primarily *about* Nurse. This is confirmed when we notice that the later poem is half the length of the earlier and that, by disregarding the colloquy between the nurse and the children, it parodies only what the nurse says. Blake wisely limited his satire to the nurse herself. Experience would hardly want to satirize the playing of children on the green, since that is just what children ought to be doing instead of going up to the church to pray.

In order to direct his satire more effectively at the speaker of the poem, Blake has made the children she nurses older. Instead of laughing on the hill, she hears whisperings in the dale—the conspiratorial whisperings of adolescents—and this recalls the days of her "youth." It is the memory of her youth—not her childhood—that turns her face "green and pale" with Urizenic jealousy. What she says to the children is therefore a disillusioned projection of her own failure to "pluck fruits before the light" (Rossetti Manuscript, No. 24):

> Your spring & your day are wasted in play
> And your winter and night in disguise.

*Her* spring and day were wasted in whisperings and coy flirtations rather than open gratification of desire, and consequently her winter and night are now wasted in Urizenic disguise—that is, in hypocritical pieties that mask secret sexual longings. The poem is thus a satirical exemplum against the repression of natural instinct that makes the same point as "The Angel" and No. 68 of the Rossetti Manuscript:

> An old maid early—e'er I knew
> Ought but the love, that on me grew;
> And now I'm cover'd o'er & o'er
> And wish that I had been a Whore.

Blake plays the symbolism of the *Innocence* version and this version against one another. In the original the nurse's empathy with the children prompted a resurgence of innocence and blessedness within herself. This continuation of innocence in the adult was paralleled by the continuation of the sun's light after it had set. In the later poem the sunset parallels the nurse's later life in a different way, though the words are the same as before:

> Then come home my children the sun is gone down,
> And the dews of night arise.

Her sun, having been wasted in play, has gone down, and the dews of her night have arisen in the form of a Urizenic "disguise" that Blake has lifted.

*The Design.* A buxom but jealous looking nurse of about forty combs an adolescent boy's hair, while an adolescent girl, seated, is visible behind them. The picture supports the idea that the "children" of the poem are nubile and that Blake's primary notion of "wasted day" is repressed sexuality.

## THE SICK ROSE

"The Sick Rose" is sometimes read as an account of Beauty destroyed by Evil—a reading that gives the sexual imagery of the poem an appropriate sinisterness by suggesting the fatal attraction felt by evil for the innocent, passive, helpless, and beautiful. Such a reading for all its attractiveness is not entirely accurate. The rose is being satirized by Blake as well as being infected by the worm. The idea of sickness is the imaginative center of the poem, and part of the rose's sickness is her ignorance of her disease. Her ignorance *is* her spiritual disease because in accepting "dark secret love" she has unknowingly repressed and perverted her instinctive life, her "bed of crimson joy." The rose's sickness, like syphilis, is the internal result of love enjoyed secretly and illicitly instead of purely and openly. The repressive order which causes "holy men" to pluck fruits by night also corrupts the lady who accepts the hypocrisy. Secret love under the night-time coverlet produces the same internal disease that has infected the speaker of "A Poison Tree." The rose is the type of female who, enjoying the outward show of modesty (the rose and the sheep in "The Lilly") promotes the repressive and hypocritical customs of the "Father of Jealousy":

> Why darkness & obscurity
> In all thy words & laws,
> That none dare eat the fruit but from
> The wily serpent's jaws?
> Or is it because Secrecy gains
> females' loud applause?

[Rossetti Manuscript, No. 21. For other relevant examples see
pp. 89–91]

In this poem the inward harm that is done to the applauding female is the main theme, as it is also in "Nurse's Song" (*Experience*) and "The Angel."

Implicit in this idea of sickness is the idea of perversion. Secret, nocturnal love is particularly perverse because it changes what is life-giving into a disease that is

life-destroying. The perversion lies not just in the destructiveness of secret love but in its unnaturalness. Just
as there is no tree of mystery in nature ("The Human
Abstract"), so there is no invisible worm. He is an invention of the "human brain." What brings him to the
rose is the howling storm—the setting for man's perversion of the natural order in this poem as in *Lear*. The
perverted human order is contrasted with the open, natural order; dark secrecy with crimson joy, sickness with
health.

What Blake shows in this poem, then, does have a
connection with the theme of Beauty destroyed by Evil.
Natural joy is corrupted by stolen and perverted joy. It
is another of Blake's naturalistic versions of the Fall.
"Worm" is traditional for "serpent," and before Milton's
serpent perverted Eve he flew through the howling storm
of chaos and old night. In the traditional version sexual
shame was a consequence of the Fall; in Blake's it is the
agency of it. The rose existed in her natural paradise of
crimson joy before the advent of the corrupting worm
(Joy is crimson only in daylight), but that paradise was
not abstemious; it was crimson; it showed the "lineaments of Gratified Desire" (K.180). Finally, then, it is
right to respond to the profound suggestiveness of the
poem by recalling the insidious love that Evil bears to
Innocence and Beauty. In this case the evil is within
the rose as much as in external forces, and Blake satirizes
her as much as he regrets her fatal sickness.

*The Design*. Above the text on the branches of a rose-
bush two human figures are draped in attitudes of pain
and distress. A caterpillar eats one of the leaves. Below
the text is a large rose, into the center of which a caterpillar insinuates itself, while a female figure with arms
outstretched emerges. As secret love enters, life and joy
depart.

## THE FLY

I have shown at some length that Innocence accepts both the evils of actual life and the fact of physical death, which is for it a fulfillment rather than a loss. Experience, on the other hand, being entirely this-worldly, finds its fulfillment in actual life or not at all. The Piper looks upward; the Bard of Experience gazes straight ahead with vigorous expectation. The fact of death, therefore, presents Experience a knotty problem which, on the whole, it is not particularly eager to face. If fulfillment resides entirely in this life, death must appear to be negation, total extinction, and loss. "The Fly" is the one poem Blake wrote in the 90s which wrestles with the problem of death. "Wrestling" is the proper term to describe the false starts and alterations that appear in the manuscript draft of the poem, and, considering the perplexing quality of death for the viewpoint of Experience, it is not surprising that this draft should betray greater uncertainty than the draft of any other poem by Blake.

The first lines he wrote down were a false start:

> Woe, alas! my guilty hand
> Brush'd across thy summer joy;
> All thy gilded, painted pride
> Shatter'd, fled . . .

That is the response to death we would expect from Experience. The accidental or purposeless destruction of vitality and joy is an irrecoverable loss, and the hand responsible for it is "guilty." On the other hand, the point in wrestling with the problem of death is to be able to salvage a victorious affirmation of life in spite of death. It is therefore necessary to make a more propitious beginning. Blake's new start is conceived in a shorter and brighter rhythmical pattern:

> Little fly
> Thy summer play
> My guilty hand
> Hath brush'd away.

This no longer has "Woe, alas!," and the shorter verse is more light-hearted, but the hand is still guilty. That will not do, since the admission of guilt is still an admission of radical loss that requires penitence. Blake therefore deleted "guilty hand" and made a more ethically neutral substitution which converted the first stanza into its final form:

> Little fly,
> Thy summer's play
> My thoughtless hand
> Has brush'd away.

The second stanza that Blake wrote down proved to be as unsatisfactory as the first:

> The cut worm
> Forgives the plow,
> And dies in peace,
> And so do thou.

This was the way death had been confronted in the "Proverbs of Hell," which also contained the admonition: "Drive your cart and your plow over the bones of the dead." Both of these proverbs are, however, inapplicable in this poem, though Blake momentarily hoped in writing the stanza that they might lead him to the victorious conclusion he desired. The proverbs do not apply because a "thoughtless hand" is not a plow. The cut worm forgives the plow because the plow increases and renews life. The worm dies in the service of the larger processes of life. The aimlessly killed fly does not. Furthermore, the problem Blake has set himself is not to come to terms with death as a general fact; that is easily solved by pointing to the immortality of life taken in its totality:

> Pluck thou my flower, Oothoon the mild!
> Another flower shall spring. [*Visions,* plate 1, K.189]

Blake's problem in "The Fly" is individual death—the problem as viewed from the standpoint of the plucked flower itself, which is not only killed but wantonly and uselessly thrown away. Blake canceled the stanza about the cut worm and made another attempt to come to terms with the fly. This stanza was to stick:

> Am not I
> A fly like thee?
> Or art not thou
> A man like me?

The first two lines present the standard equation of men and flies in their common mortality, and Blake expands the equation in the next stanza:

> For I dance,
> And drink & sing
> Till some blind hand
> Shall brush my wing.

This establishes that a man is mortal like a fly, but what of Blake's question:

> art not thou
> A man like me?

If Blake had wanted to show that men are to the gods as flies to wanton boys, these lines would be a tactless irrelevancy. Actually, his daring reversal of the equation

238

lies at the heart of the difficult affirmation Blake wants to make.

The reduction of men to flies and the elevation of flies to men are quite different imaginative acts. It is the elevation of the fly that permits Blake his triumphant conclusion. If a fly is a man, then a fly's "summer play" has a significance that is the same as human delight. Both are manifestations of the immanent divinity of all life "where every particle of dust breathes forth its joy." (*Europe,* plate iii, line 18). The joy of a fly and the "thought" of a man are expressions of the divine impulse, and both a fly's joy and a man's thought are therefore immortal. The fly or the man may die, but what is essential to each, his joy or thought is divine and immortal. "The soul of sweet delight Can never pass away" (*Visions,* plate 1, lines 9–10). That is the importance of the word "happy" in the way the concluding stanza comes to terms with the death of a fly or a man:

> Then am I
> A happy fly,
> If I live
> Or if I die.

In his original draft Blake wrote down this affirmative conclusion immediately after he had admitted that

> some blind hand
> Shall brush my wing.

But while the logic of his conclusion, as described above, was obvious to Blake, it was not, he realized, obvious in the poem as it stood. An explanatory stanza had to be introduced before the concluding affirmation. Blake therefore proceeded to explain:

> *Thought* is life
> And strength & breath;

239

> But [i.e. "only"?] the want
> Of thought is death.

By equating a human attribute, "thought," with vitality, Blake implicitly confirms that the fly is "A man like me." For "thought" is simply a higher and more obviously incorporeal version of the vitality that is in the fly. The vital principle in both is immortal. Thus the conclusion to Blake's draft version of the poem now stood:

> Thought is life
> And strength & breath;
> But the want
> Of Thought is death.

> Then am I
> A happy fly
> If I live
> Or if I die.

The unmistakable implication is that my thought, and therefore my happiness, continues whether I live or die, and this is the implication Blake meant to convey.

At a later date, however, Blake, using a broader pen, altered the penultimate stanza to its final form with disastrous results. He tried to strengthen the logical connections between the two last stanzas by converting them into a single if-then sentence:

> If thought is life
> And strength & breath
> And the want
> Of Thought is death

> Then am I
> A happy fly,
> If I live
> Or if I die.

This is unobjectionable so long as we, like Blake, understand his point, but it has been enormously confusing and has caused no end of trouble to readers who do not. They quite understandably construe the sentence as equating two quite different conditions:

(1) If Thought is life
and

(2) If the want of Thought is death
then

(1) If I live (have thought) I am happy
and

(2) If I die (want thought) I am happy.

This construction is plausible but, as should now be obvious, is incorrect.

*The Design.* Below the text, a mother is helping a very young child to take its first steps. An older child is hitting a shuttlecock with a racquet. No fly is illustrated; what we see is the "summer's play" of human beings. The joyous vitality of the child who hits the shuttlecock is also the *élan vital* surging through the child who is beginning to walk. Both are carrying forward the undying spark of energy, the soul of delight that "can never pass away."

# THE ANGEL

Like the "Nurse's Song" (*Experience*) this is a poem in which the speaker is made to satirize herself, and like the rose in "The Sick Rose," the speaker is not even aware that she is sick. The poem is an uncompromising satire, too, on all the props of innocence—dreams, guardian angels, tears, and naïveté ("witless woe"). The speaker is an innocent who still believes in the "fairies and elves" that Blake disdainfully rejected in his "Motto" (Rossetti Manuscript, No. 56). She dreams she is "a maiden Queen." The tone of uncomprehending naïveté is established in the first line:

> I Dreamt a Dream! what can it mean?

Her impercipience is accompanied by a boundless faith in the sanctity of childlike ignorance:

> Witless woe was ne'er beguiled.

So she thinks, but her witless woe is less protective than she counts on, since her faith that God protects the meek and tearful is fostered by the same delusive propaganda that forms the artificial world of dreams, guardian angels, and maiden queens. The nice twist of Blake's satire is that her dream discloses a deeper and truer source in herself than she is conscious of—which is why she cannot understand what the dream means.

As it turns out, the real meaning of her dream is that her "Angel mild" is not, after all, an illusionary, fairy-tale angel from the "allegorical abode where existence hath never come," but a real angel who, unknown to her, represents her repressed instincts of life and joy. He is not one of those angels who "pitying stand and weep," but one who is driven away by weeping. He is repelled by the hypocrisy which "wishes but acts not." He is repelled by her weeping ("So he took his wings and fled") because it is based on the cunning idea that witless woe is never beguiled and also on the unhappiness that comes from repressing natural instinct:

> And I wept both day and night
> And hid from him my heart's delight.

## The Angel

The source of her unhappiness is precisely her hiding or repressing of natural joy. She perversely turns the world into the vale of tears which is so consoling to the pious souls who repress natural joy. At this point in the poem the speaker still has delight to hide. She is still struggling against her best instincts.

With time this hypocrisy passes into habitual prudery —into a proud sanctimoniousness that no longer weeps and no longer even desires help in warding off the joys and desires of instinctive life:

> I dried my tears, & arm'd my fears
> With ten thousand shields and spears.

We have descended from the early stage of her fall, when she at least had tears to be wiped away, to an irredeemably fallen state in which she no longer has anything to regret. When the angel returns—that is, when the spark of life tries to flare up once more:

> I was arm'd, he came in vain.

The encrustation of Urizenic customs and habits is now heavy as frost and deep as life. And, at the same time, the spark of life has dwindled:

> For the time of youth was fled,
> And grey hairs were on my head.

The chance is permanently gone. The speaker is beyond redemption. The poem is an exemplum as well as a satire—an exemplum that affirms the holiness of natural desire, and which corresponds to the biblical admonition: "Why tarriest thou? arise and be baptized and wash away thy sins," or better, "Awake, arise or be for ever fallen."

*The Design.* Above the text, the "maiden queen"

243

pushes away her good angel, and averts her face from him. The angel is trying his best to make the maiden turn around to look at him. Her willful perversity is Urizenic hypocrisy.

## THE TYGER

This greatest of Blake's poems displays his most distinctive characteristic as a lyric poet: the contrast between his vividly simple language and his immense complexity of meaning. If this is a richer poem than "The Lamb," it is not because its language is more difficult. Verbally, the most daring phrase of "The Tyger" is "forests of the night," which is not different in kind from "clothing of delight" in "The Lamb." The great distinguishing mark of "The Tyger" is the complexity of its thought and tone.

Like "The Lamb," which it satirizes, it begins with a question about the Creator:

| | |
|---|---|
| Little Lamb, who made thee? | Tyger, Tyger! burning bright |
| Dost thou know who made thee? | In the forests of the night |
| Gave thee life, & bid thee feed | What immortal hand or eye |
| By the stream & o'er the mead? | Could frame they fearful symmetry? |

While "The Lamb" answers the questions it poses, "The Tyger" consists entirely of unanswered questions. In this simple fact lodges much of the poem's richness. The questions it asks are ultimate ones, and while the answers are implicit in the poem, they cannot be pat answers because, no matter how the reader construes its implications, the poem remains a series of questions. The way each question is formed makes it also an answer, but still the answer is formed as a question, and neither is resolved into the other. All the complexities of the poem are built on this doubleness in its rhetoric, and every aspect of the poem partakes of this doubleness.

Blake's first intention in forming such a poem was no doubt to satirize the singlemindedness of "The Lamb," a poem which excluded all genuine terror from life and found value only in what is gentle, selfless, pious, and loving. It is true that the *Songs of Innocence* as a whole do not exclude cruelty and terror. In "Night," "wolves and tygers howl for prey," and in other poems there is a sufficiency of pain and tears. But cruelty and terror are presented as aspects of life that are to be finally overcome and therefore have no permanent reality or value. In "Night" the lion is ultimately transformed into a loving guardian; in Eternity he lies down with the lamb. Thus, while *Innocence* acknowledges tigerness, it entertains two reassuring ideas about it: that it is temporary and transcended, and that it is directly opposite to true holiness, which consists entirely of the lamblike virtues of Mercy, Pity, Peace, and Love. These are the two ideas that "The Tyger" satirizes as illusions. To the idea that the terrors of life will be transcended, the poem opposes a tiger that will *never* lie down with the lamb. He is just as fundamental and eternal as the lamb is. To the idea that only lamblike virtues are holy, the poem opposes a God who is just as violent and fiery as the tiger himself. He is not a God whose attributes are the human form divine, but a God who is fiercely indifferent to man. Thus, to the singlemindedness of "The Lamb," "The Tyger" opposes a double perspective that acknowledges both the human values of Mercy, Pity, and Love, and, at the same time, the transhuman values of cruelty, energy, and destructiveness.

For this reason "The Tyger," is not primarily a satirical poem. It submerges its satire beneath its larger concerns. It counters "The Lamb" by embracing both the lamb and the tiger, and it accomplishes this by embracing two attitudes at once. That is the brilliant service performed by the device of the question. The first stanza, for example, really makes two statements at once. The speaker's incredulity when confronted by a tiger who is just as fundamental as a lamb is the incredulity of one who is still close to the standpoint of *Innocence*. Could *God* have made this ferocity? Is there, after all, radical evil in the world? Can it be that the God who made the tiger is a tiger-God? The speaker's astonishment is that of a man who confronts for the first time the possibility that what is divine may not be what is reassuring in terms of human values, may indeed be entirely evil from the exclusively human perspective. All sympathetic readers of the poem have experienced this evocation of an evil that in human terms remains evil. Blake meant us to experience this, as we know from such phrases in the first draft as "cruel fire," "horrid ribs," and "sanguine woe."

Nevertheless, Blake canceled these phrases because they interfered with an equally powerful affirmative motif in the poem. This is easily seen when the moral astonishment of the question is transformed into something quite different by converting the question to a statement:

> Tyger, Tyger burning bright
> In the forests of the night
> None but immortal hand or eye
> Could frame thy fearful symmetry.

That would simplify the poem quite as much as "horrid ribs" and "sanguine woe," but it would also show that the *language* of the poem makes an affirmation that is just as powerful as its horrified confrontation of radical evil.

That is because the tiger is not simply burning; he is burning bright. His ferocity and destructiveness are not diminished by his brightness, but transfigured by it. His world is the night—dangerous, and deadly—but "forests," like "bright" transfigures all that dread. Blake's usual word for a tiger's habitat was "desart" ("The Little Girl Lost") and it was the word normally used by Blake's contemporaries, if we may judge from Charles Lamb's misquotation of the line: "In the desarts of the night." [1] "Forests," on the other hand, suggests tall straight forms, a world that for all its terror has the orderliness of the tiger's stripes or Blake's perfectly balanced verses. The phrase for such an animal and such a world is "fearful symmetry," and it would be a critical error to give preponderance either to that terror or that beauty.

Nor should we regard the image summoned up by the incantation of the first line as anything less than a symbol of all that is dreadful in the world. For the terror of the vision corresponds to the terror of the created thing itself—the *felis tigris*. No other animal combines so much beauty with so much terror. The symbol of the natural fact is grounded in the natural fact. The speaker's terror thus constitutes an insight that is just as profound as the poet's admiration of the tiger's beauty, and to disregard that terror is to trivialize the poem. "The Tyger" is not about two modes of looking at a tiger but about the nature of the creation.

1. See Lamb's letter to Barton, May 15, 1824: "Blake is a real name, I assure you, and a most extraordinary man if he be still living. He is the Robert Blake whose wild designs accompany a splendid folio edition of the 'Night Thoughts.' . . . His poems have been sold hitherto only in Manuscript. I never read them; but a friend at my desire procured the 'Sweep Song.' There is one to a tiger which I have heard recited, beginning:

> Tiger, Tiger burning bright,
> Thro' the desarts of the night."

In the "Proverbs of Hell," Blake had celebrated the divinity of natural strife and energy, and in the revision of *There Is No Natural Religion* he had stated quite unambiguously: "He who sees the Infinite in *all* things sees God." There can be no doubt that "The Tyger" is, among other things, a poem that celebrates the holiness of tigerness. This aspect of the poem is reminiscent of one of the Proverbs of Hell: "The roaring of lions, the howling of wolves, the raging of the stormy sea, and the destructive sword, are portions of eternity too great for the eye of man." But the poem is a far greater statement of this religious faith than the proverb, because the mere assertion that the terrors of creation have a holiness transcending the human perspective is too complacent to be believed. How can this confident assertion be too great for the eye of man? Though the raging of the sea may be holy, it is merely terrible to the man at sea, unmitigably evil and malignant. Blake's accomplishment in "The Tyger" is to preserve the divine perspective without relinquishing the human. The union of terror with admiration makes the general tone of the poem that of religious awe, but this general tone is compounded of two attitudes that never altogether collapse into one another.

In the second stanza, Blake continues to evoke the doubleness of the tiger in images which suggest equally God and the Devil:

> In what distant deeps or skies
> Burnt the fire of thine eyes?

Is the tiger's fire from the deeps of Hell or the heights of Heaven? Whether good or evil, the fire has a provenance beyond the realm where human good or evil have any meaning.

> On what wings dare he aspire?
> What the hand dare seize the fire?

Did the immortal dare to fly like Satan through chaos?
Did he dare like Prometheus to bring the fire from
Heaven?

As the God begins to form the tiger, the immensity of
his power takes precedence over the daring of his exploit:

> And what shoulder and what art
> Could twist the sinews of thy heart?

The twisting shoulder of the god forms the twisting
sinews of the tiger's heart. This imaginative identification of the tiger and the god carries the same kind of
double-edged implication as the preceding images. The
identification of the tiger and his creator turns the god
into a tiger: if that shoulder could make that heart, what
must be the heart of the god? The divine artist plays
with ferocity out of ferocity. Yet if the god is a tiger,
then the tiger is a god. The fire of those eyes is the spark
of divinity. As the astonished and uncertain mind of the
speaker shifts alternatively from god to tiger he lapses
into an incoherent confusion that makes no literal sense
(The couplet is an unassimilated vestige from an earlier
draft) but makes good dramatic sense:

> And when that heart began to beat
> What dread hand and what dread feet?

Finally, the creation of the tiger is seen not as an
act of ruthless physical daring and power but as an act
of fiery craftsmanship in a fantastic smithy. This is
Blake's favorite image for artistic creation, whether it be
the creation of a tiger, a world, a religion, or a poem.
The fiery forge is a place where incandescent energy
and artistic control meet, just as they meet in the fearful
symmetry of the tiger. As the rhythmic pulses of the

verse fall like hammer blows, the speaker looks alternatively at the maker and the thing made, in an ecstasy of
admiration and empty horror:

> What the hammer? What the chain?

[The hammer is wielded by the god, the chain is beaten
by the hammer.]

> In what furnace was thy brain?
> What the anvil? What dread grasp
> Dare its deadly terrors clasp?

These staccato beats of controlled fury are succeeded
by a stanza of immense calm that enormously widens the
imaginative range of the poem. It is a highly compressed
and difficult stanza, but it is perhaps the finest moment
in Blake's poetry:

> When the stars threw down their spears,
> And water'd heaven with their tears,
> Did he smile his work to see?
> Did he who made the Lamb make thee?

The effect of the last two lines is to throw into clear relief the unresolved conflict between the divine perspective that has been implied all along in the poem, and
the speaker's terrified and morally affronted perspective.
The god smiles, the man cowers. (Of course, God smiled,
and the answer to both questions is, "Yes!" The entire
stanza is formed from traditional biblical and Miltonic
imagery, and within that tradition, "God saw everything
that he had made and behold it was very good.") But
while the man cowers, he has a growing sense of the reason for God's smile. It could be a satanic and sadistic
smile, but it could also be the smile of the artist who
has forged the richest and most vital of possible worlds, a
world that contains both the tiger and the lamb.

This broader perspective is introduced in the first two, highly compressed, lines of the stanza. "When the stars threw down their spears" is an allusion to the angelic fall as presented by Milton:[2]

> They astonisht all resistance lost,
> All courage, down their weapons dropt.
>
> [*P.L.* VII. lines 1838 f.]

The defeat of the rebellious angels is followed by their being cast into Hell, which is followed in turn by the creation of the world. That moment of the angelic defeat is therefore a decisive moment in the divine plan. The fall of the angels is the prelude to the fall of man, and in the tradition it is thus the prelude to the bringing of death into the world and all our woe. This moment begins the catalogue of evil and cruelty that will include the tiger. Yet the angelic fall was also "his work." To smile at that is to smile at the tiger.

But why does Blake call the rebellious angels "stars"? His reason belongs to the central conception of the poem, and it is given in the next line: "And watered heaven with their tears." The defeat of the angels caused them to weep tears, and these tears, left behind as they plummeted to Hell, became what we now call the stars. The angels are named "stars" proleptically to explain the name now given to their tears. The immediate result of the angelic defeat was therefore the creation of the stars, just as its indirect result was the creation of the world. No doubt, the God whose "work" was the angelic fall is a terrible and inscrutable God, but however terrible his work is, it is sanctified by vitality, order, and beauty. The stars of night are part of the same awesome design as the forests of the night and the fearful

---

2. Blake recalled this image of the angelic fall in his later description of Urizen's Fall, *The Four Zoas*, V, lines 220–25, K.310–11.

symmetry of the tiger. When, therefore, the poet repeats the questions of the first stanza, it is with no less terror but with increased awe. The question is no longer how *could* a god—physically and morally—frame such *fearful* symmetry, but how *dare* God frame such *fearful symmetry*. The last line now emphasizes the artistic daring inherent in a creation that is incredibly rich, and terrifyingly beautiful, and is like God himself beyond human good or evil.

While "The Tyger" expresses a religious affirmation that is common to all of Blake's poetry in the 90s, it is the most comprehensive poem Blake produced in that period. Philosophically, of course, it is no more inclusive than "The Clod and the Pebble," *The Marriage,* or *The Book of Urizen,* but in tone it is the most inclusive poem Blake ever wrote. It celebrates the divinity and beauty of the creation and its transcendence of human good and evil without relinquishing the Keatsian awareness that "the miseries of the world Are misery." For all its brevity, its spiritual scope is immense.

*The Design.* To the right of the text is the trunk of a large tree. Below the text, Blake has drawn a tiger which some critics have found to be rather tame. Obviously these critics have consulted only the earlier issues or reproductions of them. In the opaquely colored later issues Blake's tiger is quite ferocious. It is only to be expected that a tiger colored with light watercolor washes will be less terrifying than an opaque tiger with yellow about the eyes and vigorous mottles of dark green, dark brown, and yellow. Furthermore, the expression on the tiger's face varies considerably from copy to copy. The line of the mouth in the lightly colored copies appears to be smiling. In the opaquely colored ones, where Blake could cover the lines etched on the plate, the mouth is snarling.

## MY PRETTY ROSE TREE

Since this is the first poem Blake wrote down in the Rossetti Manuscript, his earliest impulse to write lyric poetry in the 90s was apparently the impulse to blow off steam. The poem has the flavor of autobiography—not because we have extrinsic information that William and Catherine were having a spat—but because the poem attaches so much bitterness of emotion to what is, even in symbolic terms, a rather trivial incident. It is just the sort of incident in domestic relationships that appears more comic than bitter to an outside observer. The subject matter is, after all, a theme for comedy rather than philosophical satire: "A pretty girl flirted with me, but I resisted temptation because I had a pretty rose tree at home. And what did my faithfulness win me, when I triumphantly announced it, but suspicion and jealousy?" Since this is precisely what the speaker should have expected, his shock does not carry the satirical weight it is meant to carry. Blake would probably not have written the poem if the intensity of domestic frustrations had not called for a timely utterance to give the thought relief. There is likewise a highly personal flavor to the second poem of the Manuscript, which also bitterly presents the futility of openness in love. This theme runs like a thread through the collection, particularly in "I asked a thief," "I fear'd the fury of my mind," "Silent, Silent night," "I slept in the dark," "I walked abroad," and "The look of love alarms." The personal and *parti pris* tone of these poems accompanies their broader, satirical implications, and is an important part of their meaning as poems.

On the other hand, the author does satirize himself as well as his pretty rose tree, and in doing so he gives the satire the kind of general implication that is found in other poems of *Experience* like "The Garden of Love" and "The Lilly." Mr. Gleckner quite rightly points out that Blake satirizes not only female irrationality but also the speaker's adherence to conventional morality.[1] Why should a man—or a woman—be constricted by the marriage ring? This Godwinian view of marriage is quite un-Godwinian in its motivation. It is founded on the principle not that men and women should form and dissolve unions on the basis of rational analysis, but that they should follow their natural bent. Blake's iterated pleas for openness in love, besides suggesting the romantic idea that man is unfallen and Eden at hand, also implies that the instincts cannot betray. The instincts are, in fact, holy. The poem, therefore, for all its autobiography and triviality, satirizes a double crime against the divine—the speaker's for not following instinct, and the rose tree's for not advocating, like Oothoon, "Love free as the mountain wind." The ideal that Blake portrayed in Oothoon, was, we recall, that of a woman who not only wanted Theotormon to have other girls, but actively fetched them for him and watched with delight "their wanton play."

*The Design.* On this plate Blake also etched "Ah! Sun-Flower" and "The Lilly," but only this poem is illustrated. Immediately below it and above the other two poems Blake has drawn a picture of a woman. She lies on the ground in an attitude of complacent self-approval that resembles the attitude of the woman in the design to "The Angel." To her left sits a male figure, head in his arms as though in despair. The thorns of the pretty

1. See R. F. Gleckner, "Point of View and Context in Blake's *Songs*," reprinted in *English Romantic Poets. Modern Essays in Criticism,* ed. M. H. Abrams (New York, Oxford University Press, 1960), pp. 68–75.

rose tree are graphically associated with self-regard and
Urizenic hypocrisy.


## AH! SUN-FLOWER

This fine poem is, except for the "Introduction," the
only poem of the original *Songs of Experience* which
does not appear in the Rossetti Manuscript, and like the
"Introduction" belongs to the period in late 1789 and
early 1790 when Blake stood poised between the sacramental transcendentalism of *Innocence* and the revolutionary naturalism of *Experience*. It is as much a poem
of Innocence as of Experience. It is the one poem in
*Experience* which Blake might have transferred to *Innocence* after 1805, but that was impossible, since "Ah!
Sun-Flower" had been etched on the same plate with
"The Lilly" and "My Pretty Rose Tree." On the other
hand, the poem displays several themes of Experience.
The "Youth" and the "Virgin" are sexually mature. He
has pined away with desire *because* she is shrouded in
Urizenic snow. The resolution of their unhappiness is a
fulfillment in the realm beyond this life. This allusion
to Eternity is, of course, quite uncharacteristic of Experience, which has plenty of figures who are disillusioned with life but none who want to leave it. The only
canonical poem of *Experience* that deals with death—
"The Fly"—is a poem that, like the little girl in "We
Are Seven," does not really admit the fact of death. In
"Ah! Sun-Flower" Blake has preserved the Christian
Eternity of *Innocence* but has relinquished all the Christian doctrinal trappings. Here the longing for Eternity
does not belong to the special province of the Christian
imagination but is grounded in nature itself—in the
Sunflower as well as in Man. In a moment of perfect

spiritual balance between Innocence and Experience Blake composed one of the best poems of the *Songs*.

Part of its beauty lies in this spiritual balance. The first stanza affirms both the traveler's journey and also the realm he seeks:

> Ah, Sun-flower! weary of time,
> Who countest the steps of the Sun,
> Seeking after that sweet golden clime
> Where the traveller's journey is done:

To seek the golden clime beyond is also to follow the golden sun here and now. The same double value adheres to the youth and virgin, whose *Sehnsucht* is both earthly ("desire") and heavenly ("aspire"). Their desire is for the sweet golden clime and for each other.

*The Design.* See the commentary to "My Pretty Rose Tree."

## THE LILLY

"The Lilly" belongs to the large group of satirical poems in *Experience* and the Rossetti Manuscript which contrast the open, daytime expression of natural instinct with its night-time perversions in coyness and secrecy. The apparent approval of modesty and humility in the first lines is highly ironical:

> The modest Rose puts forth a thorn,
> The humble Sheep a threat'ning horn.

Why should modesty express itself by a thorn, or humility by a threat? Because this is the way hypocrisy betrays itself. In the draft version, the Rose was at first "lustful" and her thorn "envious," while the sheep was not humble but "coward." Both the Rose and the Sheep have the divine, vital force, but in their external obedience to

the Urizenic system they have repressed and perverted
it. Blake's first impulse was to suggest that open love
had been perverted to lustfulness and cowardice. The
revision makes the poem more subtle and ironical. A
maiden is modest because she is retiring and shamefast;
she blushes at any open acknowledgment of sexuality.
This kind of modesty blushes, however, not because it
dislikes sexuality (the rush of blood betrays the contrary)
but because it prefers to preserve an appearance that
belies the reality in order to enjoy secret pleasures under
a coverlet in the dark. "Modest" also means "humble," but
when humility exhibits itself publicly by thorn or horn
it really expresses pride in the appearance of humility.
This humility is the same kind of hypocrisy as the modesty that walks chaste in the daylight and unmasks its
lust in the night. The two kinds of hypocrisy go together, and Blake exposes them as not simply lies but
as life-denying perversions that breed pestilence.

The Lilly, on the other hand, *is* modest and humble,
because she makes no attempt to appear as something
she is not. Her purity, while not that of the infant or
lamb, is no less perfect than theirs—another example
of the innocence celebrated in *Experience*. Her white-
ness is not "stained" by the sin of hypocrisy but is preserved by the cleansing fires of "sensual enjoyment" and
by the divine grace of "gratified desire." Her joys are
therefore vigorous; she "shall in love delight." Blake's
use of "shall" (not "doth") has the biblical ring of re-
warded righteousness and reminds us again of the religious fervor that underlies his naturalism:

> Blessed is the man
> That walketh not in the counsel of the ungodly,
> Nor standeth in the way of sinners,
> Nor sitteth in the seat of the scornful.
> But his delight is in the law of the Lord;
> And he shall be like a tree planted by the rivers of water,

That bringeth forth his fruit in his season,
His leaf also shall not wither;
And whatsoever he doeth shall prosper.


*The Design*. See the commentary to "My Pretty Rose Tree."


## THE GARDEN OF LOVE

"The Garden of Love" presents no real difficulties, but does have a "prophetic" dimension that is not usually noticed. The poem, first of all, uses as its satirical standard what I have called the innocence of Experience. The speaker had been an innocent like the Lilly and the Little Vagabond, and the joy of life in him had been strong enough to keep him unaware of the mind-forged manacles that are instituted to repress desire. He is thus like the chimney sweeper who used to be happy on the heath ("I used to play on the green") but has now been taught to sing the notes of woe. But it is wrong to suppose that the speaker has entirely lost his innocence. In being victimized by "God and his priest and king," he preserves the feeling that his earlier sense of life was right and the priests in black gowns wrong. His attachment to his earlier, innocent, values is the source of his indignation. The poem is a confrontation between natural innocence and cunning repression. That is the basic sense of the poem, but what I alluded to as the prophetic dimension is equally strong. The poem describes a Fall from a garden to a graveyard, and while this can apply to the history of the young man's disillusionment in the social order, it applies also to the history of mankind as Blake had presented it in the Lambeth Books. The Garden of Love (or Eden) used to exist for man before he was separated from nature by the imposition of pharisaical religious institutions. The priests in black gowns, making their pointless rounds, have clothed all of us in the clothes of death, have substituted tombstones for flowers and fetters for freedom. It is they who have written "Thou shalt not" over the door. This image of a Golden Age followed by a Fall is part of Blake's effort in these satirical poems "to Restore what the Ancients call'd the Golden Age." (*A Vision of the Last Judgment*, K.605). The "I" of the poem is a disillusioned young man and also briar-bound humanity. The poem is thus a satire on the Urizenic order, and also, implicitly, an injunction to return to natural innocence.

*The Design*. Above the text three figures are kneeling in a churchyard. One of them, a priest in a black gown, reads from a book before an open grave. Beside him, a youth and a maiden bend their heads downward and hold their hands together in prayer. These two young people ought to be embracing one another or driving a cart and plow over the bones of the dead. The priest is a death figure, both concerning himself with death and extinguishing the holy vitality of others.

## THE LITTLE VAGABOND

When Blake in *The Marriage of Heaven and Hell* asked Isaiah and Ezekiel "how they dared so roundly assert that God spoke to them," Isaiah's answer, which is also Blake's in the *Songs of Experience*, appeared on the surface to be remarkably arbitrary:

> "As I was then perswaded, & remain confirm'd, that the voice of honest indignation is the voice of God, I cared not for consequences, but wrote."

> Then I asked: "does a firm perswasion that a thing is
> so, make it so?"
> He replied: "All poets believe that it does."

The apparent arbitrariness of Isaiah's answer suggests,
as Blake means it to, that all deities reside in the human breast, but the answer also implies another quite
clear and consistent poetic-prophetic principle: strong
feelings signify a divine source and therefore can never
betray. This is the principle of imaginative authenticity
for all the romantic poets, but it is not, of course, a satis-
factory principle of rhetoric. Isaiah, when he comes to
the point, does not authenticate his words with "thus
saith the voice of honest indignation," and Blake is
aware that strong emotion is no rhetorical substitute
for "thus saith the Lord." One of Blake's most consistent
devices for authenticating either the vision of Eternity in
*Innocence* or the vision of the natural paradise in *Experience* is to make the dramatic speaker of his poem a
child whose innocence and direct access to the divine
guarantee the truth of what he says.

The little vagabond is one of several innocents in both
books of the *Songs* who, like the little boy in the story
of the Emperor's new clothes, speaks a truth that no
adult can utter. These children have an insight which is
not yet clouded over by "life's pelting storm" (Innocence)
of Urizen's "cunning wiles" (Experience). In their lack
of corruption and purity of heart they have direct access
to a God who is a loving, not a threatening, father:

> And the Angel told Tom if he'd be a good boy,
> He'd have God for his father, & never want joy.

> ["The Chimney Sweeper," *Innocence*]

> And God, like a father rejoicing to see
> His children as pleasant and happy as he.

> ["The Little Vagabond"]

But it is precisely at this point of similarity that the innocent truths of *Experience* show themselves as contraries to the truths of *Innocence*. While the child of *Innocence* imagines a distant world that has all the most glorious and delightful aspects of this one, the child of *Experience* imagines how delightful *this* world would be if every church were an alehouse and every priest an innkeeper.

The little vagabond envisages, in *his* version of paradise, a perfect happiness that is possible in the actual world:

> Then the Parson might preach, & drink, & sing,
> And we'd be as happy as birds in the spring;
> And modest dame Lurch, who is always at church,
> Would not have bandy children, nor fasting, nor birch.

In the ironic use of the word "modest" and in the robust confidence in the beneficence of natural delight, the little vagabond speaks with the voice of the bard. This poem presents one of the clearest instances of the difference between Innocence and Experience. It is not, fundamentally, the difference between naïveté and sophistication, or illusion and reality, but the difference between a religious faith expressed in an apocalyptic vision of Eternity and a religious faith expressed in an apocalyptic vision of the natural paradise.

*The Design.* Blake stresses the closeness of the little vagabond to God. Above the text in a wood, God and the little vagabond embrace. Below the text, various blankly etched human figures stand and sit around a campfire. As in the right-hand design of "London," men must seek the fire outside the Urizenic establishment. There is no fire in the church.

## LONDON

This will no doubt remain one of the best city-poems ever written, and will always stand as a memorable expression of the kind of human degradation and misery that is peculiar to large cities. But it is not an anti-city poem. Blake has no interest in pointing to Surrey and the Cotswolds as redemptions from the "sorrow barricadoed evermore within the walls of cities," because, for all the horror evoked by his brilliant verbal daring, the implicit alternative to this London is another quite different London. It is not a poem against a large collection of people or even against the industrial revolution, but against chartered lives and mind-forged manacles, against all the tyrannies and unnatural repressions that breed pestilence. The city of London is a symbol of the way the deluded Urizenic inventions of the "human brain" have brought man to his fallen state. The bitter, ironic tone of the poem is established by the repetitions in the first stanza of "charter'd" and "marks," repetitions which emphasize the ironic senses Blake attaches to these words. "Charter'd" means, first of all, "hired out":

> There souls of men are brought & sold,
> And milk fed infancy for gold;
> And youth to slaughter houses led,
> And beauty for a bit of bread.
>
> [Rossetti Manuscript, No. 28]

This kind of hiring-out is so universal that even the streets and the river are enslaved:

> I wander thro' each charter'd street,
> Near where the charter'd Thames does flow.

The first irony is that the Thames—gliding at its own sweet will—is an image of freedom. It is the attitude of the Londoners which turns everything to constriction and commerce. But the repetition suggests another irony. Englishmen (including Blake himself in *King Edward the Third,* line 9) were fond of boasting of their "charter'd liberties"—the rights guaranteed by Magna Carta. But, in fact, these chartered liberties are chartered (sense one) slaveries. That the *Thames* is chartered in this way shows the mind-forged arbitrariness of the Englishman's slavery and the idiocy of his brag. In the same way, the marks which Blake marks are not only symptoms of weakness and woe but also markings on the human lineaments by weakness and woe, the causes as well as consequences of human fallenness.

Both chartered streets and marks of woe are therefore "mind-forg'd." The bitterness of the poem is directed against a fallen state that need not exist. Behind the passionate irony and the uncompromising accusation of the poem lies Blake's revolutionary faith in a possible transformation of the human spirit. The one thing needful in achieving this transformation is the removal of the mind-forged manacles of the institutional tyrannies —marriage, the church, and the king. The imagery of "London" is easily translatable into the imagery of revolutionary enthusiasm:

> Remove away that black'ning church:
> Remove away that marriage hearse:
> Remove away that man of blood
> You'll quite remove the ancient curse.

> [Rossetti Manuscript, No. 33]

Because every face Blake sees in London is marked by weakness and woe, every sound he hears must be a clink of the mind-forged manacles. "Every ban," for example, is a multiple clank of the awful trinity of king, priest, and marriage. A "ban" is:

1. A summons to arms (king).
2. A formal denunciation or curse (church).
3. A proclamation of marriage.
4. A prohibition, "Thou shalt not" (king, church, marriage).

In the third and fourth stanzas Blake explicitly connects the sounds he hears with these three Urizenic principles:

> How the Chimney-sweeper's cry
> Every black'ning church appalls.

The cry appalls (dismays, horrifies) the church not because the church pities the plight of chimney sweeps, nor because what blackens chimneys also blackens churches, but because it is the church that has caused chimney-sweepers to exist:

> "Where are thy father & mother? say?"
> "They are both gone up to the church to pray."
>
> ["The Chimney Sweeper," *Experience*]

Blake's technique throughout is to compress the horror and its cause into a single image that enforces a grim justice by showing the way in which the horror appalls, defaces, and blights the very tyranny that has caused it. Thus:

> the hapless Soldier's sigh
> Runs in blood down Palace walls.

Blake reserves the worst example of this grim justice for the last.

> But most thro' midnight streets I hear
> How the youthful Harlot's curse
> Blasts the new born Infant's tear
> And blights with plagues the Marriage hearse.

264

It is the marriage hearse that breeds youthful (and thus potentially innocent) harlots, by creating the necessity for prostitution. If there were no marriage, there would be no ungratified desires, and therefore no harlots. Thus it is ultimately the marriage hearse itself and not the youthful harlot which breeds the pestilence that blights the marriage hearse. The incidental victim of this vicious cycle is the newborn infant whose tear and cry of fear are both consequences of Urizenic perversions, whether in the form of a scary bogeyman like Nobodaddy or of a loveless and diseased parent. The youthful harlot, like the chimney-sweep and the soldier, is a victim of the mind-forged manacles. She too is chartered. And she is bought and sold under the gospel of the pharisees as well as the gospel of mammon.

*The Design.* Above the text a hoary old man on crutches makes his way down a London street, led by a little boy. To the right of the text, a naked child warms his hands before a fire. The crippled old man is a replica of Urizen. The weakness and woe he symbolizes is also the weakness and woe he has caused. Like the poem, the design telescopes cause and effect.

## THE HUMAN ABSTRACT

This poem is as central to the *Songs of Experience* as "The Divine Image" (the poem it satirizes) is to the *Songs of Innocence.* It begins as a point-for-point refutation of the touchstones of Innocence—Mercy, Pity, Peace, and Love—but moves quickly beyond this limited satire to present a bitter mythical account of the way the delusive values of Innocence have caused the Fall of man. The opening stanza, one of Blake's best attempts to satirize an earlier poem, should be read as if one of the

Swedenborgian "Angels" were speaking. (One draft version, No. 8 of the Rossetti Manuscript, explicitly gives the lines to an "Angel.") In defending the values of Innocence, the Angel damns both them and himself:

> Pity would be no more [pronounced
> as an unthinkable calamity]
> If we did not make somebody Poor.
> And Mercy no more could be [an even
> greater calamity]
> If all were as happy as we.

In accepting that this is an ineluctably suffering world, Innocence had celebrated the sacramental quality of Mercy and Pity. But the love from which these divine attributes arise demands more than passive sympathy with another's sorrow; it demands active alleviation of sorrow as well, and this was a point that Innocence had failed to urge with sufficient force. It thus left itself open to the accusation that it valued pious complacency and self-gratulation above active social betterment. The accusation is not altogether fair, and since Innocence was to have the last word in Blake's final version of the *Songs,* it should be pointed out that the accusation is itself rather vulnerable. When all men are released from the Urizenic bonds, will there be no more misery? If you abolish poverty, do you really abolish the need of pity? Even though the cut worm forgives the plow, is there to be no compassion for pain? for failure? old age? death? The underside of Blake's attack is the sanguine and touchingly naïve revolutionary faith that all would be "as happy as we" if only the whole unnatural edifice built with Mercy and Pity and the rest were to crumble.

In the second stanza Blake quickly drops the angelic mask and converts the two remaining divine attributes of Innocence to something overtly sinister:

And mutual fear brings peace
Till the selfish loves increase.

The dropping of the mask is preparation for Blake's naturalistic myth of the Fall, which like the traditional
myth involves a tree. Blake was fond of allegorical trees.
The symbols of roots, branches, fruits, and roosting
birds are all to be found in *Poetical Sketches* ("Love
and Harmony Combine") and the association of the tree
with the Fall is central, of course, to "A Poison Tree."
Blake preserved his favorite images, but the fallacy of
attaching the same kind of meaning to each recurrent
use of them should be apparent to anyone who compares
the symbolic tree of this poem with that of "Love and
Harmony Combine." Blake's tree also illustrates the
pointlessness of insisting that his poetry is "mythic,"
which is to say trans-intellectual, archetypal, and, in
short, good, rather than "allegorical," which is to say
intellectual, self-conscious, and, in short, bad. Blake's
tree, like most images in his poetry, is mythical and allegorical at the same time. Like any poet risen above the
level of primitive culture, Blake attaches definite con-
ceptions to his myths and thereby converts them to alle-
gories.

In this poem every image has precise conceptual corre-
spondences. The seed of the fatal tree is "Cruelty"—the
cruelty implied in the Angel's desire to keep people
poor and unhappy. Within the trap he has baited,
Cruelty waters with crocodile tears the seed he has
formed. Blake's horticultural knowledge was precise.
First the root forms from the seed—the root of "Humility"—but it is the false humility of the "humble sheep"
who displays a "threat'ning horn" ("The Lilly"). Then
the epicotyl develops into leaves and branches—into the
dismal shade of Mystery. Next

the Catterpiller and Fly
Feed on the Mystery.

The priestly caterpillar who benefits from human repression has been encountered before:

As the catterpiller chooses the fairest leaves to lay her eggs on, so the priest lays his curse on the fairest joys.

["Proverbs of Hell"]

Then, the stage of flowering being wisely skipped over, the tree

bears the fruit of deceit
Ruddy and sweet to eat.

Of course, the fruit is sweet, just as Eve's apple was, but its sweetness is entirely in its secret, hypocritical, and mouth-watering voluptuousness. Finally, the denizen of this tree is the Raven—the symbol of death, for the tree is the epitome of all that is life-denying and life-destroying.

Blake calls this image a "Human Abstract" because it is the history of an illusion. The tree of religion is an entirely human invention, like Locke's philosophy. It is a "cloven fiction" built up by dividing the mental from the actual, the human from the natural. The tree is thus "abstract" in the same way that to Wordsworth and Coleridge the false, secondary powers of the mind are abstract. Blake is giving his own version of the distinction between "fancy" or "understanding" on the one side and "imagination" on the other, between operations of the mind in disconnection and isolation, and operations which are in alliance with the larger reality. Imagination or vision, being a fusion of the mind with this larger reality, is authentic and true, while fancy or abstraction is unauthentic and false. To put the matter as simply as possible, Blake calls the tree of religion an "abstract" because it is the consequence of the mind's turning, like Urizen, upon itself. The concrete reality Blake opposes to this abstract is Nature. His statement is as explicit as possible:

> The Gods of the earth and sea
> Sought thro' Nature to find this Tree.
> But their search was all in vain.
> There grows one in the human brain.

The appeal to Nature had been implicit from the beginning of the poem. That pity should be no more is a natural condition, because pity is founded on an artificiality. We "make" somebody poor. Our trust in instinct and the natural order is perverted by "mutual fears." And all the components of the tree—Humility, Mystery, Deceit—are unnatural in precisely the same way. They create a separate human world that has nothing to do with the fundamental reality—the universal, exuberant, self-delighting impulse of life. That reality is what Blake has in mind when he says, "every thing that lives is holy." That reality is also what he means in this poem when he uses the word "Nature."

This satire of "The Divine Image" thus turns out to be a poem that affirms a religious faith as powerful as the one expressed in the poem it satirizes. And the faith it expresses was derived from the very religion against which it directs its irony. The subject of "The Divine Image" had been the indwelling presence of the divine:

> Where Mercy, Love & Pity dwell
> There God is dwelling too.

Now, abandon the idea of a mediating Christ, and leave out of account the transcendent reality that sanctions this immanental faith, and the result is the conviction that

All deities reside in the human breast.

That statement implies, among other things, that the "human brain" can choose to make the world the glorious place it implicitly is, or can create a falsely isolated and therefore fallen world. It can make a god that is repressive of holy instincts or it can make a god out of those holy instincts themselves. The deity that resides in the human breast *can* be the true deity—that is, the divine life in man and nature. "The Human Abstract" is not just a satire of "The Divine Image" but also a naturalization of it. The same immanental faith runs through both, and this is important to notice because it discloses one of the main currents in the astonishing spiritual development to which we owe the existence of the *Songs*.

*The Design.* Below the text, Urizen squats on the ground as if rooted there. Out of his head grow ropelike branches that appear to hold him prisoner as his hands struggle against them. As in the design to "London" Urizen is both the cause and the victim of his bondage.


## INFANT SORROW

This contrary to "Infant Joy" was originally the beginning of a much longer poem (Rossetti Manuscript, No. 13). The title "Infant Sorrow" was added later with a different pen. The poem is therefore an example of the way Blake manufactured some of the contrary songs out of materials that originally lacked dialectical implications. In this case, Blake's transformation of the poem was highly successful, mainly because the shortened poem brings into relief elements that were already implicit in the original.

In the longer draft version the two stanzas served as

an introduction to a history of the speaker from birth to
old age. The idea dramatized by this history was that
repressive social customs will defeat life, energy, and joy
unless "youth" arises to oppose these repressions. Thus
in the original context the first two stanzas—which now
constitute the etched poem—described the first stage in
the speaker's failure. In infancy, man is too weak to
overcome repression and therefore learns early that the
best course is deceit:

> When I saw that rage was vain
> And to sulk would nothing gain,
> Turning many a trick & wile
> I began to soothe & smile.

This stratagem works effectively as long as the speaker
confines his desires to what is socially acceptable. But as
soon as he feels the sexual urge he finds himself baffled:

> My father then with holy look,
> In his hands a holy book,
> Pronounc'd curses on my head,
> And bound me in a mirtle shade.

In a state of frustration, the speaker finds himself close
to the mirtle blossoms, but unable to pluck them. The
priests, on the other hand:

> Like to serpents in the night,
> They embrac'd my blossoms bright.

The revelation has now occurred, and all the speaker's
repressed energies are aroused in his indignation; he
breaks his bonds and smites the holy men. But it is too
late:

> The time of youth is fled
> And gray hairs are on my head.

The poem has turned out to be an exemplum showing the pestilence that is bred by not plucking fruits before the light, and thus belongs with "Nurse's Song," "An old maid early ere I knew" (No. 58), and "The Angel" (which borrows its last two lines). Blake in "Infant Sorrow" excises the introduction to this exemplum in order to make a different, though related point.

The willful perversity of the rebellious infant in "Infant Sorrow" is his mark of excellence and divinity. His uproar makes him seem a veritable fiend—a devil—but the devils of *Experience* are, of course, angels, because the divine substance is life and energy. The infant's sorrow is owing not to his innate waywardness but to the repressive forces of the world into which he has thrust himself. This point of similarity between the original poem and the new one allows Blake effectively to exploit his draft version for use in the *Songs*. By showing the vigor of infant sorrow, he makes the poem a contrary to the passivity and gentleness of infant joy.

But in satirizing the earlier poem, Blake does not misrepresent it. What he satirizes is not passivity and gentleness as such, but only a one-sided version of human babies and human nature. Babies not only smile, they enter the world piping loud, and they continue to pipe loud as frequently as they smile. Blake uses this commonsensical corrective to *Innocence* as the basis for a broader philosophical corrective. The new poem does not repudiate the blessedness of infant smiles; it confronts us with the contrary to them—the divinity of infant screams. The two poems belong together in the way that "The Lamb" and "The Tyger" belong together. The new poem is added so that "Infant Joy" and "Infant Sorrow" may combine to celebrate the dialectic of opposite forces in man and the cosmos. Taken together, the two poems have the same implications as "The Clod and the Pebble." Infant joy makes a heaven in hell's despite, and infant sorrow a hell in despite of heaven. As fundamental aspects of the vital natural order, this heaven and this hell are equally divine. And even though the point is totally irrelevant to the original impulse of "Infant Joy," the dialectic Blake now imposes makes "joy" feminine and "sorrow" masculine (the opposite to the arrangement in the "Proverbs of Hell": Joys impregnate. Sorrows bring forth").

The contrast of masculine and feminine is an important element in "Infant Sorrow"—particularly as represented in the contrast between "mother" and "father," the two forces that the rebellious infant must cope with:

> My mother groan'd! my father wept.
> Into the dangerous world I lept:
> Helpless, naked, piping loud:
> Like a fiend hid in a cloud.
>
> Struggling in my father's hands
> Striving against my swadling bands,
> Bound and weary I thought best
> To sulk upon my mother's breast.

The first mention of "mother" and "father" refers to the pain of childbearing. The father presumably weeps in sympathy with the mother's groans, and their sorrow is the first expression of the natural enmity that arises between child and parent. This enmity, another version of the terrible but glorious strife of contraries, explains why the world into which the infant leaps is "dangerous." It is not an entirely pejorative word, for it describes the same awesome, cruel, and beautiful world evoked in "The Tyger." Because the world is dangerous in this sense, the rebellious energy and self-seeking autonomy of the infant have positive value. The first bonds the infant knows are male—those of the father, who bends the struggling infant to his active will. Then the infant experiences the female bonds of the mother (symbolized by the swaddling bands and the devouring embrace) who invites the infant to trade his active vigor for clodlike passivity and acceptance. Having failed in his helplessness to break these bonds, he finds it "best" to act the lamb and suck at his mother's breast, though he is really a tiger in disguise who is "sulking" at the breast—waiting, like Orc, for the moment when he will grow strong enough to break the fetters.

"Infant Sorrow," is, then, a highly affirmative poem. If human babies were exclusively docile and smiling they would become sterile and lifeless adults. The human world would be nothing but "the same dull round over again," lacking the productive energy of the tiger and the plow that cuts the worm. By embracing both the smiling and the screaming babe, Blake is affirming the rightness and divinity of actual life. Behind the satire of Innocence lies his celebration of the holiness of the natural order.

*The Design.* Only a small space on the upper left is allotted to the text. The rest of the plate is filled with an interior scene. A mother stretches her arms toward a baby who appears to be twisting and turning. The baby's body is muscular and energetic. Like the poem, the design stresses his great vitality, not his "sorrow."


# A POISON TREE

As any reader of "London" may notice, Blake was capable of great verbal daring, but the hallmark of his lyric poetry is the contrast between the simplicity of his language and the complexity of his symbolic implications. Each image of this poem, each line, and even each main rhythmical beat stands out in perfect relief, and displays the same clarity of outline that Blake demanded in pictorial art. The symbolic implications of the poem are no less clear, but they are much less straightforward.

To give outlet to emotion is natural, to repress it unnatural. To nurse unacted desires breeds pestilence. On the other hand, the unnaturalness of the spiritual disease that grows to fruition in the poem is made to seem all the more unnatural by being described as a natural growth. This is the same effective technique used in "The Human Abstract." All the images are those of natural life-processes—rain, sun, fruition—but the tenor of the images is sickness and death. The speaker of the poem is delighted with his self-contemplating horticultural prowess, and that is the measure of his spiritual sickness. He, like the sick rose, or the speaker in "The Angel," is unaware of his disease, and thus exists at the bottom of what constitutes for Experience the fallen state.

Yet it is not the speaker who eats the apple that is symbolic of this Fall. The apparent confusion that arises here is really the most brilliantly imaginative aspect of the poem. Both the speaker and his foe are fallen—the speaker in his "soft deceitful wiles" and his *Schadenfreude,* the foe in his equally deceitful stealing into the garden in the dark of night. The poem does not confine itself to an attack on unacted desires or hypocrisy. It attacks the entire structure of a social order represented by the speaker and his foe. It describes not only a particular instance of man's spiritual self-destruction, but also the causes and characteristics of human fallenness. It thus resembles "The Human Abstract" not only in its horticultural imagery but also in its wider symbolic implications.

*The Design.* The foe lies on his back, outstretched beneath a tree. The back of his head is in the foreground and almost masks his body, which lies beyond on the line of vision defined by the reader's eye and the head.

This design, which resembles Montagna's perspective studies of the dead Christ, has a powerful impact.

## A LITTLE BOY LOST

This little boy is not lost in the wilderness but lost to the world after being immolated (whether spiritually or corporeally is irrelevant) on the Urizenic altar. The poem is in no significant sense a satire of "The Little Boy Lost," nor did Blake add his title (see the Rossetti Manuscript, No. 35) until long after he had written the poem. Interestingly, he did not etch it for the original issue of *Experience*, and it first appeared in copy B, the copy to which Blake also added his general title page. Quite probably, the more philosophical and less satirical conception of the *Songs* implied by the title page allowed Blake to take a looser view of what was required in a contrary to a poem of *Innocence*. It was then possible to present a contrary poem that was neither a parody nor a direct satire of an earlier poem, but rather a vigorous and bitter counterweight to the spirit, not the theme of its gentle pieties.

While the poem does oppose "The Little Boy Lost" in this general way, it also develops an idea that was latent in Blake's earlier insistence on the humanness of God. In urging the divine humanity Blake held that we can only honor what is like ourselves, for what we love must correspond to something that is at least latent in us. This early idea, which took its first form as the humanization of God, grew more comprehensive in Blake's thought, until it finally embraced the humanization of all reality (see letter to Butts, 2 Oct. 1800 and elsewhere). It is a profound idea that in its epistemological form corresponds to the pre-Socratic principle: only like can know like. In the 90s this leitmotif in Blake's thinking underwent a very special, "hellish" transformation. From the principle that you cannot love what is unlike yourself he arrived, in the period of *Experience,* at the idea that you cannot love another as much as yourself:

> Naught loves another as itself
> Nor venerates another so.

Blake shows the origin of the thought in the next lines:

> Nor is it possible to Thought
> A greater than itself to know.

The second idea is a repetition of the earlier assertion of God's humanity. The interesting point is that the two ideas presented by the little boy are far from being corollaries of each other. Man cannot know anything greater than man, but this does not logically imply that he cannot love another as much as he loves himself. Blake, in repudiating Innocence, has added something new.

The new element is a consequence of Blake's shift of allegiance from the universal brotherhood of man ("all must love the human form, In heathen, turk, or jew") to the universal selfhood of nature. I have discussed this concept at length in commenting on *The Marriage of Heaven and Hell* (see above, p. 63–64) and need only repeat here that Blake's affirmation of pebbles, tigers, and other ruthless self-seekers implies an affirmation of the divine substance—life. Obviously, everyone loves himself best and seeks out his own self-fulfillment. That is "nature's holy plan." Clods please themselves best, as it happens, by "seeking not themselves to please," and Pebbles please Clods by caring only about themselves. While the interaction of selves is not always so convenient as this, even the war of selves results in a vigorous, "dangerous," and "fearful" world that is also a "symmetry" and a harmony. "All discord harmony not understood." It is the vital harmony of polyphony rather than the dull unison of the plain song.

The little boy of the poem is an innocent like the other children of *Experience,* and therefore what he says is authentic and true. Furthermore, the boy's pronouncement, while infuriating to the priest, is really much gentler than Blake's similar pronouncements in "The Tyger" and *The Marriage of Heaven and Hell.* The little boy does not insist that everyone should love only himself. In fact, the little boy equally affirms the universal bond of love that exists between everything that lives. That is the other side of his shocking revelation:

> And Father, how can I love you
> Or any of my brothers more?
> I love you like the little bird
> That picks up crumbs around the door.

To love oneself first and to love all of life as one loves one's brothers is to follow the divine commandment and fulfill "nature's holy plan." This Wordsworthian phrase again obtrudes itself because the little boy expresses the gentler, Wordsworthian side of Blake's naturalism. One first eats one's own bread, and the crumbs that are left over can go to the little birds. The image is highly reminiscent of Wordsworth's Old Cumberland Beggar, whose palsied hands shook out the crumbs that became the "destined meal" of the small mountain birds.

While Blake employs heavy artillery in having the little boy burned at the stake "in a holy place, Where many had been burned before," his image is justified by the fact that the little boy truly belongs in the tradition of religious martyrs. Blake suggests the harmlessness of the child in the brilliantly ironic "all admir'd the Priestly care," but the priest, as regards his self-preservation, is well advised to burn this heretic whose antihypocritical and naturalistic religion is, like the religion of the early martyrs, subversive of the established order.

*The Design.* Below the text, the little boy's family kneel in mournful attitudes while the sacrificial flames shoot out from the left.

## A LITTLE GIRL LOST

Since this poem is neither in the Rossetti Manuscript nor in copy A, it was possibly, except for "To Tirzah," the last composed of the *Songs*. On the other hand, the tone of the poem is in places similar to "The Little Girl Lost" and "Ah! Sun-Flower," while the first stanza bears similarities to "The Voice of the Ancient Bard" and "Introduction." It is therefore more probable that this is Blake's first unqualified poem of Experience. The only quite certain assertion that can be made regarding Blake's inclusion of the poem is that its title discloses the broader, philosophical conception of the contrary poems introduced into copy B, the copy in which this poem and the general title page were added for the first time. The poem is not a parodic contrary to "The Little Boy Lost." Its nonce title as well as its inclusion in the *Songs* were made possible by the broadening of Blake's conception of the *Songs* between copy A and copy B.

Blake calls the page he has etched "indignant." His indignation is not only against the Urizenic order, where Love is "thought a crime," but also against the fact that this age is not "the future Age." For it is only artificial repression which prevents immediate and universal beatitude. The poem is not difficult, but it has one or two cruxes that can be resolved as soon as we recognize in in it the pattern that underlies most of Blake's poetry, the pattern of Golden Age, Fall, Resurrection. The cruxes arise from Blake's unacknowledged shifts of perspective from one moment of this cycle to another. The second stanza is entirely in the Golden Age:

> In the Age of Gold,
> Free from winter's cold,
> Youth and maiden bright
> To the holy light,
> Naked in the sunny beams delight.

The story that is narrated in the subsequent stanzas apparently begins in this Golden Age:

> Once a youthful pair,
> Fill'd with softest care,
> Met in garden bright
> Where the holy light
> Had just remov'd the curtains of the night.

Now, in a sense this scene *is* in the Golden Age. The time is dawn, and the "youthful pair" meet in a "garden." However, we soon discover that we are witnessing a re-enactment of the Golden Age within the present fallen world, where "strangers" and "Parents" do not approve of such open "play," and where the maiden at first feels "fear":

> There, in rising day,
> On the grass they play;
> Parents were afar,
> Strangers came not near,
> And the maiden soon forgot her fear.

Blake has very neatly shown that under these special circumstances, when innocent youth is free of Urizenic restrictions, the Golden Age is possible within the present world. The Fall is nothing but an artificial imposition of restrictions on natural instinct. Therefore, the "future Age" can arise as soon as men throw off these restrictions.

The rest of the poem shows how the present order corrupts the natural innocence of the youthful pair. The first corruption is their being forced into night-time secrecy:

> Tired with kisses sweet,
> They agree to meet
> When the silent sleep
> Waves o'er heaven's deep,
> And the weary tired wanderers weep.

And the final corruption is Ona's terror and guilt before her Urizenic father.

The confusion of perspectives between the Golden Age and the present fallen age is now seen to be deliberate. Fallenness is something that exists only "in the human brain." The poem has traced the true meaning of the Fall in the story it relates, and it has implied that the Future Age will arrive whenever men choose to behold it. The future readers of this indignant page are therefore told of a horror they will not have the misfortune to experience, and present readers are told of a horror they need not tolerate.

*The Design.* The text is decorated with vegetation. On the right the branches of a tree follow the contours of the text.

## TO TIRZAH

This poem, so utterly unlike any of the other *Songs,* was added to *Experience* approximately ten years after the publication of the combined *Songs.* This astonishing fact cannot easily be explained on aesthetic grounds, since the poem conflicts thematically with the other poems of *Experience*. Nor can it be explained on systematic grounds, since the poem is in no way a contrary to *Innocence*.

Sampson dates "To Tirzah" ca. 1801–03, and Keynes accepts this conjecture, which coincides very well with the general view of Blake's development advanced in this book. However, an even later date is more probable. Erdman and Margoliouth have argued convincingly that Blake's last additions to *The Four Zoas* are no earlier than 1804, and it is in these last additions that "Tirzah" makes her first appearance in *The Four Zoas*.[1] The probable date of "To Tirzah" is 1804–05.

Blake derived the symbolic figure Tirzah from the Bible by an ingenious and imaginative combination of allusions. As the "Mother of [our] Mortal part," Tirzah is the counterpart to Jerusalem, the mother of our immortal, spiritual part. Since Jerusalem, in Blake's later mythology, is both a woman and a spiritual city, her counterpart ought to be a woman and a city. For some reason—possibly because the word had undesired associations—Blake did not follow John in opposing Babylon to Jerusalem. Instead he chose the capital of Israel, Tirzah. The logic of the choice is that the kings of Israel "did evil in the sight of the Lord" (I Kings 15:34), while the opposing kings of Judah, whose capital was Jerusalem, "did that which was right in the eyes of the Lord" (I Kings 15:11). In this poem "Tirzah" represents the natural, physical world and the natural, physical aspect of man belonging to that world.

The poem is best discussed stanza by stanza.

1. Erdman and Margoliouth are agreed that the latest stratum of *The Four Zoas*, including all of "Night the Eighth," must be dated 1804 or later. See *Prophet against Empire*, pp. 369–74, and *Blake's "Vala,"* pp. 174–75. An earlier dating is advocated in John Sampson, ed., *The Poetical Works of William Blake*, London, 1913, p. 96.

## To Tirzah

Whate'er is Born of Mortal Birth
Must be consumed with the Earth
To rise from Generation free:
Then what have I to do with thee?

The repetition of Christ's words to his mother at Cana
conveys the soul's ruthlessness toward everything that
interferes with God's work. Tirzah, the mother of our
mortal, physical part must be cast aside as the mother of
Christ was cast aside. Blake does not, however, conceive
of man's spirit as a vague and vaporous cloud inhabiting
the body. The soul is the "human form divine," a form
clear in outline, like Blake's pictorial art, and complete
in sentience. This is evident from stanza three, in which
the human soul is given all the human senses except the
sexual and totally physical sense of touch.[2] What is
being repudiated in the first stanza is the constriction of
the human form by the body and also the spiritual constriction that accompanied this incorporation of the soul.
"Mortal Birth" or "Generation" is therefore something
which confines and imprisons, while the casting aside of
Tirzah is something which makes us "free."

When Blake foretells that the physical side of man
"must be consumed with the Earth," he means exactly
what he says. It is only fair, however, to present to the
reader the usual explanation of such lines in Blake's

2. See *Milton,* plate 27, K.514. The best commentary on "To Tirzah" in the rest of Blake's work is also found in *Milton,* and was
probably composed at the same time:

These are the Sexual Garments, the Abomination of Desolation,
Hiding the Human Lineaments as with an Ark & Curtains
Which Jesus rent & now shall wholly purge away with Fire
Till Generation is swallow'd up in Regeneration [plate 41, K.533]

Compare also the fulmination against

Ulro, Seat of Satan
which is the False Tongue beneath Beulah: it is the Sense of Touch.
[plate 27, K.514]

later poetry. According to the standard account, Blake is prophesying the annihilation of the physical world in a purely Pickwickian sense. His pronouncements are taken as referring only to the kind of psychological apocalypse Blake prophesied in *The Marriage of Heaven and Hell* (plate 14). Now the idea of an inner apocalypse is one of Blake's most consistent themes. It is implicit, as I have suggested, in the *Songs of Innocence*; it is explicit in *The Marriage of Heaven and Hell;* it is explicit in *A Vision of the Last Judgment* and *Jerusalem*. Thus: "Whenever any Individual Rejects Error & Embraces Truth, a Last Judgment passes upon that Individual" (*VLJ,* K.613). Another version of the psychological apocalypse extends the Last Judgment to a whole nation or civilization:

> The Last Judgment is an Overwhelming of Bad Art & Science. Mental Things are alone Real; What is call'd Corporeal, Nobody knows of its Dwelling Place: it is in Fallacy, & its Existence an Imposture. Where is the Existence Out of Mind or Thought? Where is it but in the Mind of a Fool? . . . Error or Creation, will be Burned up, & then, & not till Then, Truth or Eternity will appear. It is Burnt up the Moment Men cease to behold it. [*VLJ,* K.617]

I have quoted Blake at some length on this point because I by no means want to suggest that this psychological apocalypse is absent from "To Tirzah." Indeed, that is precisely the kind of apocalypse he implies in the line "The Death of Jesus set me free." As an individual, the speaker is "free" and therefore risen "from Generation free," in spite of the fact that Tirzah has "betrayed" him to mortal life. The speaker of the poem has had his Last Judgment and already exists spiritually in Eternity. But, that being true, why does he regard his being "set free" as a future event?

## To Tirzah

Whate'er is Born of Mortal Birth
Must be consumed with the Earth
To rise from Generation free.

The obvious and most probable explanation is that Blake imagines a cosmological as well as a psychological apocalypse. Even more important, Blake's private, psychological apocalypse would be impossible without his confidence in the final cosmological one it prefigures. Blake can give the "Last Judgment" an inward meaning because the inward experience is a sacramental re-enactment of something beyond individual experience. The pattern of Blake's sacramental imagination here is the same as in the *Songs of Innocence*. Eternity is both within and beyond.

In Blake's later thought, then, there are three apocalypses: the annihilation of "Error" in an individual, the overcoming of "Error" by an entire civilization, and the literal annihilation of the temporal world, after which the New, wholly incorporeal Jerusalem will descend. Blake derived the idea of the individual apocalypse from Swedenborg, but he derived the idea of the other two apocalypses from the Book of Revelation. John's first apocalypse was to bring the Millennium to mankind, but his second was to annihilate the physical world. All of Blake's late apocalyptic pronouncements, whether individual or millennial, have this final apocalypse as their model and justification. It is only because the created world is ultimately ephemeral that an individual can reject it. While Blake sometimes insisted that the created world does not even exist, his repudiation of the world was based not on his quite late reading of Berkeley, but on his reading of John. In "To Tirzah" the argument is not Berkeleian at all. The argument is that since the physical world has no permanent existence, it has no real existence. That is the logic of the first stanza: everything physical is mortal and will be consumed; *therefore* what have I, who am immortal, to do with thee, the "Mother of my Mortal part?" If we take Blake's words literally, the argument is perfectly logical. If we do not, the argument makes no sense.

In the first stanza Blake rejected everything in man that belongs to the physical, natural world. At the same time, he implicitly identified that world of generation with fallenness. It is something from which we must "rise." In the second stanza Blake proceeds to show how this Fall into corporeality occurred:

> The Sexes sprung from Shame & Pride,
> Blow'd in the morn; in evening died;
> But Mercy chang'd Death into Sleep;
> The Sexes rose to work & weep.

This highly compressed account of the Fall accomplishes in four lines what Blake was later to expand into the first ninety-eight plates of *Jerusalem*. Originally, before the Creation (which is the Fall), man existed as a purely spiritual being whose perfect self-unity was sexless. By making Shame and Pride the spiritual corruptions that produced the Fall Blake consolidates the biblical and Miltonic accounts. Satan and his hosts fell from pride; so, in a more complex way, did Eve and Adam. And the first effect of this fall was Shame—the shame of nakedness which, in Milton at least, led directly to concupiscence and thus to sexuality. In Blake's myth all this is converted into a fall from spiritual unity to corporeal sexuality. But the springing of the sexes also brought death into the world: "Blow'd in the morn; in evening died." And that death would have been the end of man, the just consequence of his sins, had not mercy (Christ) changed death into sleep. When Adam and Eve awoke, in Blake's version, they found themselves in the world

as we know it: "The sexes rose to work and weep."
Rescued from non-entity, they must now eat bread in
the sweat of the face and bring forth children in sorrow.

Why has Blake contrived this new version of the Fall,
differing not only from the account in "The Human
Abstract" and the other poems of the 90s, but also from
the traditional account? In one sense the equation of the
Fall with sexuality is a development of the elaborate
male-female oppositions in *The Four Zoas,* where the
Fall was conceived in part as a quarrelsome disunity between each Zoa and his female Emanation. But in *The
Four Zoas* the Fall was characterized by lover's quarrels
between male and female, not by an original division
into sexes. In the new version of "To Tirzah" the original unity is not harmony between the sexes but complete
sexlessness. Furthermore, the lapse into sexuality is now
an event which accompanies the lapse of the spiritual
paradise into the physical world. Thus, fallenness is
both sexuality and the creation, and this is so because
Blake now regards sexuality and the created world with
vigorous repugnance. He has turned violently against his
previous celebrations of sexual drives and natural strife
in the *Songs of Experience* and the other works of the
90s.

Having presented this general account of Creation
and Fall, the poem returns to the situation of the individual soul within the fallen world of Generation:

> Thou, Mother of my Mortal part,
> With cruelty didst mould my Heart,
> And with false self-deceiving tears
> Didst bind my Nostrils, Eyes, & Ears:
>
> Didst close my Tongue in senseless clay,
> And me to Mortal Life betray.

Because of the Fall, each man is now betrayed to mortal
life; each soul must be "vegetated." The first corruption

of physical life is the corruption of the heart to "cruelty." It is the cruelty that necessarily resides in physical life, where each self, like the Pebble or the Tiger, satisfies his corporeal desires of sex and hunger at the expense of other selves. The vital strife of nature has now a purely negative value, and the attack on natural life ironically reverses the pattern of Blake's attack on "unnatural" life in "The Human Abstract." There "cruelty" had been the first of corruptions, but it was the cruelty of institutional Christianity which kept people physically miserable by promises of spiritual blessings. There, too, the agent of the Fall had shed false tears, as a sign of hypocritical pity, Tirzah's tears are "self-deceiving," however, because they are directed to the deceiving realm of natural life and have no relevance to the reality of spiritual life which is joyous and immortal.

The image of nostrils, eyes, ears, and tongue being bound in "senseless clay" is peculiarly Blakean. This is another inheritance from the earlier work, in which Blake had similarly conceived of the Fall as a constriction of the senses. That constriction, however, was an entirely psychological limitation of energy and instinct through Urizenic repressions, whereby the living, infinite world was converted to a dead and limited world. In "To Tirzah" the constriction of the senses is a constriction of spiritual, not natural, energies, and it occurs not through institutional repressions but through physical existence itself. The senses are betrayed to mortal life. And all of them, except the "created" sense of touch, will achieve their redemption when they rise from Generation free. Accordingly, the best commentary on the physical constriction of the senses is Blake's prophecy in *Jerusalem* of their apocalyptic liberation:

South stood the Nerves of the Eye; East, in Rivers of bliss,
  the Nerves of the

## To Tirzah

Expansive Nostrils; West flow'd the Parent Sense, the
    Tongue; North stood
The labyrinthine Ear: Circumscribing & Circumcising the
    excrementitious
Husk & Covering, into Vacuum evaporating, revealing the
    lineaments of Man.                    [plate 98, K.745]

This final apocalypse guarantees that the true self is
the spiritual not the natural man. We were betrayed into
natural life by the sins of Shame and Pride, but because
of Christ's atonement each man can be free of those
inherited sins and therefore free of the inherited physical world:

> The Death of Jesus set me free.
> Then what have I to do with thee?

Thus, by an extension of the divine Mercy which transformed Death into Generation, we can, in spirit, transcend Generation until the annihilation of the natural
world sets us free forever. But until that final apocalypse,
our individual transcendence of the world occurs within
the world, and exists "in Spirit but not in the Mortal
Body." Blake's explicit words on this point are worth
quoting:

> Many Persons, such as Paine & Voltaire, with some of the
> Ancient Greeks, say: "we will not converse concerning
> Good & "Evil; we will live in Paradise & Liberty." You
> may do so in Spirit, but not in the Mortal Body as you
> pretend, till after the Last Judgment; for in Paradise they
> have no Corporeal & Mortal Body—that originated with the
> Fall & was call'd Death & cannot be removed but by a Last
> Judgment.                              [VLJ, K.616]

Blake's addition of "To Tirzah" to the *Songs of Innocence* is to be explained as an act of penitential self-
correction. It is a repudiation, like the opening lines of

*Milton* (probably composed at about the same time) of the false, vegetated tongue that had celebrated the natural world:

> even till Jesus, the image of the Invisible God
> Became its prey.

When the poem is thus understood, its artistic relevance to the other *Songs of Experience* becomes clear. It stands to *Experience* as *Experience* stands to *Innocence*. Christ's words to his mother at Cana are not just Blake's words to Tirzah but also his address to the earlier Blake of the *Songs of Experience*: "Then what have I to do with thee?" When Blake composed the poem and placed it at the end of the *Songs*, he implied a sweeping repudiation of all the preceding poems of *Experience*.

*The Design.* Two women support a limp and semi-recumbent man while a hoary figure holds toward him a revivifying pitcher. The hoary figure is God as Christ, and the scene represents the raising of Lazarus from the dead. This symbolizes, of course, Christ's raising of man from Generation which "was call'd death." Etched vertically on Christ's garment are the words from I Corinthians "It is Raised a spiritual Body." The poem will be illuminated by quoting Paul's words in full:

So also is the resurrection of the dead. It is sown in corruption: it is raised in incorruption: It is sown in dishonour; it is raised in glory: it is sown in weakness; it is raised in power: it is sown a natural body; it is raised a spiritual body. There is a natural body, and there is a spiritual body. And so it is written, The first man Adam was made a living soul; the last Adam was made a quickening spirit. Howbeit that was not first which is spiritual, but that which is natural; and afterward that which is spiritual. The first man is of the earth, earthy: the second man is the Lord from heaven. As is the earthy, such are they also that are earthy: and as is the heavenly such are they also that are heavenly. And as we have borne the image of the earthly, we shall also bear the image of the heavenly. Now this I say, brethren, that flesh and blood cannot inherit the kingdom of God; neither doth corruption inherit incorruption.     [I Corinthians 15:42–50]

## THE SCHOOLBOY

This was one of the poems that Blake later transferred to *Experience*. He probably composed it late in 1789, and in his final ordering of the combined *Songs* he took cognizance of its mediation between Innocence and Experience by placing it, along with "The Voice of the Ancient Bard," at the end of the work. The poem is distinguished from the canonical poems of *Innocence* by its images, which hark back to the secular pastorals of *Poetical Sketches*. There as here we find, for example, birds on trees ("Love and Harmony Combine") a huntsman ("To Morning"), a bower ("When Early Morn" and a caged bird ("How sweet I roam'd"). The schoolboy is unlike the other children of Innocence in feeling the stirrings of resistance and rebellion. He is beginning to think for himself (cf. the "Motto," Rossetti Manuscript, No. 56), and he expresses Blake's own growing resentment of repressive customs and institutions.

Like "The Little Girl Lost" and even possibly "A Dream," this poem expresses Blake's incipient naturalism, and shows that the seeds of the new faith lay in *Innocence* itself, where a pastoral nature echoed childish joy and foreshadowed Eternity. In this poem we find more than sympathetic echoes; the schoolboy and nature are identified:

> And the sky-lark sings with me.

The imagery is far more naturalistic than that of the canonical poems. To be in school is to droop like a flower, be caged like a bird, be rained on by a "dreary shower." It is to be nipped in the bud or to have one's petals blown away. The boy is a "tender plant" and the time of his youth "the springing day." In the final stanza the whole of human life is identified with the succession of the seasons, just as in the "Proverbs of Hell." It is true that other poems of *Innocence* associate human life and death with night and day, but that is quite a different matter, since the times of day have a symbolic meaning that reaches beyond nature. Here nature itself is the sanction for Blake's appeal. The joy that is to preserve us "when the blasts of winter appear" is the primal joy in being alive. It is not the inborn sense of a better world than this. The poem is far closer to "The Little Vagabond" and "The Chimney Sweeper" of *Experience* than to other poems of Innocence.[1]

*The Design.* The margins are decorated with twisted stems. On the right, two boys are climbing the stems and one sits above, reading. Below the text, three boys are playing marbles. The boy who reads a book has Blake's approval, along with the others, for he does not object to a child's studying outside the classroom. The images of natural growth in the poem and the design imply the superiority of original instinct and genius to learned rules:

> Thank God I never was sent to school
> To be Flog'd into following the Style of a Fool.

> [Rossetti Manuscript, ca. 1808–11]

## THE VOICE OF THE ANCIENT BARD

This was the terminal poem of the earliest known *Songs of Innocence* and it became, in Blake's final ordering,

1. See further comments above, pp. 49, 159.

the terminal poem of the combined *Songs*. It is clearly a transitional poem, belonging to late 1789, and is the only poem of Innocence etched (like the second version of *There Is No Natural Religion*) in italic script. The transitional character of the poem is discussed in detail above, pp. 47–49, and Blake's reasons for making it the final poem of the whole work are discussed on pp. 161–62.

This, like the other transitional poems, displays characteristics of both series, though Blake persisted until about 1815 in regarding it as a poem of Innocence. Before that time he may have preserved it in *Innocence* simply because he had already etched a similarly prophetic poem of Experience—the "Introduction"—and did not want to include another. Blake's final solution of the problem—to make this the terminal poem of all the *Songs*—was one that remained true to the original impulse of the poem, for it belongs neither to Innocence nor to Experience. Like "The Schoolboy" it was placed after "To Tirzah," to stand as reconciliation of the two states and an affirmation of what is true in both of them.

This mediating use of the poem was made possible by the vagueness of its prophecy. The "opening morn" and the "image of truth new born" could serve equally well as intimations of the imminent terrestrial paradise or of Blake's final concept of the spiritual millennium—the city of true biblical art, Jerusalem. Certainly, the latter is meant in the final edition of the *Songs*. In this final use of the poem, however, Blake's mellow self-forgiveness led him to imply that even the "mistaken" prophecies of the early 90s, of which this poem was the precursor, had a kind of truth—the truth of honest prophetic fervor which Blake in the end saw to be the unifying impulse of all his work:

The Nature of my Work is Visionary or Imaginative; it is an Endeavor to Restore what the Ancients call'd the Golden Age.    [*A Vision of the Last Judgment*, K.605]

*The Design.* Below the text, a venerable bard stands in the foreground plucking a harp and singing. Around him youths and maidens are standing and sitting. On the left a youth and maiden embrace. They are drawn like the two figures on the first plate of "The Little Girl Lost," which was also probably composed and etched in late 1789. The embrace foreshadows the tenor of the writings to come. His hand is on her buttocks.

*Appendixes*

# I. The Two Versions of
## *There Is No Natural Religion*

When Blake etched the first version of this work, he no doubt planned to publish a number of copies. The incisive logic and satirical skill of his presentation indicate great care in composition. In fact, however, there is no extant copy of this work alone. All of the twelve known copies are amalgamations of the first and second versions. This suggests that Blake altered his ideas and etched a new version fairly soon after completing the first. If, as seems likely, Sampson and Keynes are right in dating the first version 1788, then the second probably belongs to 1789. Internal evidence suggests a date in late 1789 or early 1790. Also the script of the first version is that of *Innocence*; the script of the second that of *The Marriage*.

Since I have asserted that the differences between the two versions demonstrate the kind of change Blake's thinking underwent between 1788 and 1790, the best way to support this view is to analyze each short work in detail. By "natural religion" Blake means the deistic view that religious faith comes from natural experience, not from revelation or innate ideas. The philosophical basis for the form this religion took in Blake's day was Locke's *Essay on Human Understanding*.

### FIRST SERIES

*The Argument*. Man has no notion of moral fitness but from Education.

On the surface this is a concession to Locke. The moral sense is not inborn; it has to be learned. See Locke's *Essay on Human Understanding*, I.2.2–14. Blake is willing to speak as a disciple of Locke because his method will be to assert various Lockean premises and then suddenly turn on them to unmask their self-contradictions.

Naturally he is only a natural organ subject to Sense.

To the deist and the Lockean what man is "naturally" is what he is truly. The "only" is accepted by the deist as a noble and tough-minded assertion. The statement itself is pure Locke, for whom sense perception is the "inlet of all knowledge in our minds" (*Essay*, II.9.15, II.1.2–11).

I. Man cannot naturally Perceive but through his natural or bodily organs.

A complacently and again ironically stated Lockean truism; see *Essay*, II.1.

II. Man by his reasoning power can only compare & judge of what he has already perceiv'd.

A firm tenet in Locke. See *Essay*, II.2.2.

III. From a perception of only 3 senses or 3 elements none could deduce a fourth or fifth.

This indeed follows. Blake carefully uses the terms "senses" and "elements," which are fundamental in Lockean philosophy. They cannot be reduced to simpler components in sense data, and therefore cannot be derived or deduced from other simples. Thus Locke: "Our specific ideas of substances are nothing else but a collection of a certain number of simple ideas considered as united in one thing" *(Essay,* II.23.14). Yet in spite of this, Locke elsewhere says that we can have ideas of spiritual and imperceptible beings on the basis of "sensation and reflection" alone *(Essay,* II.23.36). Blake thus unerringly finds the central contradiction in the Lockean-deistic position. This proposition is, very neatly, the turning point of the work, which now moves from mock affirmation to refutation. It may be observed parenthetically that Blake's acute logical talent caused him to precede Coleridge's similar attack on this contradiction by twenty-seven years. The *locus classicus* of the refutation is in Coleridge's *Biographia Literaria*:

> The existence of an infinite spirit, of an intelligent and holy will, must, on this system, be mere articulated motions of the air. For as the function of the human understanding is no other than merely (to appear to itself) to combine and to apply the phaenomena of the association; and as these derive all their reality from the primary sensations; and the sensations again all *their* reality from the impressions ab extra; a God not visible, audible, or tangible, can exist only in the sounds and letters that form his name and attributes. If in *ourselves* there be no such faculties as those of the will, and the scientific reason, we must either have an *innate* idea of them, which would overthrow the whole system; or we can have no idea at all.
>
> [Shawcross, ed., *1,* 83]

That is precisely the objection Blake proceeds to make:

> IV. None could have other than natural or organic thoughts if he had none but organic perceptions.

This directly subverts the favorite idea of natural religion that we progress from sense data to the "moral sense" and the idea of God. The statement strictly follows, however, from proposition III.

> V. Man's desires are limited by his perceptions, none can desire what he has not perceiv'd.

This is the most loosely stated of Blake's propositions. Nevertheless, it is a condensed and perfectly correct statement of implications in the Lockean position. It is really another corollary of proposition III: A man cannot desire what he has no idea of, and he cannot have an idea that is not compounded of "elements" from previous sense perceptions.

> VI. The desires & perceptions of man, untaught by any thing but organs of sense, must be limited to objects of sense.

But man does desire non-sensible objects. This was admitted in the apparently innocent *Argument,* which any Lockean would have acceded to. Man has notions of "moral fitness," gained only from "Education." But a notion of moral fitness is not a concatenation of sense elements. How did this leap from the sensible to the non-sensible occur? It is impossible to reach the final rung of Hartley's ladder. Since, as has been granted, the moral sense has been acquired by "Education," and since Education means learning through perceptions, the "notion of moral fitness," which is a non-sensible notion, must be learned through non-sensible perceptions. Thus a religious idea has to be gained by extra-organic perceptions. And since man does have religion and a moral sense, he must have more than "organic perceptions." There is religion, but there is no natural religion, Q.E.D.

> *Conclusion.* If it were not for the Poetic or Prophetic character the Philosophic & Experimental would soon be at the ratio [i.e. common denominator] of all things, & stand still, unable to do other than repeat the same dull round over again.

The *Conclusion* is the positive result of the attack. Because man's desires and ideas reach beyond sense, he must have perceptions beyond sense. He must therefore have a non-sensible faculty of perception, which gives him knowledge beyond philosophic (or Lockean) and experimental (or Newtonian) knowledge. Under the philosophic and experimental alone, all things would soon be reduced to various combinations of sense impressions, and these would recur with monotonous regularity, like the aimless circuits of Newtonian astronomy. The faculty in man that reaches beyond this to what is genuinely new and vital must be that faculty from which poetry and prophecy, both expressions of new truths beyond sense, arise. Blake's identification of poetry and prophecy, a very important and consistent motif in his work, is based on their common perception of a divine and extrasensory dimension of reality.

### SECOND SERIES

> I. Man's perceptions are not bounded by organs of perception; he perceives more than sense (tho' ever so acute) can discover.

While Blake begins here where he left off in the earlier version, he changes his mode of approach. He says nothing in this version about the special poetic-prophetic faculty. Man's perceptions are not "other than" sense, as in the first version, but "more than sense." Although this difference in phrasing need not necessarily imply a difference in meaning, the way the argument proceeds indicates that it in fact does.

> II. Reason, or the ratio of all we have already known, is not the same that it shall be when we know more.

This proposition breathes that spirit of "futurity" found in "The Voice of the Ancient Bard" and the first two stanzas of "The Little Girl Lost." We *shall* know more. But Blake's assumption in the first version was that we have always known more, have always had religion and morality. Blake is not concerned to subvert Lockean religion in order to plead the cause of revealed religion; he is concerned to foresee the better time when we shall know more. Blake's emphasis on "more" rather than "other" is again apparent, although what he means by this "more" is not yet certain.

> III. [This proposition, if it was ever etched, is lost.]
> IV. The bounded is loathed by its possessor. The same dull round, even of a universe, would soon become a mill with complicated wheels.

Here is the first unambiguous indication of the new impulse that caused Blake to revise his tractate and convert "other than" to "more than." Man is dissatisfied with the world of the philosophical deists not because it cannot account for the spiritual dimension of experience, but because it creates a bounded world. The "same dull round" of the first version was unsatisfactory because it brought nothing spiritual to knowledge, nothing other than repeated sense impressions. Now it is unsatisfactory because it is bounded.

> V. If the many become the same as the few when possess'd, More! More! is the cry of a mistaken soul; less than All cannot satisfy Man.

If the possession of many things is as unfulfilling to man as the possession of a few, then merely to ask for and obtain more is to remain unsatisfied. In the first version, the ideal of human fulfillment is the *perception* of the spiritual; here it is the *possession* of the infinite. The difference between perception and possession is the difference between an ideal that can never exist entirely in actual experience and one that can be possessed here and now.

> VI. If any could desire what he is incapable of possessing, despair must be his eternal lot.

But despair is not man's eternal lot even though he desires "All." Therefore Man must be capable of "possessing" the infinite.

> VII. The desire of Man being Infinite, the possession is Infinite & himself Infinite.

The logic here is far from being as elegant or compelling as that of the first version. Since man desires All, he is himself infinite. The implication is that only an infinite being can desire the infinite, which does not follow. Nor does it follow that the desire of the infinite entails its possession. At this point it has become apparent that Blake has abandoned logic in favor of enthusiastic affirmation. He is no longer concerned to prove the existence of spiritual perceptions, and, therefore, revealed religion. He wants to affirm the infinitude and thus the divinity of the actual world. This is his explicit conclusion:

> *Application.* He who sees the Infinite in all things sees God. He who sees the Ratio only, sees himself only.

The significance of Blake's shift from "other than" to "more than" is now fully laid out. The divine is not separate from and beyond sensory experience; it is "in all things." To see the infinite is to see that all life is holy: it is to cleanse the doors of perception, not to bring a special transorganic faculty into play. These first two sentences of the *Application* precisely parallel two sentences from *The Marriage of Heaven and Hell*: "If the doors of perception were cleansed every thing would appear to man as it is, infinite. For man has closed himself up, till he sees all things thro' narrow chinks of his cavern." Blake's new emphasis on the holiness of all life is, as I have shown in some detail, a development from and naturalization of his earlier, immanental Christianity. His concluding sentence discloses the pietistic origins of his new naturalism, just as the "Argument" to *The Marriage* does, and it is confirming evidence that this revision belongs with "The Little Girl Lost" and "The Voice of the Ancient Bard" in the transition period of 1789–90.

Therefore God becomes as we are, that we may be as he is.

## II. *The Book of Thel* and *Tiriel*

Since *The Book of Thel* is the only etched work of Blake's that bears the same date as the *Songs of Innocence,* one might expect it to shed light on the *Songs.* In fact, it sheds very little. The poem in *Innocence* that it most resembles in tone is "The Little Girl Lost," and while *Thel* is less ambiguous than "The Little Girl Lost," it displays a similar imaginative uncertainty. It is primarily a poem of Innocence. Yet it is also an attack on the sort of Innocence that retreats from actual life. I think it must have been both composed and etched in the same year as "The Little Girl Lost"—1789.

"Thel's motto" is a series of questions which suggest the moral necessity of immersion in life, but, at the same time, the distastefulness of the immersion:

> Does the Eagle know what is in the pit?
> Or wilt thou go ask the Mole?
> Can Wisdom be put in a silver rod?
> Or Love in a golden bowl?

Since the Eagle does not know what is in the pit, one has to ask the Mole, and in order to ask him one must go to the pit. But the Eagle is so much more glorious than the Mole that one wonders why it is desirable to know what is in the pit. The answer to this is implied in the next two questions. Wisdom can *not* be put in a silver rod, nor Love in a golden bowl. Both the rod and the bowl are beautiful artifacts, separate from life and antithetical to its passion and suffering. To learn Love and Wisdom it is necessary to go to the pit:

> If God is anything he is Understanding. . . . Understanding . . . is acquir'd by means of suffering & Distress & Experience.     [Annotations to Swedenborg, ca. 1788, K.89]

The disvaluation of life implied by the words "pit" and "mole" is an acknowledgment of "suffering & distress." But the value of learning what is in the pit is implied by the words "Love" and "Wisdom," words which Blake elsewhere in the annotations to Swedenborg associates with "understanding" (K.96 and passim).

The idea that underlies the "Motto" and the whole poem is a tradition sort of theodicy. Life is a vale of tears, a "pit" of suffering and distress. These evils are part of the divine plan under which we suffer and mourn in the world, so that we may become as God is; for "if God is anything he is Understanding."

> And we are put on earth a little space,
> That we may learn to bear the beams of love;
> And these black bodies and this sunburnt face
> Is but a cloud and like a shady grove.

> For when our souls have learn'd the heat to bear,
> The cloud will vanish; we shall hear his voice,
> Saying: "Come out from the grove, my love & care,
> And round my golden tent like lambs rejoice."

I have quoted from "The Little Black Boy" to emphasize that the basic idea of *Thel* is implicit in the *Songs of Innocence*. This is a necessary reminder because *Thel* does attack the kind of Innocence that wants to remain forever laughing on the echoing green. Thel is an inhabitant of such a land. She dwells in the vales of Har, a pastoral realm of "Seraphim" and "sunny flocks," and she is quite unwilling to leave this happy, child's world:

O life of this our spring! why fades the lotus of the water,
Why fade these children of the spring, born but to smile &
    fall?

Thel's lamentations are always recording her distress with the mutabilities of life and the inevitability of death. She has not gained "understanding" and does not want to gain it.

Her first teacher and comforter is a lily of the valley who explains to Thel that even such a lowly creature as a flower is "visited from heaven" and is cared for by God. When she dies she will go "to flourish in eternal vales":

Then why should Thel complain?
Why should the mistress of the vales of Har utter a sigh?

Thel's reply shows that her unhappiness is caused by her separateness from life. She sees that the Lily of the Valley has gained Love and Wisdom by becoming a part of life:

Thel answer'd: "O thou little virgin of the peaceful valley,
"Giving to those that cannot crave, the voiceless, the o'ertired;
"Thy breath doth nourish the innocent lamb, he smells thy
    milky garments,
"He crops thy flowers while thou sittest smiling in his face,
"Wiping his mild and meekin mouth from all contagious taints.
"Thy wine doth purify the golden honey; thy perfume,
"Which thou dost scatter on every little blade of grass that
    springs,
"Revives the milked cow, & tames the fire-breathing steed.

"But Thel is like a faint cloud kindled at the rising sun:
"I vanish from my pearly throne, and who shall find my place?"

Because of her concern with mutability Thel is next gently lectured by a cloud who is happy to "fade away," because he knows that he will go to eternity, "link'd in a golden band and never part." Thel's reply again shows that her uselessness is the source of her unhappiness:

I fear that I am not like thee,
"For I walk thro' the vales of Har, and smell the sweetest flowers,
"But I feed not the little flowers.

.     .     .

"And all shall say, 'Without a use this shining woman liv'd.
" 'Or did she only live to be at death the food of worms?' "
The Cloud reclin'd upon his airy throne and answer'd thus:
"Then if thou art the food of worms, O virgin of the skies,
"How great thy use, how great thy blessing."

After speaking to a worm and then to a clod of clay, Thel learns that "we live not for ourselves," and that God blesses even the earth, the mother of his children. Finally, the clod of clay invites Thel to enter "the land unknown," of "sorrows & of tears." This land is the symbol of that immersion in life that causes us to undergo "Suffering & Distress & Experience." The voice Thel hears in that land issues from a "pit," but she is so frightened by what the voice says that she rushes away without having learned "what is in the pit":

"Why a Tongue impress'd with honey from every wind?
"Why an Ear, a whirlpool fierce to draw creations in?
"Why a Nostril wide inhaling terror, trembling, & affright?
"Why a tender curb upon the youthful burning boy?
"Why a little curtain of flesh on the bed of our desire?"

The voice issues from Thel's "own grave plot," and expresses her own antipathy to the horrors of physical life. The little curtain of flesh is the physical body that curbs and debases the spiritual desire of the youthful burning boy. The soul is degraded by being "placed on earth." That is, of course, Thel's fundamental mistake. She did not learn her lesson from the flower, the cloud, the worm, and the clod of clay—all of whom live on earth a little space to serve others and gain understanding. Instead of following them, Thel retreats back to an Innocence that is not the Innocence of the *Songs,* but rather a Dantean antechamber reserved for those who are neither saved nor damned.

The ambivalence of the poem resides in its poise between an affirmation of actual life and a devaluation of it, between an affirmation of Innocence as embodied in the clod of clay and the lily and a rejection of Innocence as embodied in Thel. That timid maiden exposes the spiritual danger that lurks in a too exclusive repudiation of life's adult complexities. It was a danger that Blake was beginning to find in his own writings. If *Thel* was written before July 1789, it shows that Blake was in any case moving toward a poetry that would celebrate Experience, though it would be the kind of Experience commended by the clod of clay and the other innocents in *Thel.* It would honor the "Distress & Suffering & Experience" of the annotations to Swedenborg. If, on the other hand, Thel was written in late 1789, the moral imputation directed against the vales of Har would signify not only Blake's rejection of a too exclusive Innocence but also the dim beginnings of his rejection of Innocence altogether.

In interpreting the poem it does not matter which of these possibilities one accepts, since the positive figures in the poem celebrate the same kind of religious acceptance that is found in *Innocence.* On the other hand, the vales of Har are attacked in another poem of this period in a way that foreshadows Blake's later repudiations of

*Innocence.* It is *Tiriel,* a poem that exists only in manuscript. Sampson considered the work to be earlier than
*Thel,* since *Tiriel* contains the line "Can wisdom be put
in a silver rod, or love in a golden bowl?" Keynes accepts
this relative chronology, but I cannot. The line in question could just as probably have been borrowed from
*Thel* as vice versa. That *Tiriel* was never etched does
not mean that it was early. It might, with greater probability, mean that it was written when Blake was less
certain of his appropriate idiom than when he wrote
*Thel,* and thus would belong to the transition period,
late 1789–early 1790.

This is supported by internal evidence. Tiriel is a
hoary old autocrat whose children have rebelled for the
same reason that Urizen's children rebel in *The Book
of Urizen.* They cannot keep his iron laws. The violent
and rebellious spirit of the work belongs to Blake's
later manner. So does the phrasing:

Why is one law given to the lion & the patient Ox?

[cf. *The Marriage,* plate 24, K.188]

. . .

Some close shut up
In silent deceit, poisons exhaling from the morning rose.

[cf. Rossetti Manuscript, poems]

. . .

And why men bound beneath the heavens in a reptile form,
A worm of sixty winters.        [cf. *Europe,* plate 5, K.240]

For convenience, I have taken these examples from a
single manuscript page, no. 8, K.109–10.

Tiriel is very clearly the precursor of Urizen. His
death, which is the final event of the poem, corresponds
to the collapse of Urizen's power after his sons and
daughters have wrecked the orderly world he had
planned (*Urizen,* plate 23, K.234–35):

## *"The Book of Thel"*

"Such was Tiriel,
Compelled to pray repugnant & to humble the immortal spirit
Till I am subtil as a serpent in a paradise,
Consuming all, both flowers & fruits, insects & warbling birds.
And now my paradise is fall'n & a drear sandy plain
Returns my thirsty hissings in a curse on thee, O Har,
Mistaken father of a lawless race, my voice is past."
He ceast, outstretch'd at Har & Heva's feet in awful death.

The death of Tiriel is the passing of the old Urizenic order. The vales of Har to which he returns are in the pastoral land of *Innocence*. Since that is the land Blake associated with the old order of Tiriel-Urizen, it is fitting that the bitter old tyrant should die there, cursing its inhabitants.

# III. "The Mental Traveller"

This magnificent nightmare belongs to that period of Blake's profound despair when he had given up *The Four Zoas* in a state of acedia and had not yet begun its revision. "The Mental Traveller" was probably composed in the years 1799–1800—July 1800 being the date of Blake's report to George Cumberland that he had begun to emerge from his "Deep pit of Melancholy" (K.798). As usual, Blake generalizes about the spiritual history of mankind out of the experiences of his own spiritual history. The best comment on the universal implications of the poem is one of the earliest, that of W. M. Rossetti:

> The "Mental Traveller" indicates an explorer of mental phaenomena. The mental phaenomenon here symbolized seems to be the career of any great Idea or intellectual movement—as, for instance, Christianity, chivalry, art, etc.—represented as going through the stages of— 1. birth, 2. adversity and persecution, 3. triumph and maturity, 4. decadence through overripeness, 5. gradual transformation under new conditions, into another renovated Idea, which again has to pass through all the same stages.[1]

1. Quoted in A. Gilchrist, *Life of William Blake, "Pictor Ignotus"* (London, 1863), p. 98.

Blake's mental traveler is thus an olympian observer of the human spirit, but he is also one who has himself traveled the terrifying and tragic journey he describes. The poem begins with "I," and Blake is both the poet and the subject of the poem. As in a nightmare, the transformations the mental traveler observes are also transformations he experiences.

The first stanza gives the setting of the tragedy in very precise terms:

> I travel'd thro' a land of Men
> A Land of Men & Women too,
> And heard & saw such dreadful things
> As cold Earth wanderers never knew.

The land is the realm of the mind—as the title explains. The men and women in it are symbolic figures whose sexual distinctions represent the distinction between two different sorts of spiritual ideals. The sexual distinction also represents the distinction between the mind and the ideal it sets before itself. The "dreadful things" seen and heard by the mental traveler are the painful histories of human ideals, and these remain unknown to "cold Earth wanderers," because men who remain in "Newton's sleep" and the concerns of the physical world are not even aware of man's tragic spiritual history. They are wanderers on earth, just as the poet is a wanderer in the realm of the spirit.

In the next stanza Blake makes the distinction between these two realms emphatic by showing the precise inversion of natural phenomena that occurs in the transnatural realm of the mind:

> For there the Babe is born in joy
> That was begotten in dire woe;
> Just as we Reap in joy the fruit
> Which we in bitter tears did sow.

In the physical world the babe is brought forth in sorrow that was conceived in physical delight. But in the mental realm the first conceiving of a new ideal arises out of pain and dissatisfaction. It is sown in bitter tears. But when it comes to fruition when it is realized, it is reaped in joy.

After this introduction to the mental world, Blake begins his first history. As it happens, he begins with the history of a male ideal, but the significance of the "if" should not be overlooked. The first history to be traced could just as well be that of a female ideal:

> And if the Babe is born a Boy
> He's given to a Woman Old,
> Who nails him down upon a rock,
> Catches his shrieks in cups of gold.

Now the male babe is the ideal of an earthly paradise, while the female babe, as Blake will go on to show, is the ideal of an inward, spiritual paradise. When the boy is first born, the earth is a woman old. That is, in fact, why the boy is born; his purpose is to renew Earth. At this point in the poem Blake's treatment is totally objective, so that the Orcan, male figure represents, as Rossetti suggested, a new religious ideal shared by men. On the other hand, the identification of the ideal and the men who hold it is implicit, since the old woman is not an ideal at all but the world that the ideal is to transform.

When the redeeming boy vision is born, he is at first persecuted—thus the allusions to Christ and Prometheus. The persecution of the new ideal by the old, fallen world symbolizes the world's opposition to a new faith and also its recalcitrance to being transformed. In her fallen state the old woman is therefore the type of the religious

314

persecutor and also the type of fallenness and corruption:

> And the woman was arrayed in purple and scarlet colour and decked with gold and precious stones and pearls, having a golden cup in her hand full of abominations and filthiness of her fornication. And upon her forehead was a name written, MYSTERY, BABYLON THE GREAT, THE MOTHER OF HARLOTS AND ABOMINATIONS OF THE EARTH. And I saw the woman drunken with the blood of saints, and with the blood of the martyrs of Jesus.
>
> [Revelation 17:4–6]

But the persecutions of the new vision by the corrupt world do not destroy the ideal; they cannot. The cutting out of the boy's heart, like the exposing of Prometheus' liver, cannot kill something that is no cold earth wanderer. In fact, the tortures make that heart feel both cold and heat; they make the boy come to practical terms with the matter he will transform. Thus the ideal matures in wisdom and practicality, but at the same time this gruesome intercourse gradually rejuvenates the world and thereby accomplishes the purpose for which the ideal was born:

> Her fingers number every Nerve,
> Just as a Miser counts his gold;
> She lives upon his shrieks & cries,
> And she grows young as he grows old.

At last the purpose is accomplished. The world, or so it appears to those who hold this revolutionary ideal, is redeemed, and the terrestrial paradise has arrived:

> Till he becomes a bleeding youth
> And she becomes a Virgin bright;
> Then he rends up his Manacles
> And binds her down for his delight.

He plants himself in all her Nerves,
Just as a Husbandman his mould;
And she becomes his dwelling place
And Garden fruitful seventy fold.

The scene is a precise re-enactment of the apocalyptic moment in the Preludium to *America* when Orc binds down the Nameless Female and restores the naturalistic Golden Age. The symbolism is rich and appropriate. The image of the apocalypse—a sexual act—is also the image of the restored paradise—an "improvement of sensual enjoyment" within a fruitful garden. To turn earth into this garden it is only necessary to "plant" the vitality of the naturalistic ideal, just as a gardener incorporates "mould" into the soil. Agricultural imagery is the proper vehicle for the kind of paradise to be realized.

But the garden did not, after all, thrive. At the high point of the naturalistic ideal, the apocalypse was imagined, not achieved. Hope and expectation and desire outstripped reality, just as the present tense in which the apocalypse was described in *America* outstripped subsequent events:

The stern bard ceas'd, asham'd of his own song, enrag'd he swung
His harp aloft sounding, then dash'd its shining frame against
A ruin'd pillar in glitt'ring fragments; silent he turn'd away,
And wander'd down the vales of Kent in sick & drear lamentings.                                                    [K.196]

These are the lines Blake added to *America* after his own disillusionment in its prophetic present tense, and the word "wander," the symbol of journeying without faith or goal, describes what also happened to the boy ideal, whose failure is symbolized by his growing old:

> An aged Shadow, soon he fades,
> Wand'ring round an Earthly cot,
> Full filled all with gems & gold
> Which he by industry had got.

The Earthly cot that is no longer an earthly paradise is like the ruined pillar on which the bard breaks his harp. The failed ideal is now very obviously the man who held the ideal, grown old in spirit and faded in spiritual substance.

But the ruined cottage *is* filled with the gems and gold he had got by the industry of artistic creation. These riches are the works of art that the momentary flash of hope and faith had inspired. Autobiographically, they are the works Blake had produced at the height of his apocalyptic naturalism: *The Marriage, Visions, America, Europe, Urizen,* the *Songs of Experience:*

> And these are the gems of the Human Soul,
> The rubies & pearls of a lovesick eye,
> The countless gold of the akeing heart,
> The martyr's groan & the lover's sigh.

The stanza is a parody of the now ruined hopes that had inspired these works, particularly a parody of a little poem Blake had composed at the height of those hopes:

> Riches
> The countless gold of a merry heart
> The rubies & pearls of a loving eye,
> The indolent never can bring to the mart,
> Nor the secret hoard up in his treasury.

> [Rossetti Manuscript, No. 49, K.181]

While the poet's parody of his own former inspiration bitterly rejects his ruined hopes, he realizes that the works of art he had forged can still provide spiritual nourishment for himself and joy for others. But their joy is in poignant contrast to the poet's own despair. In more general terms, Blake also implies that the husks of a failed religion—like the books of the Bible—can still supply spiritual nurture even after the primal inspiration of the religion has decayed:

> They are his meat, they are his drink;
> He feeds the Beggar and the Poor
> And the wayfaring Traveller
> For ever open is his door.
>
> His grief is their eternal joy;
> They make the roofs and walls to ring.

During the last three stanzas, which have recorded the failure of the boy-ideal or terrestrial paradise, the female figure has faded entirely from sight. If Blake had mentioned her at all, he would have had to depict her as growing old again. But he is no longer concerned with Earth, the Nameless Female. He is concerned to show a tragic and meaningless inevitability in the historical cycle of human religious ideals. And the ideal that must inevitably be born out of the ruins of earthly hopes is a spiritual ideal, here symbolized by the birth of a girl:

> Till from the fire on the hearth
> A little Female Babe does spring.

The inevitability of the new birth is suggested by the apparent continuation of the process in which the Woman Old was growing young. Yet, though the spiritual process is continuous, the female babe has nothing to do with the Woman Old. She springs from the fire of creative intellect, and nothing earthly can touch her nor torture her:

> And she is all of solid fire
> And gems & gold, that noe his hand
> Dares stretch to touch her Baby form,
> Or wrap her in his swaddling-band.

She is an inner paradise that comes like grace to those whom the earth has failed, and her first task is to drive out the earthly ideal:

> But she comes to the Man she loves,
> If young or old, or rich or poor;
> They soon drive out the aged Host,
> A Beggar at another's door.

But the earthly ideal, grown old, is also the man, grown old in hope, who had believed in it. And so, to describe the way the new ideal will win the visionary to a new faith, Blake picks up the mental traveler's story from the point, five stanzas before, when the aged shadow wandered round his earthly cot. Still identified with his old ideal, he still wanders, but no longer round the old ruins. His wandering is a seeking for some different, unknown, and better faith which will renew him:

> He wanders weeping far away,
> Untill some other take him in;
> Oft blind & age-bent, sore distrest,
> Until he can a Maiden win.

In his wandering he has become like the poor who visited *his* cottage for meat and drink, but now he has found new spiritual sustenance at another's door. Consequently, the little female babe has grown up into the maiden he was seeking. And at their first embrace, the old, earthly ideal totally vanishes:

> And to allay his freezing Age
> The Poor Man takes her in his arms;

> The Cottage fades before his sight,
> The Garden & its lovely Charms.

The first effect of this banishment is to alienate the mental traveler from all things outside his new, totally inward ideal. He is even alienated from other men ("The Guests," who had visited his door and who are guests on earth):

> The Guests are scatter'd thro' the land,
> For the Eye altering alters all.

That the altering of Blake's eye was at first accompanied by a feeling of melancholy and of alienation from men is confirmed by his retrospective letter to Cumberland, which spoke of his emergence from a "Deep pit of Melancholy":

> I hid my face for not being able to abandon as a Passion which is forbidden by Law & Religion, but now it appears to be Law & Gospel too, at least I hear so from the few friends I have dared to visit in my stupid Melancholy. Excuse this communication of sentiments which I felt necessary to my repose at this time. I feel very strongly that I neglect my Duty to my Friends.      [2 July 1800, K.798]

The initial alienation from men corresponds to an initial alienation from everything else. The next lines are, no doubt, a good description of what Blake's melancholy had been like:

> The Senses roll themselves in fear,
> And the flat Earth becomes a Ball;
>
> The stars, sun, Moon, all shrink away,
> A desart vast without a bound,
> And nothing left to eat or drink,
> And a dark desart all around.

This initial moment of alienation passes when the mental traveler is renewed by the positive fulfillments of the inward paradise or Beulah. The next stanza summarizes the spiritual movement he has just passed through as well as the one he is about to experience. It is a foreshadowing stanza that gives a synopsis of the whole history of the female ideal. She begins as an infant, and he ends as one:

> The honey of her Infant lips,
> The bread & wine of her sweet smile,
> The wild game of her roving Eye,
> Does him to Infancy beguile;

That this stanza summarizes what is about to happen is indicated by the explanatory "For" which introduces the more detailed account that follows:

> For as he eats & drinks he grows
> Younger & younger every day;
> And on the desart wild they both
> Wander in terror & dismay.

The world in which they wander is still a "desart" because the new, inward vision has not yet removed the feeling of alienation and terror from the outward world.

Gradually, however, her attractions begin to make the world more habitable; her maidenly fear plants "many a thicket" in the desert:

> Like the wild stag she flees away,
> Her fear plants many a thicket wild;
> While he pursues her night & day,
> By various arts of Love beguil'd,

Yet the positive benefits of planting thickets are qualified by the increasingly sinister character of the maiden. She is coyly flirtatious; she beguiles; she uses "arts of love." The world is made habitable through an ideal that is not altogether innocent or true. The love that has beguiled the desert to bring forth is a "wayward Love":

> By various arts of Love & Hate,
> Till the wide desert planted o'er
> With Labyrinths of wayward Love,
> Where roam the Lion, Wolf & Boar,

At this point, the *femme fatale* has achieved her purpose. She has lured the mental traveler into altering his eye once more. The outer world, where predatory beasts roam, is no longer terrifying. He has become a fearless infant once more, and she, having served her purpose, has become a woman old.

> Till he becomes a wayward Babe,
> And she a weeping Woman Old.

Her tears are the false, deceiving tears of the three virgins in "The Golden Net," because they are "tears & sighs" for "the woe that Love & Beauty undergo." That is to say, the ideal of Beulah is young and healing until one discovers that it is no escape from the terrors of life. Then it grows old. The man who holds this ideal is reduced to a "wayward Babe," someone who has been renewed by a false ideal.

The words, "wayward" and "weeping" are, however, proleptic. The moment of disillusionment has not yet arrived, and the next six lines are devoted to describing the momentary fulfillment of the female ideal, just as in the previous cycle eight lines were devoted to the momentary fulfillment of the male ideal.

> Then many a Lover wanders here.
> The Sun & Stars are nearer roll'd.

## "The Mental Traveller"

The trees bring forth sweet Extacy
To all who in the desert roam;
Till many a City there is Built,
And many a pleasant Shepherd's home.

This is the state Blake later called Beulah. It is an inward state that is at home in the natural world because it filters out everything violent or unpleasant in nature. It is the spiritual domain of the pastoral, which welcomes "many a Lover" and sheep, but not lions, boars, and wolves. It is not a natural paradise but a pastoral land created by the human mind from the gentler aspects of the natural world. It does not contain a fruitful garden or an earthly cot, but "many a city" and "many a pleasant Shepherd's home." The trees bring forth a spiritual fruit to those who roam in the desert of the natural world, just as the trees brought manna to the Jews wandering in the wilderness.

But there is something suspicious about all this—to use Blake's word, something "wayward." It is suspiciously like the pastoral land that had been the realm of the *Songs of Innocence*. That is why the babe is wayward; the new ideal has turned out to be nothing but that old illusion of "allegorical abode[s]" (*Europe,* plate 5, K.240), the repressive religion which had turned earth into the Woman Old who appeared at the beginning of the poem. The wayward Babe has turned out to be the Christ child of pharisaical religion.

Suddenly, therefore, the Babe becomes a frowning and pestilential force corresponding to the repressions of the Urizenic order:

But when they find the frowning Babe,
Terror strikes thro' the region wide:
They cry "The Babe! the Babe is Born!"
And flee away on Every side.

323

For who dare touch the frowning form,
His arm is wither'd to its root;
Lions, Boars, Wolves, all howling flee,
And every Tree does shed its fruit.

The withered limbs, the banishment of lions and wolves, the shedding of fruit—all belong to the negative imagery of Blake's poetry in the early 90s. Beulah has turned into Priestcraft, as it had to, because the spiritual ideal always collapses into "State Religion"—Blake's phrase in 1798 (K.385 ff.). Consequently, earth grows old and corrupt once more. In order to overcome MYSTERY, BABYLON THE GREAT, another Orc must be born, and so the "frowning Babe" of the churches turns into the new ideal of Revolution and natural renewal; and all's to do again:

And none can touch that frowning form,
Except it be a Woman Old;
She nails him down upon the Rock,
And all is done as I have told.

# IV. Blake's Works Arranged by Period

Some of the points I have made in this book can be conveniently summarized in a chronological list. At some points I have departed from Keynes' conjectural dates, though not, of course, from his firmly established ones. My departures are based on internal evidence.

I. Poetic apprenticeship, 1769–1783.
*Poetical Sketches* (pub. 1783, composed 1769–83).
"Then she bore pale desire" (ante 1777).
"Woe cried the muse" (ante 1777).

II. Period of the *Songs of Innocence,* 1783–89.
Poems written in a copy of *Poetical Sketches* (ca. 1783).
*An Island in the Moon* (ca. 1784–85).
*There Is No Natural Religion,* first version (1788).
*All Religions Are One* (1788).
Annotations to Swedenborg's *Wisdom of Angels Concerning Divine Love and Divine Wisdom* (ca. 1788).
*The Book of Thel* (1789).

*Songs of Innocence* (pub. 1789, composed 1784–89).

III. Period of Transition, late 1789–90.
Annotations to Lavater's *Aphorisms on Man.*
*Tiriel.*
*There Is No Natural Religion,* second version.
Late *Songs of Innocence* and early *Songs of Experience:* "The Little Girl Lost," "The Little Girl Found," "The Schoolboy," "The Voice of the Ancient Bard," "Introduction" to *Experience,* "Ah! Sun-Flower."
"Argument" to *The Marriage of Heaven and Hell.*

IV. Naturalistic Period, 1790–95.
Annotations to Swedenborg's *The Wisdom of Angels Concerning Divine Providence* (ca. 1790).
*The French Revolution* (1791).
*The Marriage of Heaven and Hell* (1790–93).
Poems from the Rossetti Manuscript (1792–94).
*America, a Prophecy* (1793).
*Prospectus, to the Public* (1793).
*The Book of Urizen* (1794).
*Europe, a Prophecy* (1794).
*Songs of Experience* (pub. 1794, composed 1790–94).
*The Song of Los* (1795).

V. Disillusionment, 1795.
*The Book of Ahania.*
*The Book of Los.*

VI. Threefold Vision, 1796–99.
Annotations to Watson's *Apology for the Bible* (1798).

"The Smile."
First versions of *The Four Zoas* (1796–99).

VII. Repudiation of Threefold Vision, 1799–1800.
"The Mental Traveller."
"The Crystal Cabinet."
"The Land of Dreams."
"To My Friend Butts I Write" (Oct. 1800).
"A Divine Image" (a precursor of "To Tirzah"
having similiarities with "The Golden Net."

VIII. Return to Innocence, 1801–04.
"Now I a four fold vision see" (1801).
Second version of *The Four Zoas* (1801–04).
"My Spectre around Me."
"Mock on, Mock on."
"The Grey Monk."
"The Golden Net" (composed in this period,
but like *The Four Zoas* refers to period VII;
thus Blake puts it in the Pickering Manu-
script as the second poem).
"Auguries of Innocence."
Annotations to Bacon's *Essays*.
Annotations to Boyd's translation of *The In-
ferno*.
Most of *Milton*.

IX. Last period, 1805–27.
"To Tirzah" (ca. 1805).
Last additions to *The Four Zoas* (ca. 1805).
Additions to *Milton* (1805–18).
Last fragments in the Rossetti Manuscript (ca.
1808–11).
*A Descriptive Catalogue* (1809).
Public Address (ca. 1810).
*A Vision of the Last Judgment* (1810).

*Jerusalem* (1804–20).
*For the Sexes: The Gates of Paradise* (ca. 1818).
Annotations to Berkeley (ca. 1820).
*The Laocoön* (ca. 1820).
*The Ghost of Abel* (1822).
Annotations to Wordsworth (1826).
Notes to the illustrations to Dante (1825–27).
Annotations to Thornton (1827).

# *Index*

# Index

# Index

# Index

"Welcome, stranger, to this place," 24

Whatman, J., 73

"When early morn walks forth," 291

"When silver snow decks Sylvio's clothes," 24

Wicksteed, Joseph, 7, 8

Wolf, Edwin, II, ix, 20n, 72n, 81n, 97n, 107n, 150

Wolstonecraft, Mary, 49

Wordsworth, William, 4, 34. 40, 43, 49, 50, 66, 74, 110, 119, 128, 147, 268, 328; "Intimations of Immortality," 34; "The Old Cumberland Beggar," 278; *The Prelude*, 34, 50, 74n; "We Are Seven," 255

Yeats, W. B., 4

Young, Edward, *Night Thoughts*, 108–09, 170, 247